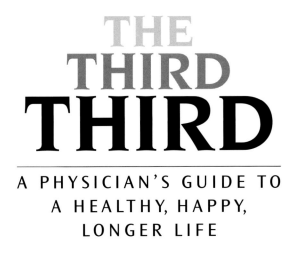

THE THIRD THIRD

A PHYSICIAN'S GUIDE TO A HEALTHY, HAPPY, LONGER LIFE

N. Thomas Connally, M.D.

bright sky press

Albany, Texas • New York, New York

ꞵ

BRIGHT SKY PRESS
Albany, Texas
New York, New York

Medicine is an ever-changing field. Many recommendations in this book may be replaced as new scientific data is accumulated. More importantly, this is not intended as a guide to self-diagnosis, treatment, or medication. It is meant to help you work with your own doctor. One of the major points in most chapters is that advice on both prevention and treatment has to be individualized. You must consult your doctor about specific medical problems.

In the interest of page economy and readability, only the most frequent side effects of drugs or drug families have been mentioned. Readers are advised to check the product information currently provided by the manufacturer of a drug to be administered to verify the recommended dose, method of administration, contraindications, and side effects. You must work with your doctor for all your medications.

Neither the publisher nor the author assumes responsibility for injury to persons who do not follow this common-sense advice.

Library of Congress Cataloging-in-Publication Data

Connally, N. Thomas (Nathaniel Thomas), 1936-
The third third : a physician's guide to a healthy happy longer life / N. Thomas Connally.
p. cm.
Includes bibliographical references and index.
ISBN 0-9704729-2-7 (alk. paper)
Aged—Health and hygiene. I. Title.

RA777.6.C68 2001
613'.0438—dc21
2001037841

Book design by Oksana Kushnir
Cover design by Karen Ocker
Illustrations by Stephen R. Wagner
Editors: Constance Buchanan and Bob Somerville

Distributed by: Sterling Publishing Co., Inc.

Printed in China

CONTENTS

This book is about you and your health in the third third of life, from the age of sixty onward. It is the product of thirty-three years of practice as a general internist in Washington, D.C. While I'm not a geriatrician per se, longevity eventually caught up with me, and I now have three patients over one hundred years old, forty patients over ninety, and over three hundred patients in their late eighties. These senior citizens make me look like a spring chicken at sixty-four years old, and sometimes I have to remind myself that I'm actually four years into the third third myself. To paraphrase Pogo, "I have looked at the patient, and he is me."

What I present here is mainstream American medicine as it is in the year 2001. The word doctor comes from the Latin word *docere*, meaning to teach. In my opinion, the most important role a primary care physician can perform is to teach his or her patients how to take care of themselves, and to explain to them why certain medical tests or treatments are being advised. I respect the intelligence of my patients. They're more comfortable following advice when they understand why it is given. Knowing that bone is a living tissue, for example, or how blood vessels contract, enlightens them about osteoporosis and high blood pressure. My hope here is to convey to a larger audience what I've tried to teach my patients, and to share any wisdom I may have gained through years of helping people and interacting with them.

We don't know precisely what causes aging. Certainly, longevity as well as disease incidence and patterns are influenced by both heredity and environmental factors. Aging itself — defined as cell death, cell loss, or loss of cell function — makes us less functional and less able to fight off disease by the time we reach our mid-eighties. Some things just inevitably deteriorate, including our all-important first line of defense, the immune system. That's not to say that older people who take care of themselves can't fare better than younger patients who don't. An eighty-year-old who exercises regularly may have just as strong — or stronger — a heart than a sedentary forty-year-old.

When age does catch up with us, it is in the form of specific illness. Some physicians occasionally write "old age" on a death certificate, but I've never had a patient die of something other than a disease. The disease ultimately wins because of reduced immune resistance, environmental factors, or bad habits. This book is about postponing the day disease catches up with us. It isn't a medical encyclopedia; it concentrates on the most common major health problems older people face.

The first part, "Beating the Odds," is about reducing the risk of disease ending your life early, or about postponing the time that disease descends on you. One of my patients, in thanking me and the attending surgeon for the early diagnosis and successful removal of a cancerous colon growth, wrote, "Life isn't much fun when you're dead." I want to help keep you alive to enjoy the rich rewards of the third third of your life.

Part 2, "Staying on Top of Your Health," is about quality of life in the middle portion of the third third. It deals with illnesses and conditions that affect how you feel and how you function, such as osteoporosis, depression, and sexual dysfunction, and suggests how you might avoid, postpone, or at least tolerate them. This part of the book also highlights the value of exercise, the single most important factor in keeping people vibrant and functioning into their nineties.

In part 3, "Coping and Caring," you'll find information geared toward people in the final stretch of life. This is written both for them and for their families and caregivers. It discusses how to live with certain serious diseases like congestive heart failure and how to understand treatment options. I focus on the more common problems encountered in the very old and very frail, those with cognitive impairment and those who are virtually bedridden. Here you'll come across advice about how to work with the doctor or the health team to promote comfort and avoid complications or disasters. You'll also get some tips about working with the doctor to ensure that during a terminal illness, you or your loved one will be comfortable, and no treatment options will be taken against you or your family's wishes.

Although some of what I write here will have to be modified as new drugs, new techniques, and new clinical epidemiological studies change our concept of mainstream medical practice, much of it should stand the test of time. Bear in mind that my advice is based not just on personal observation of patients but also on studies of large groups of people over several years. The public often gets conflicting recommendations from different publications or from year to year about what is good or not good for human health. "Eggs are out; eggs are in." "Vitamin E is in; vitamin E is out." "Very rigorous exercise is what you need; moderate exercise is just as good." In grappling with conflicting results from different studies, what the public may not know is that the sizes of study populations and other variables might differ — or that a given study might not be large enough to produce statistically significant results. More confusing for the public is that the press often sensationalizes a new study that runs counter to prevailing opinion. The more radical, the more newsworthy. A poorly performed study may end up on the front page. In the interest of economy, I generally present mainstream medical opinion without wading into specific controversies, but in a few instances if a controversial study is significant enough, I do mention it.

Above all, this book is meant to help you work with, not replace or second-guess, your doctor. One of the messages I've tried to get across is that advice on disease prevention and treatment has to be individualized — no author can know your problem or problems as well as your own doctor can. Consider what you hold in your hands a blueprint. It will help guide you in certain personal lifestyle choices with the aim of keeping you healthy or getting you better faster, but you should never lose sight of the fact that your primary care doctor is your most important advocate and partner-in-health during the third third of life.

To repeat, you should view this book as a blueprint that will help you work with your doctor — not as a guide to self-diagnosis or self-treatment. Keep in mind that because medicine is an ever-changing field, many recommendations in this book may become obsolete as new scientific data accumulate. One major point in most chapters is that advice on both prevention and treatment should be individualized.

In the interests of economy and readability, only the most frequent side effects of drugs have been mentioned. When taking medication, readers are advised to consult closely with their doctor, and to check product information provided by the manufacturer to verify recommended dose, method of administration, contraindications, and side effects. Neither I nor the publisher assumes responsibility for injury to persons who don't follow this commonsense advice.

Numerous times in this book, I use patient stories as a way of illustrating important points. The stories in the introduction are about real people, and their names are authentic. In the chapters themselves, however, patients' names have been changed to protect confidentiality, and some stories are composites of different patient histories, made in order to more clearly drive home certain lessons about medical care. All the patient anecdotes are specific, medically accurate examples of the diseases they portray.

One of the biggest hurdles for a first-time author is finding a publisher. I'm forever grateful to my dear friend, Rue Judd of Bright Sky Press, for giving me the opportunity to bring my work before the public, and to Kate Hartson and other staff at Bright Sky for their guidance and encouragement.

Some authors I know have told me that working with editors can be difficult. In this case, nothing could be further from the truth. Connie Buchanan and Bob Somerville were a delight to work with, and I gained enormously from their experience, cordiality, and professionalism. They helped me transform a manuscript that was all over the lot into a coherent presentation. It has also been a pleasure to work with graphic designer Oksana Kushnir and illustrator Steve Wagner, whose efforts have enhanced the teaching quality of the book. My thanks also to Celia Beattie, who proofread the final manuscript.

I also greatly appreciate the assistance of Drs. Eugene Passamani, Richard E. Waldhorn, and Christopher Wilcox, who reviewed and commented on chapters in their areas of expertise. They are all nationally recognized in their respective fields, and any omissions or errors are entirely mine, not theirs.

I am also grateful to Jennifer Krieg and Maria Souto, who have helped enormously in taking care of my patients over many years.

Most of all, my thanks go to my wife, Judy, without whom this book literally would not have been possible. She transformed my doctor's scrawl into a computerized manuscript and repeatedly kept me from drifting into incomprehensible doctor-speak. More importantly, she gave me the emotional support and encouragement to complete the project. Sharing the results with her is what has made everything worthwhile. This book is dedicated to Judy.

We all give up some things as we get older, but we have one precious gift that doesn't vanish: more time than ever. My patients over the age of sixty — those in the third third of life — who develop their hobbies and pursue their intellectual, artistic, and spiritual interests often feel more fulfilled than at any time in their lives. The third third is the season for long postponed pleasures. For relaxed visits with friends and family. For volunteer jobs that can make people feel far better about themselves than they ever felt slugging along in paid jobs year in and year out.

These three measures — contributions to society, close relationships, and personal interests — not only make the third third of life meaningful, they play a critical role in maintaining health. Various studies have shown that all three help to keep memory alive and prevent depression. The "use it or lose it" motto of athletic trainers works for the brain also.

The Gift of Time

Medical science, public health measures, and more sensible living habits have increased life expectancy to the point that most people at the age of sixty have a very good chance of living another thirty years. The percent of the U.S. population eligible for Medicare (over age sixty-five) has increased from 8 percent in 1965 to 13 percent now, and is rapidly climbing. By the year 2020, there will be more than fifty million Americans over age sixty-five. Two-thirds of all the human beings in human history who have lived to age sixty-five are alive today!

I picture a future in which our growing cadre of people over sixty become recognized as an enormous asset to society. These are people who are contributing to society, nurturing friendships, and pursuing their personal interests — people who are enjoying what is in many ways the best time of their lives.

Contributing to Society

In recent years there has been talk about a shift of national assets to seniors by means of social security, pensions, and Medicare. Certain policy makers in Washington, D.C., regard this as a bad trend. "Why shouldn't we be focusing more on helping the young?" is their question, and the implied message is that seniors are a nonproductive drain on the economy — receivers, not producers.

I agree that education, good quality childcare, and programs to stabilize families should be extremely high priorities in Washington. But I don't agree with the premise that somehow people when they reach a certain age — say, sixty-five — stop being an asset and abruptly become a liability. Nothing could be further from the truth. Many of my older patients make significant contributions to society that benefit us all, and these are the very people, I might add, who feel the most fulfilled.

Stacy and Jean Reed. I just returned from the funeral of Stacy Reed, my second oldest patient. He was 101 years old and had been remarkably healthy and active prior to developing massive pneumonia. Born in September 1899, Stacy had lived in three centuries.

He had a successful career as a lawyer and banker, but it was after he retired as a bank president that he really blossomed. For some thirty years, Stacy served as chairman of the board of trustees of Sibley Memorial Hospital, a 400-bed institution in Washington, D.C. Just after his ninety-ninth birthday he stepped down from the chairmanship, but he remained active on the board until his death. Far from being a doddering emeritus figurehead, he presided over the hospital board's decisions and talked with the administrator every day. He was revered and respected by his board colleagues and the hospital personnel from the administrator on down.

Stacy had been a wise counselor all his life, and his wisdom and judgment seemed absolutely unchanged by his age. Whenever I talked with him, his choice of words reflected the mental alertness of a fifty-year-old. During the last years of his tenure, when many of the hospitals in the area were bordering on bankruptcy, Sibley Memorial was flourishing financially. As I write this, it is being expanded with the addition of a nursing facility and a senior citizen's apartment complex.

Despite his worldly success, Stacy's public persona was not his most remarkable accomplishment. His first wife died when he was in his late seventies, and at age eighty he married Jean, a seventy-year-old widow. Stacy had no children by his first marriage, whereas Jean had three talented grown daughters. His stepchildren and step-grandchildren came to revere and love Stacy as they would a blood relative.

The marriage was a happy one. Each day Stacy would drive Jean to the Methodist Church about a mile away, leave her, and then walk home. Jean would do her group aerobics at the church and drive home afterwards. At age ninety-two she looks like a woman of sixty, radiant and straight-backed. I'm sure his last twenty-one years were the happiest of Stacy's life. He and Jean would sit and hold hands as they watched television, and because Jean's reading vision was poor, Stacy would read to her faithfully.

Edgar and Anne Steever. Edgar "Zell" Steever is in his early eighties. Afflicted with retinitis pigmentosa, an inherited condition that left him totally blind starting in middle age, Zell also has hearing difficulty in both ears. He lives in an apartment on Connecticut Avenue in Washington, across from the National Zoo. Every morning, he gets up around five and rides the bus downtown to his job running a snack bar at the Old Federal Post Office. Whenever Zell comes to my office, his younger sister Anne, retired from an administrative job at George Washington University, accompanies him. Zell is kind, good-natured, and funny, and has remarkable insight into people. He wouldn't think of giving up his job. His only complaint in life is that he wasn't given a good location for his snack bar.

Recently Zell grew a long beard, and with his six-foot-plus height and his white cane he resembles a biblical prophet. I once accused him of trying to look like Moses to scare the District administrators into moving his snack bar. He laughed, and said that even Moses would have to have the political connections to land a good spot.

Anne is truly her brother's keeper. Although he lives a remarkably independent life, she handles some of his personal business and takes care of the day-to-day details that keep him going. A few years ago, on a sunny spring day, I spotted the two of them having a picnic on a bench in a downtown park, laughing and enjoying life like two teenagers.

Zell Steever is a great man, and Anne Steever is a great woman.

The Reeds and the Steevers don't contribute much to the gross domestic product (GDP). Stacy Reed's years of high-profile volunteer work, Jean Reed's loving companionship, Zell Steever's monumental grit and determination, Anne Steever's nurturing care of her brother — none of these figure in the GDP. The only thing the economists would count is the money Zell makes in his snack bar.

To all you economists and policy wonks who doubt the usefulness of older people, I can only say this: maybe when you're older you'll see things differently. Most of my senior patients and my older friends are contributing to their communities in enormous ways. The volunteers who bring elderly people to my office, the volunteers at the hospitals I use, and the volunteer doctors in the free clinic where I work are predominantly seniors. None of them get credited in the GDP. And yet these people, and people like the Reeds and the Steevers, are some of this country's greatest resources.

Nurturing Friendships

The two things my patients fear most about getting older are loneliness and inability to take care of themselves. Alzheimer's or a disabling stroke is a far more frightening prospect than death, a heart attack, or even cancer. Some in their late eighties and nineties confess that while they can put up with the physical problems that come with aging, the death of loved ones and close friends is much more difficult to cope with.

Certainly elderly people who have a living spouse or a lot of family living nearby are better off, but this isn't always, or even often, the case. The successful upper-agers I've known have had warm relations with family members but have also cultivated a set of friends. Many are fortunate to have a circle of friends from years back; others have to seek out new friendships.

Mildred Hunter. "Millie" Hunter died in August 2000 at age ninety-four of coronary artery disease. Like so many older women, she came to Washington, D.C., during World War II. She had no children and her husband, who was a journalist, died in the 1960s. For many years — until she was well into her seventies — Millie worked as a salesperson in a clothing store.

Millie was quite ill during the last fifteen years of her life. She had angina, congestive heart failure, high blood pressure, an irregular heart rhythm, several intestinal problems, arthritis, and severe osteoporosis. But she didn't let bad health or disappointment bother her any more than was necessary to get medical help. Millie had just enough chutzpah to get along and not bother people, and enough kindness to make everybody like her. She would sit in the small lobby of her apartment and meet and greet people. She kept up a prodigious correspondence with foreign students who had lived there. On one hospitalization, the woman in the bed next to Millie's was also my patient. They became fast friends and Millie called her almost every day. She was a strong Democrat and the other woman had once been an active Republican. The two of them loved a good-natured argument.

In her last years, Millie would always bring me something when she came to the office, *Life* magazines from the Kennedy era, coins from the Franklin Mint, old Norman Rockwell prints she had bought from *The Saturday Evening Post*. She had few worldly possessions, but she wanted me and my family to have some of what she valued. She knitted afghans for my grandchildren — how she could do that with her tremulous, arthritic hands I'll never understand. She kept up with everything. She would stand in my office and talk politics, then sit down and tell about her medications and symptoms.

On her birthday, my wife and I would take her to the little restaurant across from her apartment. She would dress to the nines, chatter with everyone in the restaurant, and always say she had a "fabulous time."

As she became increasingly infirm, she got wonderful help from IONA House, a volunteer organization that helps frail older people in her part of the city. The volunteers would bring her to my office, obviously charmed by her. Millie's "regular" chauffeurs were the president and vice president of IONA House.

Early in 2000 Millie called, very excited, to announce that she was going to be on national television that night. Somehow CNN had heard about her, and when President Clinton introduced legislation to have drug costs included in Medicare, she was the administration's poster girl. They filmed her in her apartment, hobbling to her medicine bottles and telling how much each one cost. Though I gave her an enormous number of samples that the pharmaceutical detail people had left in my office, her medicine bills still left her three or four hundred dollars poorer each month. At the end of the interview Millie looked straight in the camera, raised her fist, and said, "I don't care if you're a Democrat or a Republican, you're going to be old yourself some day — I hope you don't have to pay for your medicine like I do." Millie was a piece of work.

In spite of pain, near poverty, and a remarkable number of illnesses — how she survived her many brushes with death is a mystery — the smallest thing in life gave Millie pleasure. Her cheerfulness attracted people, and the friendship of the people she attracted must have been what kept her going.

Pursuing Personal Interests

When a patient of mine died at home of longstanding prostate cancer, I stopped by his home to do a legal death pronouncement. Although he was clearly dead, I performed the time-honored doctor's task of checking for pulse or breathing. As I did, I spotted a book in his open hand and picked it up: *How to Improve Your Short Game: Tips Around the Green,* the title read.

On hospital visits to near terminal patients, I always pay attention to what they're reading. I used to wonder what I would read if I knew I had a short time to live. Then I began to realize that my time is limited — just a few decades left, if I'm lucky. I have a long list of books I want to read, some of them classics, some of them volumes on science and philosophy. I'll never finish them all, but as soon as I retire I'll have the time to read.

Socrates said a life unexamined is not worth living. I look on the third third as an opportunity to become a wiser person. At last, I'll have time to reflect — one of the most valuable activities in life. And I'll go back to "college." I just discovered some audiotapes from an organization that records college-level lectures delivered by renowned professors on history, philosophy, literature, and music. It'll be a luxury to take a course without having to worry about a grade, whether I've got a date for the weekend, and whether I'll be invited to join the fraternity of my choice. I'll be able to pursue my interests free of the pressures of youth.

Sidney Bechet, the great jazz musician, once said, "We are born alone, we die alone, and we spend a lot of time alone in between." No matter how big your family, or how wide your circle of friends, there will be time in the third third when you're all alone, and you might as well make the best of it — whether that means reading, puttering in your garden, bird-watching, refinishing furniture, or poring over the latest baseball statistics.

Sherwood Smith. Sherwood Smith was a retired engineer. He died at ninety-three following a hip fracture. Prior to the fracture Sherwood had had no significant health problems other than angina, which dramatically improved after an angioplasty. He had nursed his wife through terminal cancer. He had a daughter in Philadelphia, a son in the Washington area, and another son who had died of a cardiac arrhythmia. In addition to family, Sherwood had friends who enjoyed and admired him. But most of the pleasure he got out of life came from his own activities. He learned French in his eighties and read everything he could get his hands on. He was extraordinarily knowledgeable about health policy and advances in medical technology, and his comments on politics, history, and religion were profound. During his final illness, Sherwood knew he might die. He wasn't afraid, just disappointed that he couldn't keep on learning. Socrates commented that you die a good death if you've finally figured things out — and that one of the things you've figured out is that you don't know everything. Sherwood Smith had a good life and a good death.

Your Third Third

Contributing to society, building close relationships, following personal interests — these are all things you can look forward to in the third third of life. But if you're sick or disabled, it can be difficult if not impossible to pursue such activities. This book is about staying alive and healthy so the third third is the best third of your life.

In my opinion, the most important role a primary care physician can perform is to teach his or her patients how to take care of themselves. That's the role I performed with Stacy and Edgar, Millie and Sherwood, and all the hundreds of others whose paths I've been fortunate enough to have cross my own. And what I shared with them, I now hope to share with you in the pages that follow.

PART ONE

BEATING THE ODDS

ONE THING IS ABSOLUTELY CLEAR from recent census and mortality statistics: more and more people are beating the odds and living to an older age. In 1900 in the United States, life expectancy at birth was forty-seven years. Now it's approximately seventy-six years for men and seventy-nine years for women. People who reach age sixty in decent health can reasonably expect to live into their late eighties or early nineties.

Much of the gain came in the early part of the twentieth century, thanks to public health measures and better nutrition, and in midcentury with the introduction of antibiotics. Infant mortality rates dropped, as did the number of deaths in young and middle-aged people.

The odds continue to improve, with substantial gains in life expectancy particularly in older age groups. Much of the recent progress traces to a dramatic reduction in the death rate from heart attacks and strokes. Over the past fifty years we've made enormous progress in our knowledge of what causes the arterial disease that leads to most heart attacks and strokes, and this knowledge has led to milestones in primary prevention — stopping or reversing the problem before it can do real harm. Americans are smoking less, they've got better control of high blood pressure, and they're paying more attention to their cholesterol levels.

We Can Do Better

Though many people have improved their chances of enjoying a long and healthy third third, some people still aren't trying, and others who are making some effort could work harder at it. What they need is a prod —

more information on the goals they should shoot for, and on how enormous the benefits can be.

In recent years, new techniques to treat vascular disease — coronary artery bypass surgery and angioplasty to open arteries, anticoagulants for strokes, and coronary care units — have played their part in improving the mortality statistics. Indeed, these innovations seem to be helping just as much as primary prevention measures. Unfortunately, though, many people aren't getting vascular disease diagnosed early enough to take advantage of the newest technology, nor are they paying proper attention to symptoms that may be vascular.

The most important message I can convey in this book is that no matter how old you are, when you start protecting your arteries, you'll significantly improve the statistical chances of good health well into the last years of your life.

Many older people rationalize bad habits with the philosophy: "The horse is out of the barn." They believe that decades of bad habits — smoking, inactivity, poor weight control, and poor diet — have already taken their toll and not much can be done to correct the situation. Let me assure you, nothing could be further from the truth. Recent epidemiological studies on death and disability from vascular disease in older people have shown that if you stop smoking, your risk of heart disease drops to that of a nonsmoker in about a year.

It takes longer — several years — for lung cancer risk to decline in an ex-smoker, and even after ten to fifteen years the risk is still twice that for a lifelong nonsmoker. But a twofold risk is far better than the eighteenfold risk if you're still smoking.

Equally dramatic are the statistics on the benefits of controlling weight, blood pressure, and cholesterol, and of starting a regular exercise program. Significant improvement in health can be seen within a year.

What's the Big Deal about Heart Disease?

Why am I focusing so much on cardiovascular disease? Simple: it's far and away the most common cause of death and disability in the United States and throughout the developed world. The table and chart below list the most common causes of death for Americans over sixty-five years old.

MOST COMMON CAUSES OF DEATH FOR AMERICANS
OVER SIXTY-FIVE (1996)

Cause	Total	Men	Women
All causes	1,694,000	776,000	918,000
Heart disease	615,000	272,000	343,000
All types of cancer	381,000	199,000	182,000
Stroke	138,000	51,000	87,000
Chronic lung disease	88,000	46,000	42,000
Pneumonia and influenza	74,000	32,000	42,000
Diabetes	44,000	18,000	26,000
Accidents	29,000	14,500	14,500
Alzheimer's disease	20,000	6,000	14,000
Kidney disease	20,000	9,000	11,000
Infections and septicemia	18,000	9,000	9,000

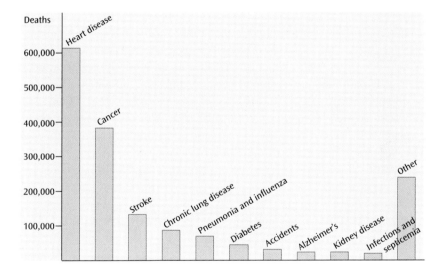

In each of these categories, a substantial number of deaths could be prevented or postponed — or, in the case of cancer, cured — through early diagnosis. In part 1, I'll discuss almost all of these causes in detail and describe how they can be prevented, postponed, or diagnosed early.

To me, the single most compelling statistic is that heart disease and stroke result in more deaths than all the other most common causes combined. (Also, take note of a fact that many people find surprising: In this age group, more women than men die of heart disease.) The majority of deaths from heart disease and stroke are caused by the same condition, atherosclerosis, which is basically a narrowing or blocking of the arteries that supply blood to the body's organs and tissues. The result can be damage to the organ or tissue.

We know a great deal about how to slow or prevent atherosclerosis, and much of the first part of this book is devoted to techniques for doing so, ranging from lifestyle changes to drug regimens. The benefits go beyond reducing your chance of dying from a heart attack or stroke. For one thing, if you slow or prevent atherosclerosis you're likely to prevent other diseases. If, moreover, in tackling atherosclerosis you avert a heart attack or stroke, you greatly reduce the chance of disability, since heart attacks and strokes are the number one and two causes of disability in developed countries.

Almost all of the things you can do to slow or prevent atherosclerosis will also make you feel better, look better, and enjoy life more. A few examples? Stopping smoking not only eliminates one of the major risk factors for heart disease, but it also reduces the likelihood of lung cancer, improves chronic lung disease, and increases your wind and endurance. Losing weight helps alleviate arthritis and improves mobility. Proper diet and careful treatment of diabetes can stave off failing vision, sexual dysfunction, and nerve degeneration in the legs. Regular exercise — the most important lesson of this book — helps prevent atherosclerosis and is also the single most important thing you can do to maintain strength, mobility, and overall physical and mental health as you age.

The Importance of Routine Maintenance

Everyone over age sixty should have a routine physical examination once every year, whether they're in good health or have a chronic medical problem requiring regular visits to the doctor. Routine tests for conditions other than a person's chronic problem need to be performed annually.

Annual evaluations are screens for many of the vascular and malignant conditions discussed in part 1. In addition to helping you beat the odds, regular visits enable you to solidify your relationship with the doctor. If you develop an acute problem or have an emergency in the intervening year, your doctor will know who you are and will have baseline data to compare with any new findings. Also, the physical exam is a good opportunity to get lifestyle recommendations on subjects such as weight loss and exercise, which will help you maintain your health and improve your quality of life.

Your annual physical should include the following:

- □ *An updated medical history.* This should include any symptoms you're experiencing, all medications you're taking whether prescribed or over the counter, and any possible bad habits you have in terms of diet, exercise, smoking, sleep, and alcohol use.
- □ *A thorough physical exam.* This should include pulse and blood pressure readings, brief nerve testing, and a look at your eyes, ears, mouth, throat, thyroid, lymph nodes, heart, lungs, abdomen, and extremities. Men and women should have a digital rectal exam; this is part of the pelvic exam for women.
- □ *An electrocardiogram (EKG).* This should be given every year if you have vascular risk factors or a previous abnormal EKG; otherwise, it can be given every two years.
- □ *A complete blood count for anemia.*
- □ *A blood profile.* I prefer the comprehensive metabolic profile that tests blood sugar and kidney and liver function.
- □ *A full cholesterol (lipid) profile.* This should be done every year unless you've had an extremely low cholesterol baseline in the past, in which case it can be done every two to three years.
- □ *A TSH (thyroid-stimulating hormone) test.*
- □ *A three-day test for hidden blood in the stool.*
- □ *A urinalysis.*
- □ *A PSA (prostatic-specific antigen) blood test (men).* This detects the presence of prostate cancer.
- □ *A breast exam and a mammogram (women).* The breast exam can be performed by a primary physician or a gynecologist. Women should also do breast self-examinations every month.
- □ *An annual pelvic exam (women).* Again, this can be performed by the primary care physician or the gynecologist. A cervical pap smear should be done unless you've had three negative tests in a row and no change in sexual partners.

In addition to the above annual tests, every three years a sigmoidoscopy should be done if you're at low risk for colon cancer, and a full colonoscopy if you're at higher risk because of family history or a history of polyps. Any positive stool test for hidden blood requires colonoscopic follow-up.

If, during your annual physical, you have unusual symptoms or report a worrisome family history, your doctor may order additional screening tests.

CHAPTER 1

HEART DISEASE

The heart is a magnificent creation — a large, muscular organ that in a long lifetime beats and pumps blood over three billion times. "The right heart" receives blood from the body and pumps it to the lungs, while "the left heart" receives oxygenated blood from the lungs and pumps it to the body. Each side of the heart has two chambers, a receiving chamber called the atrium and a larger pumping chamber, the ventricle. Valves at the outlet of each chamber keep the blood from flowing backward.

Besides making the heart a wonderfully resilient pump, some of the heart's muscle tissue has the specialized ability to initiate electrical signals and conduct them throughout the rest of the heart to keep it beating on time. Because all this is living tissue, the heart also has to have its own blood supply. The first blood to come through the aorta, immediately after it emerges from the left ventricle, flows into two moderately large arteries that supply the heart itself. These two arteries are called the coronary arteries because ancient physicians thought they looked like a crown around the heart.

What Can Go Wrong?

Lots of things can go wrong with this living pump over a lifetime. Heart disease takes various forms:

- □ *Congestive heart failure*. In this condition, the ventricle muscles weaken and fail to pump enough blood, causing it to pool in the lungs or veins.
- □ *Valvular heart disease*. One of the four valves can leak or grow nar-

rower, making the heart muscle work overtime so that it cannot keep up.

□ *Arrhythmia.* The specialized electrical tissue in the heart can become damaged, making the heart beat irregularly, or too slow or too fast for the demands of the body.

□ *Coronary atherosclerosis, or coronary artery disease.* In this chronic condition, the coronary arteries that supply blood to the heart become narrowed or blocked by patchy deposits of cholesterol called plaques *(see below)*. Atherosclerosis is the cause of the vast majority of heart disease in the United States — as much as 80 to 90 percent of all cases. Indeed, this disease often plays a role in other common forms of heart disease. It is the major cause of damage to the ventricle muscle that leads to congestive heart failure, a major cause of arrhythmia, and a cause of some valve damage.

A WORD OF CAUTION

Both because of its magnitude and because it can be successfully prevented or reversed, coronary artery disease is the prime focus of preventive cardiology. You can prevent death or disability from coronary disease in two ways: by stopping or reversing the buildup of artery-clogging plaque, or, if the condition has progressed, by recognizing the symptoms and taking appropriate action before irreversible damage occurs.

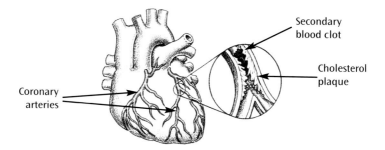

Typical atherosclerotic narrowing of a coronary artery, with cholesterol plaque and secondary blood clot, or coronary thrombosis. The two coronary arteries branch off from the aorta and wrap around the surface of the heart.

Assessing Your Risk of Atherosclerosis

Atherosclerosis can lead to acute destruction of a portion of the heart muscle — a heart attack, or as doctors say, myocardial infarction. Since the 1950s, numerous studies have investigated which factors make a person most likely to develop atherosclerosis. The research is unequivocal and has identified the major risk factors (*see below*). Moreover, evidence strongly suggests that vigorous efforts to minimize these factors — whether through specific treatment or lifestyle change — can slow, stop, or even reverse this killer disease.

The major risk factors for atherosclerosis are:

☐ Elevation of blood cholesterol or one of the cholesterol fractions
☐ High blood pressure
☐ Diabetes
☐ Cigarette smoking
☐ Physical inactivity
☐ Obesity, which increases the first three risks
☐ Heredity, especially having a close family member develop heart disease at an early age

Recent research also suggests that factors in the blood such as homocysteine and C-reactive protein may either cause coronary disease or serve as markers indicating its presence. But the preventive implications of this research are not clear.

With the exception of heredity, each of the factors in the above list can be mitigated or corrected, gaining you years of life and health. In fact, the benefits of tackling the risk factors for heart disease are potentially so great that I have devoted a full chapter to cholesterol; you will also find more information about heart disease in the chapters on high blood pressure, diabetes, smoking, and weight problems.

How Can You Tell If You Have Cardiovascular Disease?

By the age of sixty, many of us will have developed at least a mild accumulation of cholesterol plaque in some of our vessels — a process that begins for some individuals in their twenties or thirties. For most people, the accumulation is minimal and requires nothing more than careful attention to risk factors. However, it is important to know if your disease has progressed to the danger point. Why? Because you and your doctor may need to get more aggressive in treating risk factors, and because your condition may call for direct treatment of the vessels themselves.

KEY HEART DISEASE SYMPTOMS

Heart disease can progress silently, without producing any noticeable symptoms. But eventually, if left untreated, it will send you clear signals that something's gone wrong. The five cardinal heart disease symptoms are:

- ☐ Chest pain or pressure
- ☐ Shortness of breath, particularly on exertion
- ☐ Unusual fatigue on exertion
- ☐ A sense of heart irregularity or rapidity
- ☐ Severe lightheadedness, fainting, or near fainting

Chest Pain

As a coronary artery narrows, the amount of blood that can get through is usually enough to supply the heart when you are resting, but during exercise the heart muscle has to work harder and needs more blood. When it cannot get enough extra blood, you feel pain or a sensation of pressure in the chest. This is called angina pectoris, or just angina. The pain may radiate to the neck, jaw, or inside the left arm. If you experience this type of pain, report it to your doctor right away.

Heart Symptoms Other Than Pain

Shortness of breath upon exertion is another symptom of narrowed coronary arteries and may be more noticeable than angina. Report any instances of this to your doctor.

Most adults — perhaps all adults — have occasional heart "skips." These premature or early heartbeats are benign in the vast majority of cases. However, if they become so frequent they bother you, or if they seem to come in runs of several rapid beats, you should see your doctor. If you feel simultaneous symptoms such as shortness of breath or near fainting, or if rapid runs last for more than several minutes, you should get medical evaluation right away. See part 3, chapter 25, "Dizziness," for more about arrhythmia.

Tests for Heart Disease

If you report to your doctor with symptoms suggestive of heart disease, there are a number of tests that may be run.

Resting EKGs and Stress Tests

As a first step, your doctor will probably order a resting electrocardiogram (EKG), which may or may not reveal an existing abnormality. For greater accuracy, your doctor will probably request an exercise stress test to see whether exercise causes abnormal heart muscle activity — an indication that an area of the heart is receiving insufficient blood. Results are measured by either a stress test form of the EKG, an echocardiogram (ECHO), or thallium perfusion. The thallium perfusion version of the stress test relies on the injection of a radioactive material into the bloodstream just before exercise begins. The radioactive material is taken up by heart muscle tissue that is abnormal because of compromised blood flow. A detector over the chest can indicate the presence, location, and size of abnormal heart muscle.

Both the stress ECHO and the thallium test are more accurate and produce fewer false readings than the EKG stress test. But they are more difficult to conduct and more expensive, so an EKG stress test is usually the doctor's first choice.

Cardiologists are evaluating cardiac MRI (magnetic resonance imaging) as a better way to diagnose coronary artery disease. Some believe this technology may replace stress tests.

Heart Scans

Another screening test for coronary disease is called a heart scan. Extensive or longstanding cholesterol plaques in coronary arteries accumulate calcium, and a heart scan, which employs CT (computerized tomography) imaging, will detect the presence of calcium. Heart scans give only a rough estimate of the functional ability of the arteries, so a stress test may need to be done as a follow-up. Currently, cardiologists are divided on the benefit of heart scans; a large group believes they aren't accurate enough to be beneficial.

Arteriograms

If your stress test is positive, indicating that in all likelihood you do have symptomatic atherosclerosis (angina), then you may need a coronary arteriogram. This is a motion-picture X ray that follows a dye after it has been injected into the coronary arteries. A catheter is inserted into an artery in the groin and under X-ray monitoring is threaded up to the areas where the coronary arteries branch off from the aorta. The X-ray images, remarkably detailed, can tell whether surgery is needed to open the arteries or whether drug therapy to dilate the arteries will suffice.

After Diagnosis

If only one or two areas of the coronary arteries are critically narrowed, then you may be able to have angioplasty. In this procedure, the narrowed segment is dilated with a balloon — again, fed through a catheter — and then held open with a wire-mesh stent (*see below*). In case of extensive disease, however, your doctor and cardiologist may recommend coronary artery bypass graft surgery (CABG). If the main artery to the left side of the heart is narrowed, or both major branches of the left coronary and the right are clogged (three-vessel disease), standard practice is to advise coronary artery surgery.

Managing Heart Disease with Medication

If you don't have one or two specific areas amenable to angioplasty, and the other narrowed segments aren't extensive enough to warrant CABG, then the best treatment is medication to increase blood flow through the clogged arteries. Generally, treatment should include a category of drugs called beta blockers, possibly some form of nitroglycerin, aspirin, and usually an intensive drug program to lower your cholesterol. Aspirin, an anticoagulant, can prevent the formation of blood clots that are one cause of heart attacks. I advise almost all men over the age of sixty and all women who have vascular disease or significant risk factors to take an aspirin each day to prevent clots or worsening vascular disease.

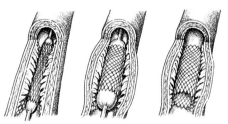

Introduction of a wire-mesh stent during balloon angioplasty. The balloon, with the stent surrounding it, is positioned at the site of plaque buildup *(left)* and inflated *(center)*. The balloon is then removed, leaving the stent in place and restoring blood flow *(right)*.

If medication leaves you symptom free or with substantially fewer and more tolerable symptoms, it should be continued. If, in spite of medication, your symptoms worsen — either gradually or suddenly (accelerated or unstable angina) — then your coronary arteriogram needs to be repeated and angioplasty or CABG should be considered again.

OF SPECIAL CONCERN

If you're being treated for heart disease, beware of the common tendency not to report a worsening of symptoms. Some patients, reluctant to acknowledge that a particular course of action may not be working, ignore or hide the fact. After each and every treatment begins, your cardiologist needs to know how you're faring so that he or she can make adjustments to improve your care. Visiting a competent cardiologist and keeping this person up to date markedly reduces your chance of having a crippling or fatal coronary attack.

What If You Have No Symptoms?

Some people with extensive atherosclerosis may have no recognizable angina symptoms. How can they be diagnosed? A resting EKG performed as part of a regular checkup may show an abnormality, but a stress test is usually more definitive. The EKG form of stress test, though not quite as thorough in diagnosing subtle narrowing as a thallium test or an ECHO test, is adequate for most people who show no symptoms.

Should you have a stress test? They are expensive and should not be considered part of a routine examination. However, if you have significant risk factors or are starting to increase your level of exercise, by all means discuss this possibility with your doctor. If, for example, you're a sixty-five-year-old man with high blood pressure and moderately high cholesterol and you want to graduate from walking to mountain hiking, you'd be wise to have a stress test first.

In Case You Have a Heart Attack

If you have a heart attack, can you do anything to minimize the damage and improve your chances of survival? Absolutely!

Some heart attacks are silent, that is, they don't generate enough chest pain to be recognized as serious. Silent heart attacks occur more often in the very old and in some people with diabetes. However, most heart attacks do cause chest pain.

The pain is most commonly a crushing or squeezing sensation, but it may feel like an ache, severe gas, or burning. It often radiates to the inner portion of the left arm, the left shoulder, or the jaw or teeth. In many cases pain is accompanied by sweating, shortness of breath, and a sense of impending doom. If you have significant chest pain that doesn't go away in three or four minutes, you may well be having a heart attack. Because time is of the essence, you need to act fast.

What to Do If You Have Chest Pain

If you have chest pain, you should take an aspirin, then get to the nearest hospital emergency room as quickly as you can. Don't drive yourself. Get help. Severe, unrelenting chest pain is a bona fide reason for calling an emergency ambulance or rescue squad (911). After hospital evaluation, it may turn out that you have indigestion, esophagitis, or a gallbladder attack mimicking a heart attack. Neither you nor a board-certified cardiologist can make this differential diagnosis without tests at the hospital. Remember, the greatest mistake is to delay and think the pain will go away.

Why Is Delay Such a Mistake?

Mel was sixty-one years old, an economist with a Washington think tank. He had moderate diabetes and mild high blood pressure and was about thirty pounds overweight. He awoke one morning and complained to his wife and daughter about chest pain. They advised him to call me or go to the hospital. He said it was just indigestion. If the pain wasn't gone after a nap he would call me. Sadly, Mel never woke up.

Leigh was seventy-one, a semiretired patent attorney. He had had a mild heart attack about eight years earlier and had since been reasonably active, walking about thirty minutes daily and doing relatively strenuous gardening without symptoms. At his office he noted a severe pressing chest pain while sitting at his desk. He took an aspirin, called 911, and was taken to the nearest emergency room, where an impending coronary heart attack was diagnosed. He had an emergency angiogram, and a single closed area in his right coronary artery was opened with a balloon and stented. The EKG changes characteristic of a heart attack disappeared, and all was normal in two days. Leigh resumed all his previous activities.

The medical team that worked on Leigh performed similar angioplasty on Vice President Dick Cheney just before he took office. Mr. Cheney, who had previously had bypass surgery, recognized cardiac pain and got immediate attention. His prompt reaction probably saved his life.

Arterial Disease in the Legs

Cholesterol plaques can clog more than the coronary arteries; they can narrow or block arteries such as those in the groin and legs. In medical parlance, this condition is known as arteriosclerosis obliterans (arteriosclerosis, a more general term than atherosclerosis, refers to hardening of the arteries). In arteriosclerosis obliterans, the arteries close and the pulse is erased or obliterated. The most common symptom of arterial disease in the legs is pain in one or both limbs, usually in the calf, coming on with walking and going away with rest. Intermittent claudication, as this pain is called, is the leg equivalent of chest pain.

If you have arteriosclerosis obliterans and it is left untreated, the symptoms will gradually get worse and you'll be more restricted in what you can do. Initially, you may have trouble walking two hundred yards on level ground or going up a steep hill. But as the condition progresses, the distance you can go without pain may decrease your mobility to just a few yards. Finally, you may experience pain even at rest: The circulation through the arteries is so restricted that the muscles of the feet and legs cannot get

Did You Know?

About a half million Americans die of heart attacks every year. Most of these deaths occur in the first hour or so because the victims don't seek immediate help. It doesn't have to be this way. The majority of heart attack deaths are caused by arrhythmias, which can be detected by heart monitoring and treated with medication to keep them from becoming fatal. Heart attacks often stem from a blood clot that forms on a rough, narrow portion of artery, blocking it entirely; today we have medications that dissolve such blood clots, and we can do emergency angioplasty and open the blocked artery. Don't forget that medication and emergency procedures grow less effective with each passing hour. Going to the emergency room with severe indigestion is nothing to be embarrassed about; not going to the emergency room with a heart attack can ruin or end your life.

enough blood to support a resting metabolism. The next stage may be gangrene, requiring amputation.

Diagnosing Arteriosclerosis Obliterans

Your doctor can usually tell if your leg pain is suggestive of this condition simply by feeling the two pulses in your feet — one on the top of the foot and one on the inside of the ankle. If any pulse is present, your symptoms probably don't come from blocked circulation. If there is no pulse, your doctor can have arterial doppler tests done to measure blood flow in the legs, but the definitive test is an arteriogram. A radiopaque dye — one that shows up on X rays — is injected into arteries in the groin or higher, where the aorta splits into two large branches going to the legs.

If the X rays indicate blockage, there are several techniques to relieve your condition. One involves a device that, in essence, reams out the artery. Surgical approaches include implanting bypass grafts to channel blood flow around the narrowed area, or stripping away the clogged lining of the vessel. If the blockage is too extensive or too far down in the leg, in vessels too small to operate on, medication may bring some improvement. The calcium-channel family of medications used for angina or high blood pressure may help by dilating the blood vessels. For reasons not well understood, the anticlotting agent Pletal (cilostazol) is also beneficial, perhaps because it reduces blood viscosity.

What Can You Do?

If you have arteriosclerosis obliterans and you smoke, quitting the habit may lead to substantial improvement. It may also help if you control your cholesterol, though no major studies have demonstrated this. Regular walking up to the point of pain, resting, and then pushing on as soon as possible can build up collateral vessels to help carry the blood. Starting with a physical therapist is a good idea, but as with most exercise programs, the goal should be to develop a program you can eventually do on your own.

Sudden pain, cooling of the foot or leg, or a whitish discoloration in your toes or foot is a medical emergency and should be evaluated immediately. It could mean a clot has formed on the rough or narrowed spot in the artery, or more likely, a clot has formed in the heart, traveled down the leg, and lodged in the artery supplying the foot. Prompt action can prevent amputation.

REMEMBER THIS

- Atherosclerosis is the number one cause of death and disability in the United States.
- Addressing the major risk factors — high cholesterol, high blood pressure, diabetes, smoking, and inactivity — is the most effective way to prevent atherosclerosis.
- Chest pain or pressure, and shortness of breath coming on with exertion and going away with rest, is usually the result of coronary artery narrowing. These symptoms require prompt investigation by your doctor.
- Severe, unrelenting chest pain should be considered a potentially fatal heart attack. Immediate ambulance transport to an emergency room for treatment can markedly reduce the chances of dying. Take one aspirin immediately.

CHAPTER 2

CHOLESTEROL PROBLEMS

In the early part of the twentieth century, the anatomical causes of heart attacks were not clearly understood. Doctors did notice, however, that in most heart attacks one or more of the coronary arteries was blocked by a blood clot — a coronary thrombosis. Then it was discovered that clots formed because the artery was narrowed and roughened from an accumulation of fatty deposits beneath its inner lining. These patchy deposits, called plaques, turned out to be predominantly cholesterol, a type of fat present in the blood. (Cholesterol plaque has nothing to do with dental plaque.) Researchers then began major studies on large numbers of people to find out the relationship between the amount of blood cholesterol and cholesterol accumulation in arteries.

The most famous of the early studies, conducted in Framingham, Massachusetts, showed unequivocally that a high level of cholesterol in the bloodstream made a person much more prone to angina pectoris (chest pain) and myocardial infarctions (heart attacks). The results were so clear-cut that high cholesterol was established as a major risk factor for heart disease.

Cholesterol and Heart Disease

Since the Framingham study, our knowledge of cholesterol and its role in coronary heart disease as well as hardening of the arteries throughout the body has increased enormously. We now know that there are several different kinds of cholesterol, some dangerous and some beneficial, and we know that lowering dangerous cholesterol can markedly reduce your chance of having a heart attack. We also know that dietary changes can help lower bad cholesterol, but that many people, no matter how hard they try, cannot achieve safe levels on diet alone.

Powerful new drugs are now available to lower cholesterol in people who cannot achieve results by way of dietary changes. And evidence suggests that extreme lowering of bad cholesterol can reverse the narrowing of blood vessels: The cholesterol in arterial plaque appears to be transported back into the bloodstream.

Now that doctors have better medications to control cholesterol, it is very important to identify and treat those people who can benefit from these drugs.

Types of Cholesterol

Cholesterol circulates in your bloodstream in several forms, two of which are heavily implicated in atherosclerosis. LDL (low-density lipoprotein) is the harmful form — the cholesterol that lodges in the walls of arteries. For most people, LDL levels are the best predictors of risk. HDL (high-density lipoprotein) is the beneficial form of cholesterol, thought to help remove LDL cholesterol from arterial plaque.

When you get your cholesterol tested, the results usually indicate levels of the following:

- Total cholesterol
- HDL cholesterol
- Triglycerides (another type of fat in the blood that can damage arteries)
- LDL cholesterol

Because LDL cholesterol is hard to measure directly, it is usually determined by a formula. Most people assume you can simply subtract HDL from total cholesterol to get LDL, but triglycerides have to be factored in as well. If triglyceride levels are in a reasonable range, below 200, LDL can be calculated by subtracting the HDL number and one-fifth of the triglycerides from total cholesterol. The formula doesn't work if triglyceride levels are higher, so some laboratories are beginning to take direct measurements of LDL — a practice that will probably soon become standard.

What Should Your Cholesterol Targets Be?

The quick answer to this question is, it depends. To begin with, doctors are paying much less attention nowadays to total cholesterol and primarily basing their advice on LDL levels, because LDL is the harmful cholesterol.

However, if HDL is very low, below 40, that in itself becomes a risk factor for atherosclerosis and must be taken into consideration. Your target LDL level depends on how many risk factors you have, such as high blood pressure, diabetes, and existing vascular disease.

The most recent advice from a National Institutes of Health expert panel on cholesterol urges the most drastic lowering of LDL for those with the highest risk: known vascular disease or diabetes. The panel also considers five other risk factors in determining who should achieve what LDL level:

- Age (men over forty-five, women over fifty-five, or any woman who has had premature menopause)
- Cigarette smoking
- High blood pressure
- Family history of early coronary disease (father or brother with coronary disease before age fifty-five, or mother or sister before age sixty-five)
- Low HDL cholesterol (less than 40)

LDL Levels and Your Risk

The following represents the most recent consensus advice from numerous large, well-analyzed population studies, tempered by my own experience of what works in practice and what people can reasonably be expected to do. The first step is to know your cholesterol, or lipid, profile. From there, you and your doctor can follow these guidelines.

No known vascular disease or diabetes, and no risk factors other than age:

LDL less than 100: Optimal. Continue diet and exercise; repeat the test in two or three years.

LDL less than 130: Near optimal. Continue diet and exercise; repeat the test in one to three years.

LDL between 130 and 159: Borderline. Pay strict attention to diet and exercise, and repeat the test in one year.

LDL between 160 and 190: Substantial risk. Follow a strict diet and reevaluate in three to six months; if there is no improvement, start treatment with a cholesterol-lowering medication.

LDL over 190: Very high risk, almost certainly requiring medication. Go on a strict cholesterol-lowering diet and repeat the test in three months. If your diet is already cholesterol- healthy, start medication right away.

No known vascular disease or diabetes, but two or more risk factors (age plus one more):

LDL less than 100: Optimal. Continue diet and exercise, and get tested in two or three years.

LDL less than 130: Acceptable. Follow a low-fat diet, exercise, and repeat the test annually.

LDL between 130 and 159: Substantial risk. Keep to a strict diet, repeat the test in three to six months; if there is no improvement, seriously consider medication.

LDL over 160: High risk, probably requiring medication. If your current diet is cholesterol-heavy, try a very strict diet for three months; if LDL doesn't fall below 130 after that, start medication.

Known vascular disease or diabetes:

LDL over 100: Very high risk. You need to get your LDL below 100; for most people, this requires adherence to a strict diet and cholesterol- lowering medication.

You're considered to have known vascular disease if any of the following conditions apply: a positive stress test, angina, a heart attack, heart surgery, angioplasty, or direct evidence of vascular disease anywhere in your body, including the legs, neck arteries, or aorta.

If you have diabetes, the most recent advice is to lower your LDL to 100. Also, if you have a strong family history of heart disease and two other risk factors, or if you have very low HDL and a family history, you probably need medication and should shoot for an LDL level under 100.

It is well worth the effort to lower

Did You Know?
The danger of multiple risk factors is more than just accumulative. For example, if high LDL cholesterol doubles your risk of a heart attack and very high blood pressure doubles your risk, the statistical increase in your risk might actually be seven or eight times greater than for a person with no risk factors.

your LDL. Reaching the appropriate LDL level for your category will reduce the chance of atherosclerosis progressing — and may actually reverse it.

Diet or Medication?

Can diet alone lower your cholesterol? Again, it depends on your specific circumstances. Let's look at two real examples, one of a man with a moderate cholesterol problem and the other of a woman with a severe problem.

Herb

Herb was a typical sixty-two-year-old man. He was twenty pounds overweight and exercised irregularly — mowed his lawn on Saturdays and played eighteen holes of golf with a cart on the weekends. He usually had cheese snacks before dinner, ate cookies and pastry, had red meat almost every night, and fish or chicken about once a week. Both his parents died of heart attacks, his father at the age of sixty-seven, his mother at eighty-three. Both had smoked; Herb didn't. His blood pressure and blood sugar tests were normal.

Herb's total cholesterol was 230, triglycerides 150, HDL cholesterol 35, and LDL 165. His age and the low HDL gave him two risk factors. Though Herb's parents had had cardiac disease, they had both developed it at an age beyond which hereditary factors seemed to play a role. Not a terrible profile, but one that put Herb in the mid- to high-range risk for developing coronary disease.

Herb basically had two options: to start cholesterol-lowering medication right away and improve his diet, or to try dietary changes alone, adding a cholesterol-lowering drug soon thereafter if no dramatic improvement occurred. He opted for the latter and went on a low-calorie, low-fat diet, reducing total calories and switching to fish, chicken, or pasta five nights a week. He gave up his golf cart and walked the course, and began doing thirty minutes on a treadmill two or three times a week.

In four months Herb lost fifteen pounds. His lipid profile was total cholesterol 205, triglycerides 120, HDL 42, and LDL 143. He had made progress: The total was down 25 points and the good HDL was up 7 points. But his LDL was still higher than it should have been. We discussed medication, but he said he would like to try diet a little longer. He was still eating a lot of cheese and some very rich cookies. Over the next two months he exercised almost every day, lost an additional five pounds, and switched to low-fat cookies and low-fat goat cheese.

At the end of the two months, Herb's LDL came in at 125 — an improvement of 40 points in six months. I told him to keep up the good work. He had reduced his risk of having a heart attack from way above average to very low. But his cholesterol would still need to be monitored carefully.

Nell

Nell was a sixty-two-year-old high school English teacher. Her father had died of a heart attack at age fifty-four, her mother of abdominal cancer at sixty-five. Nell had some blood vessel problems in her legs. She was moderately active, walking twenty to thirty minutes most days and gardening in the warm months. She avoided egg yolks and limited fats in her diet. Nell's cholesterol on her first physical in several years was 280 total, triglycerides 120, HDL 45, and LDL 215. Because of the high total and LDL cholesterol, she had a stress test, which was positive after brief exercise. Another test, a coronary arteriogram, showed almost total closure of one of Nell's main arteries, and she had an angioplasty to open it up.

Nell was started on the statin drug Lipitor (20 mg) to bring her cholesterol down. Within three months, her LDL cholesterol had fallen 90 points to 125. This would have been good enough for the average person, but not for someone with known coronary artery disease. Our target was to get the LDL under 100, so her Lipitor dose was raised to 40 mg. On this dose her LDL level fell to 88. The cardiologist and I felt we were giving her the best chance to reverse her disease.

Herb and Nell are typical examples: In one person with a moderate tendency to high cholesterol, diet and exercise suffice; in another with a severe elevation, medication is necessary.

What Is a Low-Cholesterol Diet?

If you're a careful reader of the newspapers, you know that in few areas of health is there less unanimity of opinion than in advice on diet. To begin with, reliable data are hard to come by. In large studies, for example, it's hard to verify that the participants really stick to the diets they say they do. Also, the press often focuses on a single study that runs counter to prevailing opinion. If you aren't an expert in the field, you don't know what to believe.

Let me try to simplify the matter. In this section, I'll describe in a few broad strokes a reasonable approach to dieting with the specific aim of lowering your cholesterol. Again, the information represents a compendium of advice from scientific studies and from my own experience of what patients are able to achieve. Let's begin with some background information.

Saturated Fat, Cholesterol, and Weight

First, you should know that two dietary products cause blood cholesterol to go up: saturated fat and cholesterol itself. Saturated fat sends blood cholesterol up in everyone and is a major culprit. Contrary to what most people think, however, cholesterol in food doesn't play a major role in raising blood cholesterol, nor does it raise blood cholesterol in everyone. Thus a diet to bring down blood cholesterol ought to consist of substantially less saturated fat and only moderately less food cholesterol.

FAT ISN'T ALL BAD

There are basically three kinds of dietary fat: saturated, monounsaturated, and polyunsaturated. Each of them affects your cholesterol levels in different ways, with different consequences for your health. The saturated fats — mostly animal fats or fats that are solid at room temperature, like butter — raise LDL cholesterol. Polyunsaturated fats such as corn, soybean, and safflower oil appear to lower LDL and so may actually be good for you. Monounsaturated fats such as olive and canola oil are the most beneficial; studies indicate that they lower LDL slightly and also raise HDL, the good cholesterol.

Second, you should understand that being overweight is a problem in itself. You won't help yourself merely by substituting carbohydrate calories for saturated fat calories. If you're overweight, you need to shed those extra pounds (see part 1, chapter 8, "Weight Problems").

Third, you should know that almost everyone who has high cholesterol has it partly because of diet and partly because of heredity. Herb's elevated cholesterol was mainly a result of his lifestyle, but his family history suggests that heredity may have been a minor factor. For others, heredity predominates, as it most likely did in Nell's case. In fact, I'm convinced that for many of my patients who have followed the most reasonable low-fat diet and still not achieved low-enough LDL, the failure stemmed from a hereditary predisposition. Like Nell, they needed medication.

Fourth, very few people stick to extremely low-fat, near-vegetarian diets like Dean Ornish's or the Pritikin diet. My sense is that these diets work well enough while you're at a deluxe spa, walking in the woods and eating tofu, bean sprouts, and vegetable soups; when you get back home, they're boring and practically impossible to maintain.

Fifth, people seem to fare better when they simply avoid troublesome foods rather than trying to estimate grams of fat or cholesterol for everything they eat. In my experience, very few if any patients can keep up a rigorous counting regimen.

High-Fat Foods
Too much fat in the diet is the major problem for most at-risk people. The general rule is to keep your fat intake under 30 percent of your calories, and your saturated fat intake lower than that — about 10 to 15 percent of your total calories. Saturated fats fall into three loose categories:

- Animal fat in beef, pork, lamb, and poultry (in both the poultry and the skin)
- Dairy fat in butter, whole milk, and hard cheese
- Coconut, palm, and palm kernel oils

Coconut, palm, and palm kernel oils, unlike most other vegetable oils, are saturated and are as bad or worse than animal or dairy fat. Many commercially baked products and snack foods are made with coconut or palm oil. Indeed, most cookies, pastries, doughnuts, crackers, potato chips, and other nibbles are soaking in these or the other saturated fats.

Some margarines start out as good fats (the polyunsaturates and monounsaturates) but because of processing become more like saturated fats. The "tub" oleo is much better than the stick form. Even the worst margarine is less harmful than butter, however.

All oil, even the good stuff, is high in calories, so if you need to lose weight, beware. Soaking your bread in olive oil may not directly raise your cholesterol, but it sure will pack on the pounds.

High-Cholesterol Foods
Although dietary cholesterol doesn't necessarily raise your blood cholesterol, for people with cholesterol problems, some foods very high in cholesterol are best avoided or restricted. These include egg yolks (egg whites have no cholesterol); organ foods such as liver, sweetbreads, or brains; and shellfish, especially shrimp (clams, oysters, and lobster contain less cholesterol).

Alcohol and Cholesterol
A small amount of alcohol — no more than two 3-ounce glasses of wine for men or one for women — can raise HDL cholesterol slightly. In my career I've seen so many health disasters from too much alcohol, and I've expended so much energy trying to get patients to cut down, that I'm reluctant to recommend even limited alcohol consumption. Besides, alcohol

---

SOME DIET TIPS

☐ Don't have more than six ounces of meat per day; red meat should be limited to two or three times a week. Be careful to choose lean cuts, and trim off the fat.

☐ Don't fry meat; broil it and let the juices run off. Avoid gravy.

☐ Take the skin off poultry before cooking.

☐ Don't eat prepared meats like bologna or salami; instead, choose tuna, chicken, or turkey for sandwiches.

☐ Use only skim milk, margarine or other butter substitutes, and low-fat yogurt; restrict your intake of cheese.

☐ Eat five or six servings of fruit or vegetables every day, and more if you like fresh produce.

☐ Most of your calories should come from complex carbohydrates like bread, pasta, peas, beans, and rice. Whole-grain products are the best.

---

is high in calories and makes weight loss more difficult. If you're slender and clearly in control of alcohol — if you're able to have a drink and then stop — alcohol may help your lipid profile. (See part 2, chapter 17, "Alcoholism and Alcohol Abuse.")

What If Dieting Doesn't Work?

One of the major breakthroughs in medical treatment in the past several years has been the introduction of the statin family of cholesterol-lowering drugs. These drugs block the formation of cholesterol in the liver and have been very effective in the vast majority of patients. Currently, there are several statin-type drugs available:

Mevacor (lovastatin)
Zocor (simvastatin)
Pravachol (pravastatin)
Baycol (cerivastatin)
Lipitor (atorvastatin)
Lescol (fluvastatin)

In my experience, Lipitor is the most effective and has essentially the same side effects as the others. The major side effects of statins are liver abnormalities and myositis, an inflammation of the muscles that can be severe but is rare. Generally, the liver problems are mild and reversible, but to be safe, liver function blood tests are done about three months after the drugs are started and then twice each year. Only about 2 percent of patients have had to stop statins because of liver problems. Minor side effects include headaches, insomnia, and intestinal problems such as gas, bloating, indigestion, and bowel irregularities.

If side effects are a problem, an alternative is one of the bile sequestrant drugs such as Questran (cholestyramine) and Colestid (colestipol). Cholesterol from the liver is secreted by way of bile into the intestines and then reabsorbed. These drugs work by trapping the cholesterol in the intestinal tract so it is excreted in the stool. Because they aren't absorbed, they don't cause any serious organ damage. The problem with these drugs is that they also "sequester" other substances and can keep other medications from being absorbed. They have to be given two or more times a day, so your drug dose timing can be very complicated. Also, they can cause serious constipation. Many people have to take stool softeners or bulk agents like bran or Metamucil (psyllium fiber) to maintain regular bowel movements.

Can HDL Really Be Raised?

An HDL level below 40 is worrisome no matter what your LDL. Vigorous exercise and moderate alcohol intake may bring it up slightly, but most doctors prescribe nicotinic acid, a form of niacin or vitamin B_6. This leads to uncomfortable facial flushing in most patients. The side effect can be lessened by taking aspirin and usually improves with time, but I have had many patients stop nicotinic acid because of the flushing. Liver damage is a much less frequent but more serious side effect, and has to be tested for. The drug should be discontinued if the liver tests become abnormal.

What about Triglycerides?

The other blood lipid that shows up in a cholesterol test is triglycerides. Triglycerides in the high normal range may be good because they help lower LDL. However, significant elevation of triglycerides is itself a risk. Doctors haven't yet agreed upon guidelines for when to start treating elevated triglycerides. Most laboratories list 175 or 200 as the upper "normal" level for triglycerides, but we don't know at exactly what level they become a risk in themselves. A recent study of patients in the Veterans Administration system shows that lowering triglycerides and raising HDL has a dramatic effect in reducing heart attacks, and the National Institutes of Health panel has suggested keeping triglycerides below 200.

I advise everyone with triglycerides over 250 to markedly limit sweets and be cautious with alcohol, and I strongly urge them to get their weight to the proper level. For patients whose triglycerides are above 250 and whose LDL isn't elevated, and who follow a proper diet and weight-loss regimen, I prescribe a triglyceride-lowering drug called Lopid (gemfibraozil). If the LDL is elevated also, I start with Lipitor or another statin and consider adding Lopid later. The two drugs together, Lopid and a statin, introduce a higher risk of liver and possibly muscle problems, so extra care and monitoring are required.

NEW BLOOD TESTS THAT PREDICT HEART RISKS

Recently, researchers have found that two blood tests in addition to the lipid profile can help predict the risk of atherosclerosis. The first measures the level of homocysteine, an amino acid that tends to promote the conversion of LDL cholesterol into an even more dangerous form. It is one of the easiest risks to correct: the B vitamin folic acid lowers it significantly. The other test measures the level of a recently discovered protein, C-reactive protein, which indicates the presence of inflammation somewhere in the body. Some theories hold that kidney, skin, or gum infections among others may play a role in the development of atherosclerosis. If your C-reactive protein level is up, consider it an incentive to treat other risk factors and to try to prevent or eradicate any infection. Even good dental hygiene to prevent gingivitis may be helpful in lowering this cardiac risk. High C-reactive protein should also prompt you to take aspirin daily.

If You're over Seventy-Five

We now know that no matter how old you are, correcting or eliminating risk factors — particularly smoking and high blood pressure — is beneficial. However, the data on lowering cholesterol in those past seventy-five and certainly past eighty-five are not quite as clear. At this stage, I think it's important to individualize treatment; no hard and fast rules can be set down. Generally, if you have atherosclerosis, keeping LDL around 100 is still a good idea. If you're overweight and carry other risk factors such as diabetes or high blood pressure, I would lean toward treatment as outlined above. If you have no risk factor other than age and if your HDL is high (a pattern seen in many older women), I would advise you to ignore LDL cholesterol.

I've seen some frail, underweight ninety-year-olds develop protein-calorie malnutrition partly because they thought eggs and meat were bad for them. There comes a time in life when common sense rather than adherence to general rules should tell you to eat up — anything you want — to avoid the life-threatening problems caused by too much weight loss. If you're eighty or older, ask your doctor about strict adherence to cholesterol rules; if you don't have vascular disease, you can probably pay more attention to keeping your weight and strength up than to cholesterol.

REMEMBER THIS

- Elevated LDL cholesterol is one of the most significant risk factors for atherosclerosis.
- You need to know your total cholesterol, HDL, and LDL levels.
- Guidelines can help you and your doctor decide on treatment.
- Change your diet first, but remember, diet doesn't always do the job of lowering LDL cholesterol. Many people find it hard to follow the extreme diet necessary to lower very high levels of LDL.
- If you don't meet your cholesterol targets after a reasonable trial on diet, talk to your doctor about starting medication.
- If you're overweight, calorie reduction as well as fat reduction is crucial.
- Targets for triglyceride reduction aren't firmly established, but very high levels should be treated.
- If you're over seventy-five or eighty, you may be able to relax cholesterol diet rules, but only if you don't have vascular disease or other significant risk factors.

CHAPTER 3

HIGH BLOOD PRESSURE

High blood pressure (hypertension) is one of the four major risk factors for all vascular diseases. A prominent factor in heart attacks and in narrowing of the blood vessels to the legs or kidneys, it is also the single most important risk factor for strokes and a significant cause of kidney failure. Recent data show that high blood pressure can lead to vascular dementia as well.

Roughly 60 percent of Americans over sixty have high blood pressure, about half of them women, half men. High blood pressure comes on earlier in African-Americans and is more severe and more prevalent in that population. It is the most common reason people over sixty visit their doctor. Despite the prevalence of this condition, a large number of people don't even know they suffer from it. After declining for several decades, the number of people untreated for high blood pressure crept up in the 1990s.

What Is High Blood Pressure?

Blood pressure is the pressure in the arterial side of the vascular system measured in millimeters of mercury. To measure blood pressure accurately you would have to put a needle attached to a pressure gauge into an artery itself, but the blood pressure cuff, if used properly, is an adequate measure. When your blood pressure is taken you get two figures: the top number, or systolic pressure, and the lower number, or the diastolic pressure. Systolic pressure reflects the force of the heartbeat and the elasticity or distensibility of the large and medium-sized arteries. Diastolic pressure reflects pressure or tension in the most distensible or contractile part of the vascular system — the tiniest arterioles that feed the circulatory system's smallest vessels, the capillaries. The arteriole walls are muscular and can expand and contract, and it is here that constant tension can cause diastolic high blood pressure.

For many years, our definition of high blood pressure was a systolic reading over 140 or a diastolic reading over 90. That has changed. Very large and carefully analyzed population studies have shown that an optimal blood pressure should be under 130/83. If you have diabetes, that should be even lower, 120/80, to protect the kidneys. Some data show that if there is

> **Did You Know?**
> Forty-nine percent of the reduction in death from heart attacks over the past twenty-five years derives from better blood pressure control. Even more striking, 58 percent of the reduction in death from strokes stems from detection and treatment of high blood pressure.

evidence of early kidney damage in a person with diabetes, the diastolic should be kept under 75.

New Standards for the Elderly

We have also corrected a mistaken belief that systolic pressure in older patients isn't important. Recent studies show that systolic pressure or the difference between systolic and diastolic pressure is even more important for older people than diastolic pressure, which used to be our biggest worry. If possible, your pressure should be kept under 130/80, although this can be harder to achieve in older people.

What Causes High Blood Pressure?

More than 95 percent of high blood pressure stems from essential hypertension. In this inherited condition, the biochemical mechanism controlling blood pressure is overactive and it goes up. The tiny, muscular arterioles end up in a constant state of contraction in response to a complicated interplay of certain chemicals produced by the liver and kidneys. The liver or kidneys can put out too much of these chemicals, the conversion of one of these chemicals to an active form can be too robust, or the arteries themselves can overreact to a given amount of hormone. In fact, in different people different factors may be at work, which can sometimes make diagnosis tricky.

Other things can make the tiny blood vessels tense, including:

☐ Fatigue
☐ Insomnia
☐ Too much salt
☐ Alcohol
☐ Adrenaline-type drugs

☐ Nonsteroidal anti-inflammatory drugs (NSAIDs) or other medications that cause the kidneys to retain salt.

About 5 percent of people with high blood pressure, often those with extremely high pressure, may have something wrong with a kidney or may have a tumor in the adrenal gland. Doctors only look for these unusual causes when the pressure is especially high or is not responsive to medication.

DON'T WAIT FOR SYMPTOMS

The most important lesson to remember about high blood pressure is that there are no symptoms until some organ damage has been done. Some people mistakenly think that headaches are symptoms of high blood pressure. Headaches only occur in extreme, life-threatening cases of high blood pressure. If you have the common symptoms of high blood pressure, it is late in the game — some organs are already damaged or malfunctioning. Get your blood pressure tested soon, before that happens.

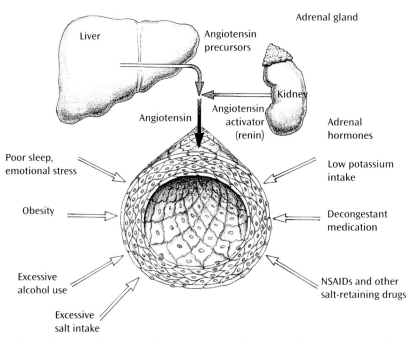

A distensible precapillary arteriole showing the wide variety of factors that can affect it. Arterioles, the smallest vessels capable of expanding and contracting, are responsible for most cases of high blood pressure.

How Does High Blood Pressure Wreak Havoc?

Elevated blood pressure tends to work in concert with high cholesterol or other irritants, like tar from cigarettes, to drive cholesterol into the walls of large and medium-sized arteries, causing them to narrow — the essential process of atherosclerosis. And if there is a congenital weak spot in the blood vessels of the brain, high pressure makes a rupture or aneurysm more likely. Also, in a vicious cycle, the constant state of tension in the tiniest vessels elevates pressure and the pressure in turn damages the vessels. So high blood pressure damages both the large arteries and the smallest blood vessels.

One way your doctor checks for signs of damage from high blood pressure is to look into the back of your eyes, where the small blood vessels are visible; he or she can see narrowing spasms and even tiny ruptures with small areas of bleeding in the retina. This is the only place in the body where the small vessels are visible, but we know that with sustained high blood pressure, the damage occurs elsewhere as well.

The two areas most seriously affected are the brain and the kidneys. The narrowing of the tiny blood vessels in the brain can cause small, asymptomatic strokes, which in the aggregate can cause dementia. An MRI (magnetic resonance imaging) scan of the brain of someone with longstanding hypertension will show a multitude of tiny areas where the brain hasn't received proper circulation. In the kidneys, damage to the tiny vessels can ultimately cause partial or total kidney failure.

If blood pressure is poorly controlled for a long time, the heart muscle may also be affected. Because it has to work harder it will thicken and dilate, raising the risk of congestive heart failure.

Getting Your Pressure under Control

One of the simplest, least expensive medical examinations is the blood pressure test. Yours should be updated and checked every time you go to the doctor for whatever reason. No person over sixty should go more than a year without a blood pressure check; if it is even borderline, it must be followed up.

The pressure should be taken with you sitting in a comfortable room that is not too cold. If your pressure is high, the test should be repeated in five minutes. Unless it is extremely high, I never start therapy based on readings from one visit. I have the patient return in a few days, and I only consider treatment if the pressure is up about the same level on the second test. Excitement, sleeplessness, or too much alcohol the previous day can create a false high reading.

WHITE COAT HYPERTENSION

It's a real thing for many people: apprehension about being in a doctor's office can artificially raise their blood pressure. If I suspect this in one of my patients, I arrange for the blood pressure to be checked at home or in some other comfortable setting.

If your blood pressure is elevated, the doctor should perform a cardio-gram or other test to evaluate heart size and function and should order a urine test and blood tests of kidney function to be sure no organ damage has occurred.

How Can You Lower Your Pressure?

Everyone with high blood pressure should make certain lifestyle changes.

- If you're overweight, go on a diet. Usually, losing ten or twelve pounds will bring the diastolic pressure down about eight points.
- Limit your salt intake.
- Consume potassium-rich foods. Bananas, citrus fruits, tomatoes, and potatoes are excellent sources of potassium.
- Limit alcohol to no more than two drinks a day if you're a man, and one a day if you're a woman. A drink is 1.5 ounces of spirits, 4 ounces of wine, or a 12-ounce beer.
- Try to alleviate stress in your job or family situation.
- Make sure you get enough rest at night.

Medication to Bring Pressure Down

If these measures don't lower your blood pressure, you need to start med-ication. A staggering number of blood pressure drugs are on the market — at least ninety-three different medications, far too many to cover here.

It's important to know what you can expect in the way of benefits and side effects from your medication, so be sure you know to which family your prescribed medication belongs. As with any therapy, your doctor will start slowly, often with weaker drugs, but will increase the dose or add a drug from another family if you need better results.

The common families of blood pressure drugs are:

- ACE (angiotensin-converting enzyme) inhibitors
- Beta blockers

☐ Calcium channel blockers
☐ ARBs (angiotensin receptor blockers)
☐ Thiazide diuretics
☐ Potassium-sparing diuretics
☐ Combined diuretics

This list doesn't include some of the older medications, which are occasionally used when the newer ones fail to benefit the patient or have untoward side effects.

ACE inhibitors. These are becoming the most frequently used group of drugs for hypertension. They work by blocking the conversion of inactive angiotensin, produced by the liver, to its active form. They are effective in lowering mild to moderately elevated pressure, but one or two more agents should be added to bring down very high pressure. ACE inhibitors are helpful in patients who also have congestive heart failure. The most common side effect is an irritative cough. If the medicine is working well people sometimes put up with the cough, but for most people it means having to switch to another drug. A hive-like skin rash can occur, and I've had five patients with a condition called angio-edema — allergic swelling around the lips and mouth — which can be severe. If you have angio-edema, the medicine has to be stopped and you may need antiswelling medication.

Beta blockers. These drugs dilate the small blood vessels. Beta blockers are reasonably powerful and are also an important part of the treatment of coronary disease and congestive heart failure. They can cause fatigue upon exertion or psychological depression, in which case they have to be stopped.

Calcium channel blockers. These drugs were introduced to treat angina because they dilate blood vessels of several sizes. Calcium channel blockers are moderately strong but in large studies have not proved all that effective in preventing the damage caused by hypertension. They come in several forms. Because the short-acting medications are less effective and perhaps deleterious, only the longer-acting drugs should be used. I prefer the other drug families.

ARBs. This is the newest family of blood pressure medicines. ARBs block the sites on the walls of the tiny blood vessels where the hormone angiotensin usually elevates pressure. These drugs have mild side effects but aren't very powerful. Most ARBs come packaged by themselves and also in a form mixed with a small amount of hydrochlorothiazide (*see below*), which makes them stronger. Many patients on ARBs need an additional drug.

Diuretics. These have been used to lower blood pressure for over forty years. The thiazide diuretics, specifically hydrochlorothiazide (HCTZ), are the most common. For mild hypertension these drugs can be used alone, but they are most frequently added in small amounts to other medications. A frequent side effect of diuretics is lowered potassium, so you may need to take a potassium supplement in pill form. If you're on a diuretic, your potassium blood levels need to be checked periodically.

Two other diuretics used to treat hypertension are triamterene and spironolactone. These are "potassium-sparing" diuretics — that is, they cause the potassium to go up rather than down. They often come mixed with HCTZ, so the potassium level still has to be monitored.

Following the Progress of Your Treatment

I find it much easier on patients if they get a blood pressure cuff and keep a record at home, bringing it to the office when they visit. If you can do this, it will make life easier and you'll be an active participant in your treatment.

A cuff with a stethoscope or a digital read-out machine can be obtained at any medical supply store. Most patients prefer the digital read-out machine, but be sure you get one that uses a cuff on the arm — finger-mounted devices are too inaccurate. You need to get a standard cuff (wide cuff if your arm is very large) and take it to the doctor's office where your technique can be observed and the cuff can be compared with the doctor's for accuracy. For people with widely varying blood pressure, or for those who may have white coat hypertension, special devices that automatically monitor pressure over the course of a twenty-four-hour period can be used at home.

Treating Blood Pressure in the Elderly

Recent studies have shown that tight control of high blood pressure in people past seventy is even more beneficial than control in younger people. The difference in the incidence of heart attacks and strokes between treated and untreated groups is more pronounced in the older population.

However, sometimes controlling blood pressure in older people is easier said than done.

One common problem in treating high blood pressure in the elderly, particularly high systolic blood pressure, is what doctors call labile (widely varying) hypertension or postural hypotension (low blood pressure when the patient stands). Blood pressure elevation in older patients tends to be systolic because the larger blood vessels are stiffer as we get older. This makes the older patient more prone to overreact to medication: it may take more to bring the pressure down, then the pressure drops so low it introduces the danger of fainting.

Ellen

Ellen was eighty-eight years old; she had had a coronary at age eighty-five and successful surgery for early colon cancer. Her blood pressure had been moderately elevated for several years, and she had tried several different blood pressure medications: ACE inhibitors, beta blockers, calcium channel blockers, and diuretics. Her pressure was only partially controlled, but she had three different episodes of fainting, all resulting in hospitalization for heart rhythm and blood pressure monitoring. In the hospital, she was taken off all medications and her blood pressure rose to 220/110 — very high. Ellen was cautiously put back on various medications, and her resting pressure was kept at about 160/90. At this level, her blood pressure would drop so low upon standing that she would have to be put back in bed.

Without treatment Ellen's blood pressure soared, and she showed signs of progressive kidney damage as a result. The blood vessels to the kidney were checked and found not to be narrowed (narrowing is sometimes a cause of severe high blood pressure). The kidney specialist and I had to compromise: We only partially treated her blood pressure, leaving it in the 170-80/95-100 range in spite of the kidney problem. To have further lowered the pressure would have left Ellen unable to stand and walk around. This is an extreme case, but I've had many patients in their eighties require similar treatment to avoid fainting spells.

Older patients with high blood pressure also have a much higher incidence of kidney disease, and too precipitous a reduction of blood pressure can lead to kidney failure. In these people, it is often necessary to compromise with less than perfect pressure control.

REMEMBER THIS

- High blood pressure is extremely common, affecting about 60 percent of older people. It is more frequent and severe in African-Americans.
- High blood pressure is a major risk factor for heart attacks, strokes, vascular dementia, and kidney failure.
- High blood pressure gives no warning. Everyone should have periodic blood pressure tests.
- Optimal blood pressure is below 130/83. The benefits of vigorously treating high blood pressure, particularly high systolic blood pressure, in older people are greater than for younger people.
- If your blood pressure is mildly elevated, weight loss, alcohol moderation, reduced dietary salt, increased dietary potassium, and a proper sleep schedule may return it to a safe level.
- If your blood pressure cannot be returned to normal, you should be on medication.
- Often a combination medication is more effective and safer than a single drug.
- Perfect blood pressure control may not be obtainable in people over eighty. A compromise is sometimes necessary to keep blood pressure as low as possible without introducing the risk of dizziness or fainting.

CHAPTER 4

DIABETES

Diabetes is the sixth leading cause of death in the United States and a contributing factor to many heart attacks and strokes. It is a risk factor for atherosclerosis in the larger and medium-sized blood vessels, and it causes a unique type of damage to tiny blood vessels that can result in blindness, kidney failure, and nerve damage. In fact, diabetes is the primary cause of blindness before age seventy-five, the main reason people have to undergo kidney dialysis, and a major cause of foot and leg amputations.

What Is Diabetes?

The pancreas, an elongated organ in the upper back part of the abdomen, has two functions. One is to secrete enzymes into the intestinal tract to help the body digest fat, starch, and protein. The other is to secrete the hormone insulin. Small islands of so-called beta cells scattered throughout the pancreas secrete the insulin, which enters the bloodstream and moves sugar from there into cells throughout the body, where it is used primarily for energy. Diabetes is an absence of insulin, or an abnormality in which the action of insulin is blocked and sugar cannot get into cells properly. In people with diabetes, blood sugar levels become higher than normal and may eventually exit the body in urine.

Did You Know?
A common medical problem in the United States, diabetes is particularly prevalent among African-Americans, Native Americans, and people of Mexican or Central American ancestry. About 16 million Americans have diabetes, and one-third of these cases go undiagnosed. The incidence of diabetes increases among people in their sixties and seventies.

The Two Types of Diabetes

There are two types of diabetes: type I, which used to be called juvenile-onset or insulin-dependent diabetes, and type II, which used to be called adult-onset or non-insulin-dependent diabetes.

Type I diabetes. In this form of the disease, beta cells in the pancreas that produce insulin are destroyed, resulting in too little or no insulin. This happens in children, teenagers, and young adults. Those affected are not usually overweight. How and why the beta cells are destroyed is not clear. Genetic factors, viral infections, and autoimmune destruction of the beta cells — in which the body's immune system attacks its own tissue — have been postulated; surgical removal of the pancreas can also cause type I diabetes. Many or most people with type I diabetes would die in a diabetic coma if they didn't take insulin.

Type II diabetes. This form of diabetes is entirely different. The beta cells produce enough insulin and may even produce a larger than usual amount, but one or more factors keep the insulin from being effective. Blood sugar cannot effectively enter the body's cells and rises to abnormally high levels, but because some does manage to get in, the condition almost never causes a diabetic coma. In rare cases, a so-called hyperosmolar coma can occur, when blood sugar skyrockets and the person becomes so dehydrated that he or she drifts into a confused stupor or coma; this is very unusual and doesn't come on as rapidly as a diabetic coma.

Because about 90 percent of Americans with diabetes, and almost all over the age of sixty, have type II, we'll limit our discussion of the effects of and treatment for diabetes to this condition.

The Insidious Effects of Type II Diabetes

The main threat of type II diabetes is long-term vascular problems. High sugar levels work in concert with high blood pressure, high cholesterol, or smoking to cause atherosclerosis in coronary arteries as well as in the arteries to the brain and the legs. People with type II diabetes have a higher incidence of resultant strokes and heart attacks. Also, poorly controlled blood sugar damages the body's tiny blood vessels, an effect that is unique to diabetes. When the damage occurs in the retina, it can cause blindness; in the kidneys, it can totally destroy the kidney, causing death or creating the need for dialysis; in the tiny blood vessels that supply nerves — the long nerves to the legs are most vulnerable — it can result in painful, burning feet or complete loss of sensation in the feet. Diabetic damage to the nerves going to the genital organs is one of the most frequent causes of erectile problems in middle-aged men (*see below*).

That's the bad news. The good news is that if diabetes is discovered and sugar levels are kept low with diet and medication, vascular disease progresses very slowly or not at all.

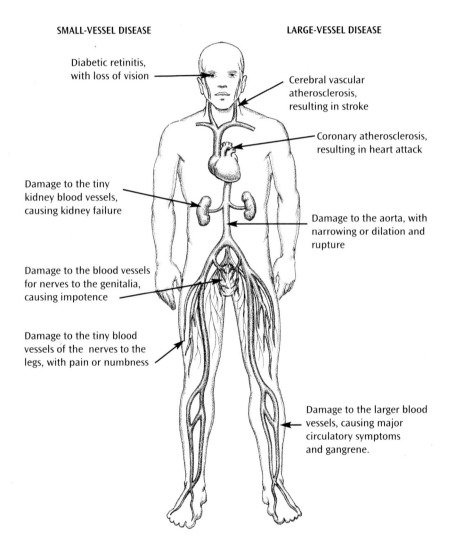

SMALL-VESSEL DISEASE

Diabetic retinitis, with loss of vision

Damage to the tiny kidney blood vessels, causing kidney failure

Damage to the blood vessels for nerves to the genitalia, causing impotence

Damage to the tiny blood vessels of the nerves to the legs, with pain or numbness

LARGE-VESSEL DISEASE

Cerebral vascular atherosclerosis, resulting in stroke

Coronary atherosclerosis, resulting in heart attack

Damage to the aorta, with narrowing or dilation and rupture

Damage to the larger blood vessels, causing major circulatory symptoms and gangrene.

The consequences of poorly controlled diabetes on small and large vessels.

How Do You Know If You Have Diabetes?

To diagnose diabetes, you need to have a fasting blood sugar test done in the morning before you've had anything to eat. I advise everyone over sixty to have a blood sugar test each year. If you aren't overweight and no parent, brother, or sister has had diabetes, then you can have it done every two years. Because you're most likely seeing the doctor for other reasons, adding a sugar test every year is easy. If you have one of the risk factors for diabetes besides your age, then you should definitely have yourself checked for this disease each year.

The risk factors for type II diabetes are:

- Age over forty-five
- Parent or sibling with diabetes
- Being overweight
- Sedentary lifestyle
- African-American, Native American, or Hispanic race
- High blood pressure
- High cholesterol
- Smoking

As I mentioned earlier, up to one-third of those with type II diabetes don't know they have it. The blood vessel damage can go on for a long time before overt symptoms occur. But there are some symptoms of moderately advanced type II diabetes: increase in frequency and volume of urine, thirst, and unexplained weight loss. Blood sugar levels rise so much that the sugar begins to come out in the urine, bringing more water with it.

Because vascular damage can occur months or years before sugar starts showing up regularly in the urine, urine tests for sugar are not good screening tests. The urine test gives only a rough approximation of the amount of sugar in the urine, and the blood level has to be quite high before any sugar shows up this way. The blood test is accurate and can show a very small, quantified rise in the sugar level.

What Happens Next?

If your fasting blood sugar level is elevated, the test should be repeated to confirm the result, and a test called glycohemoglobin should be done to help quantify the problem. Glycohemoglobin (or hemoglobin AIC) is a chemical whose levels can tell how much your red blood cells have been affected by the high sugar. The test gives an excellent estimate of sugar levels over the previous six to twelve weeks. A significantly elevated level will confirm the diagnosis. This test is even more useful in following treatment progress after diagnosis.

If your glycohemoglobin is normal or borderline and the diagnosis is still uncertain, you can have an oral glucose tolerance test, in which you're given a measured amount of glucose (sugar) by mouth, followed by blood glucose tests at standard time intervals. This test has pluses and minuses. Though much more sensitive than a fasting blood glucose test, it renders a high degree of false positives (readings that suggest a problem when there isn't one). If, for example, you've been on a reasonably low-carbohydrate diet and then take an unusually large sugar load, your glucose tolerance may suggest diabetes even though you don't have a problem.

When the diagnosis is uncertain but I suspect a patient might have diabetes, I put him or her on a weight-loss, moderate-carbohydrate, diabetes-type diet, then periodically recheck blood sugar levels two hours after a standard meal. Then if they're elevated, or if the glycohemoglobin moves up, I make a diagnosis of diabetes.

Getting Type II Under Control

To bring the disease under control, everyone with type II diabetes should:

- Lose weight if he or she is overweight. (If you're diagnosed with type II, chances are greater than 80 percent that you're overweight.) A deficit of 500 calories a day is a good diet — that will allow you to shed a pound every week.
- Start a regular exercise program. Many experts advise thirty minutes three or four times a week. I advise at least thirty minutes every day. Activity helps keep weight down and creates a steady calorie demand that facilitates accurate assessment of the effectiveness of diet and any medication.
- Learn a proper diabetic diet. It's usually best to start with a dietitian who can look at your weight and activity level and give you a reasonable daily diet prescription. Every diabetic diet should include:
  Carbohydrates (primarily starches, but also some fruit and an occasional sweet). These should account for 45 to 60 percent of your calories. The starches should be in the form of whole-grain cereals and bread, which enable the body to absorb sugar more evenly.

Restricted saturated fat and possibly an increase in unsaturated fat. You must lower your cholesterol.

Scheduled meals and planned meal sizes. These measures will help you distribute carbohydrate and caloric intake evenly throughout the day, or correlate your eating with your exercise and caloric needs. Eating most of your calories at dinner throws off the program and can be dangerous if you're on medication, as most people with diabetes are.

Many people who are overweight or sedentary can stave off the need for medication by following proper diet and exercise programs. However, a significant number of people with type II diabetes also need medication. If you have to start medication, you'll also need closer monitoring. And that means you'll have to enter into a partnership with your doctor.

HOME MONITORING

If you've been diagnosed with type II diabetes, you'll probably need to use a home glucose monitor, which you can get from your doctor's office or a diabetes teaching program at a hospital. They include a sharp stylette for pricking your fingertip and a paper test strip for collecting the drop of blood; a machine then gives you a digital reading of your glucose level. Test monitoring strips can be expensive, but most health insurance covers them. The frequency and timing of testing will depend on how severe your problem is and what degree of control you have over it.

Oral Diabetic Medications

Most type II diabetes can be controlled with oral medications. There are several families of oral agents, each of which acts a little differently to overcome the factors making insulin less effective.

Sulfonylureas

Oral therapy usually starts with one of five drugs.

Diabinese (chlorpropamide) or Orinase (tolbutamide). These two drugs, the first to be used for diabetes, are less powerful than newer drugs but rarely cause hypoglycemia (severely low blood sugar).

Amaryl (glimepiride), DiaBeta (glyburide), or Glucotrol (glipizide). These three are newer and more powerful than the older products, but can cause hypoglycemia.

Biguanides

The drugs in this family can cause kidney damage and should be restricted if you already have kidney damage. They can also cause a severe metabolic condition called lactic acidosis. They must be stopped if you're having an X ray or scan using a contrast dye.

Glucophage (metformin). This excellent medication, usually used as a second drug, is not as likely to cause hypoglycemia.

Thiazolidinediones

Actos (pioglitazone) or Avandia (rosiglitazone). These two new agents help the body utilize glucose but should be saved for unusual cases that can't be controlled on the sulfonylureas or Glucophage. One drug in this family, Rezulin, has been taken off the market because of several deaths from liver failure. Liver function has to be monitored closely on these drugs. In general, when my diabetic patients aren't well controlled on sulfonylureas or Glucophage, I refer them to a diabetic specialist before moving to Actos, Avandia, or one of the next two families.

Glucose absorption blockers

Precose (acarbose) or Glyset (miglitol). These work on the digestion of sugar in the intestinal tract, causing glucose to be absorbed more slowly and evenly so that the body won't be overwhelmed trying to move glucose into cells. They are new drugs and most internists haven't had much experience with them. Bloating and diarrhea have been such troublesome side effects that I and many of my colleagues don't use them regularly.

Meglitinides

Prandin (repaglinide). This newest diabetes medication acts like the sulfonylureas to stimulate insulin secretion by the pancreas. It has to be taken before each meal. Though promising, Prandin hasn't been used enough to enable physicians to confirm its effectiveness over long periods.

When Insulin Must Be Taken

No matter how closely they follow their diet and how diligent they are with their medications, many of my patients with type II diabetes have to start taking insulin. This is much more likely for African-Americans with diabetes.

If your sugar levels aren't being controlled, you should start on insulin either alone or added to oral drugs. There are several forms of insulin, mainly differing in their duration of action. Regular insulin is relatively fast-acting with short duration, while NPH insulin is slower-acting with longer duration. Mixtures of regular and NPH insulin are common.

Many people, particularly older people, dread the prospect of injecting themselves with insulin, and the switch from oral agents to insulin or the addition of insulin is a greater psychological blow than the initial diagnosis of diabetes. This doesn't have to be the case. With careful attention to dose and technique, taking insulin can be a very safe and easily accepted part of your daily routine.

What Are the Goals of Treatment?

Ideally, the goal of treatment is to keep your blood sugar levels as close to normal as possible. You can tell whether you're achieving your goal by way of glucose levels tested on your home monitor (just before a meal) and glycohemoglobin levels tested during periodic visits to the doctor.
Here's how to assess your blood glucose just before a meal:
  □ Normal: under 110
  □ Acceptable treatment goal: between 80 and 120
You need to adjust medications if your blood glucose is under 80 or over 140.

Here's how to assess your glycohemoglobin:
  □ Normal: under 6
  □ Acceptable treatment goal: under 7
You need to adjust medications if your level is 8 or above.

You should keep a daily record of your glucose readings and take them with you to the doctor or the diabetes specialist. He or she will do the glycohemoglobin test in the office. Because glycohemoglobin tests are more accurate, I rely mostly on them in advising treatment change.

Hypoglycemia

Hypoglycemia, or low blood sugar, is one of the most common problems in the treatment of diabetes. This condition develops much more commonly in people who have to take insulin, but it can develop in people on oral agents only. In my experience, the newer, stronger sulfonylureas (Amaryl, DiaBeta, and Glucotrol) are more likely than the older agents and more likely than Glucophage to cause low blood sugar, but anyone on any medication can develop it.

The symptoms of hypoglycemia are twofold. When blood sugar first drops, the body puts out adrenaline so you feel shaky, hungry, or anxious, and you might perspire. Later, after sugar has remained low, the brain begins to suffer, and confusion, somnolence, or unconsciousness can result.

Any of these symptoms should be recorded in your diabetic logbook and reported to your doctor. Many people with diabetes who are prone to hypoglycemic episodes have glucose or some type of sugar bar or juice available at all times to use in case symptoms suggesting hypoglycemia occur. The most frequent causes of hypoglycemia in my type II patients are late or missed meals or irregular exercise. If you're on medication for diabetes, you have to eat regular, properly spaced meals consisting of approximately the same amount of calories every day, and the amount of exercise you do should be similar from day to day. Exercise burns up glucose and can throw you into hypoglycemia if you suddenly increase your body's demand for sugar.

Follow the Rules!

I've had several patients on insulin get into trouble because they didn't follow the rules about spacing meals and maintaining regular exercise. One woman got no exercise six days a week, then would do several hours of yard work or play a long tennis match on the other day. One day, after exercising and missing a meal, she had a hypoglycemic reaction that resulted in an auto accident. Her driver's license was suspended. Don't let that happen to you — follow the rules.

Complications

All treatment of type II diabetes is directed toward preventing complications, and we know that close control is effective in preventing or postponing most of the vascular complications. But many people either can't achieve perfect control, or go so long with no control or inadequate treatment that they ultimately develop complications.

Damage to the small blood vessels in the eye is a dangerous possibility. Every person with diabetes should have an eye exam once a year. If there is evidence of damage, the use of lasers to coagulate ruptured vessels may help.

Because diabetes can block both the large vessels in the legs and the tiny vessels in the feet, foot wounds heal poorly and as a result often become infected. Any pressure sore, corn, or ingrown toenail should be seen by a podiatrist or at a medical center specializing in foot care for diabetes patients. Care in nail trimming and comfortable shoe selection is essential.

Nerve pain in the legs often occurs with longstanding diabetes. Pain or burning, particularly at night, can be a problem. These symptoms may respond somewhat to better control if the diabetes has been poorly maintained, but much of the pain will be permanent. A small dose of amitriptyline at bedtime often helps.

RECOMMENDATIONS FOR ALL DIABETICS

All diabetics should get:

- ☐ Annual eye exams
- ☐ Annual flu shots and a pneumonia vaccine every five years
- ☐ Periodic urine tests for evidence of protein, which indicates kidney damage
- ☐ Careful foot care

Flu shots and pneumonia vaccinations are important because diabetics are more susceptible to severe infections. A urine test that shows even a tiny amount of protein called albumin (microalbumin) in the urine is the first sign of kidney damage. In that case, an ACE inhibitor to lower blood pressure may protect the kidneys. The blood pressure goals for diabetics are lower than for the general population. The new recommendation for optimal blood pressure control for the general population is under 130/83 (see part 1, chapter 3, "High Blood Pressure"). For those with diabetes, however, the recommendation is under 120/80, and if you have protein in the urine or are African-American, it is 120/75.

If you have diabetes, make sure it is well controlled. If you're at risk for diabetes, be sure to get tested regularly — it can add years to your life. In the past ten years evidence for the significant benefit of carefully controlling diabetes has become firmly established. With the equipment available today for home monitoring, you and your doctor can be partners in care.

REMEMBER THIS

- Type II diabetes is a common problem in older Americans. Untreated, it can lead to serious vascular problems.
- Age, obesity, inactivity, family history, and being African-American, Native American, or Hispanic are risk factors.
- You should have a fasting blood sugar test every year if you're over sixty, particularly if you have one of the risk factors. Many diabetics — perhaps one-third — don't get treatment.
- Every overweight diabetic needs to lose weight, exercise regularly, and stay on a diet. Most require oral medication.
- If oral medications do not result in good control, you need to go on insulin.
- Home glucose monitoring as well as recording blood sugar levels and symptoms of hypoglycemia are important tools for control.
- Regular eye exams, extremely close blood pressure control, prompt attention to foot problems, and flu and pneumonia vaccinations help prevent complications.

CHAPTER 5

SMOKING: A DEADLY ADDICTION

Smoking, the major preventable cause of death in the developed world, is responsible for about 430,000 deaths in the United States each year. Despite the mountain of evidence that smoking is bad for the health, some 45 million Americans smoke — roughly 28 percent of men and 23 percent of women. The only good news the statistics reveal is that while the percentage of people who start smoking in their teens has stayed about the same over the past thirty years, the percentage of middle-aged and older people who smoke has declined.

Smoking is an addiction associated with both physiological symptoms of withdrawal and psychological dependence.

What Causes the Addiction?

Tobacco contains the chemical nicotine, which after being absorbed by the lungs is rapidly transported into the bloodstream and then to the brain. There it acts on chemical receptors called nicotine cholinergic receptors, producing a pleasant sensation. After prolonged use of tobacco, a smoker develops more nicotine cholinergic receptors and needs more nicotine to produce the sensation. Soon the smoker begins to feel bad without nicotine in the bloodstream. After just a few hours

Did You Know?
Large tobacco companies have been aware of the addictive properties of nicotine for a long time. Not only did they not publicize the facts, but they may have manufactured cigarettes in ways to make people more addicted. This is the major reason for the massive monetary settlements that have been imposed on tobacco companies in several big lawsuits.

without nicotine, the person may become agitated and restless, find it difficult to concentrate, develop a craving for food, feel a sense of foreboding, and suffer insomnia and even depression. No longer does the smoker only seek the minor pleasure of smoking; now the body needs to smoke. Nicotine addiction is similar to addiction to cocaine or opium, except that withdrawal isn't as severe.

The Damage Smoking Does

Some of what I say in the following paragraphs may seem repetitive, but to convince you of the problems you may have if you're still a smoker, I'm going to review the statistics about smoking and the problems it causes. Then we can turn to the benefits of stopping and how to stop.

Cardiovascular Disease

From the point of view of numbers, cardiovascular disease is the single greatest health problem caused by smoking. Heart attacks, strokes, and blockage of the blood vessels to the legs and pelvic area are all much more common in smokers. Smoking causes about 20 percent of deaths from coronaries, though an exact percentage is difficult to arrive at because people often have other risk factors. I've had a few patients with no other major risk factors who died of a coronary in their fifties because of heavy smoking.

The toxins in cigarettes make arterial plaque build up more rapidly in the heart. They probably do this by injuring and roughening the arterial wall, setting the stage for tiny blood clots and cholesterol accumulation. These toxins not only help clog the vessels, they also cause the vessels to go into spasms, make them less responsive to heart medication, and lower oxygen levels in the blood — all of which increases the likelihood of a heart attack.

That's the bad news. The good news is that much of the effect of smoking on the blood vessels is reversible. If you stop smoking, in a year your risk of a vascular event is practically that of a nonsmoker!

Chronic Obstructive Pulmonary Disease (COPD)

About 80 percent of chronic bronchitis, emphysema, and other conditions that obstruct the body's airways are caused by smoking. Any one of these conditions — collectively known as chronic obstructive pulmonary disease (COPD) — can make life miserable. COPD is the fourth most common cause of death.

Chronic bronchitis. Chronic bronchitis is a blockage of the airways due to excessive mucus buildup; the buildup often results from cigarette smoke irritating the cells that line the bronchial tree. A chronic cough is a hallmark, but the most troublesome symptom is shortness of breath. Secondary infections of the bronchial tree are frequent — some people seem to stay infected almost all winter. Virtually all cases of chronic bronchitis stem from smoking.

Emphysema. Emphysema refers to destruction of the tiny air passages and the microscopic sacs — the alveoli — where air in the lungs enters the bloodstream. An inherited disorder may lead to emphysema in some people who have not smoked, but people who smoke heavily can get emphysema whether they have that tendency or not. People with the tendency (deficiency of alpha 1 antiprotease) develop severe emphysema very early in life if they smoke.

Chronic bronchitis is substantially reversible in people who stop smoking. Often the cough is better or gone in two to three weeks, and breathing improves in a few months. Emphysema is a different matter. Unfortunately, the lung tissue is destroyed and cannot be replaced. For most people, though, stopping smoking does halt progression of lung destruction.

Asthma. Asthma, though not directly caused by smoking, is made substantially worse by it. For this reason, asthmatics as a group tend not to smoke.

Severe bronchial infections. Even in people with no significant chronic bronchitis, emphysema, or asthma, smoking leads to a much higher incidence of severe bronchial infections each winter.

Cancer and Smoking

The first major publicized health rap against smoking came in 1962 with Surgeon General Luther Terry's report on the causal relationship between smoking and lung cancer. Since then, some people have willfully ignored this and all the other publicized health problems associated with tobacco, rationalizing to themselves that they'll never get cancer, or they'll take their chances, or, if they develop a cough, they'll get X rays and detect it early. Believe me, it's usually too late for a cure by the time lung cancer is detected.

Sobering Statistics

If lung cancer were the only bad outcome of smoking, it would still be reason to kick the habit. Lung cancer, numerically the third worst problem associated with smoking after vascular disease and COPD, takes a horrendous toll. It is the leading cause of cancer death in men and women. In 1998 alone, about 93,000 men and 67,000 women died of lung cancer. Prostate cancer in men and breast cancer in women are more common than lung cancer, but the survival rate with lung cancer is so poor — 10 to 15 percent — that more people die from it. People who are heavy cigarette smokers (over a pack a day) have about eighteen times more lung cancer risk than nonsmokers. Lung cancer does occur in nonsmokers, but very rarely.

Vocal cord cancer is about fourteen times more frequent in smokers, and cancer of the mouth or upper throat is twenty-five times more common in smokers. Cigar and pipe smoking are major risk factors for mouth and throat cancer — with men outpacing women for risk.

Several types of cancer in other parts of the body, where the link is often to tobacco carcinogens in the blood rather than to smoke itself, are much more numerous in smokers. Cancer of the esophagus is eight times more prevalent in smokers. Leukemia and cancer of the bladder, pancreas, kidney, and stomach are all almost twice as likely to occur in smokers. Just recently, a significant risk for squamous cell cancer, the second most common type of skin cancer, has been associated with smoking.

Overall, smoking is responsible for about 30 percent of cancer deaths!

Quit Now, Not Later

One of the saddest scenarios in my practice, and it has happened many times, is telling patients I think they may have lung cancer. Often this comes after years of me warning them to stop smoking. They come in with a cough or some vague wheezing or discomfort in the chest or bronchial area, and a tumor shows up on the X ray. Typically, I ask them if they're smoking and they inform me that they stopped — *just the week before*. Too late for them, and too late for me to remonstrate — that only adds guilt to the tragic news.

Why You Should Kick the Habit

To kick the habit, you have to be very motivated. A lot of smokers past the age of sixty say, "Doctor, I've already done the damage and I'm getting too old to try and quit. What good will it do me?"

OTHER PROBLEMS FROM SMOKING

Besides the big three — vascular disease, COPD, and cancer — other health problems can develop from smoking. Smoking accelerates osteoporosis, and low thyroid is more common in women who smoke. It also increases the likelihood of erectile problems in men, an effect probably associated with smoking-related vascular disease. Last but not least, smoking makes a person look bad: it markedly increases skin wrinkling. I can look at a gray, wrinkled middle-aged woman and know she is a heavy smoker — she appears fifteen to twenty years older than her non-smoking peers.

The answer is, an enormous amount of good, even if you've been a heavy smoker for years. A pack-year means you smoke on average about a pack a day for a year. A sixty-year-old man who has smoked two packs a day since age twenty-five has seventy pack-years — needless to say, there aren't many sixty-year-olds around who have chalked up seventy pack-years. Most people who still smoke in their sixties are three-quarters to one pack a day smokers; they still run a great statistical risk.

If you stop smoking, your risk of vascular disease approaches that of a nonsmoker after about a year. If you have chronic bronchitis, that will improve dramatically even after a few weeks. Emphysema won't improve, but the rate of further lung damage will slow or stop, and symptoms won't worsen. Because chronic bronchitis and emphysema often occur together, you may well see some symptom improvement.

The reduction in risk for lung cancer is not as dramatic as that for vascular disease, but over ten to fifteen years, risk decreases from eighteen times to two times that of nonsmokers, moving lung cancer from a very common disease to an uncommon one.

Some people use fear of weight gain as a reason not to stop smoking. On average, people gain seven pounds when they stop. The downside health implications of this are minuscule compared to what you gain from stopping smoking. The weight can be slowly taken off later on anyway.

How You Can Kick the Habit

Okay, you're convinced — but you've tried to stop in the past and failed. How can you do it now?

Though it's not easy to stop an addiction to nicotine, it is possible, and there are several ways of achieving success.

Cold Turkey or Gradual Cessation?

First, you can stop cold turkey. I've had a few patients through the years who, having finally convinced themselves that smoking was really bad, stopped all at once and were somehow able to tolerate the withdrawal effects long enough to get over the physiological addiction. But they're in the minority, and as people get older the cold turkey approach seems even more difficult.

The second method is simple withdrawal: conscientiously and carefully reducing the number of cigarettes per day over a period of several weeks until you're off them altogether. For example, if you're a pack a day smoker, you go to fifteen cigarettes a day for three weeks, then to ten for three weeks, then to five cigarettes for three weeks, then stop — a two-month withdrawal program. Some of my patients have managed to quit this way, though others say it actually takes more willpower and only prolongs withdrawal symptoms. In recent years, I've recommended cold turkey and gradual cessation only to those patients who were very motivated to stop and didn't want to take medication.

A WORD OF CAUTION

Although you may think you're doing the right thing, switching to a low-nicotine cigarette may actually be a move in the wrong direction. Tobacco smoke not only contains nicotine, which causes the addiction, but also several hundred other chemicals, many of which are toxic and cause heart and lung disease and cancer. On a low-nicotine brand, you may actually smoke more to maintain the blood nicotine level that keeps you from feeling bad — and thus pump more toxins into your body!

Medications for Withdrawal and Treatment of Withdrawal Symptoms

In the past few years, two medicinal approaches have become available to help ease withdrawal symptoms. The first is a nicotine substitute in the form of nicotine chewing gum, nicotine nasal spray, and most recently, nicotine skin patches. The patches come in three sizes, and the program of withdrawal should be planned to last three or four months after you initially stop smoking.

The other approach is to calm down the hungry nicotine cholinergic receptors. Zyban (bupropion) is the drug used most often. Prescribed as an antidepressant under the name Wellbutrin, it has been around for several years but has only been recommended as an aid to tobacco withdrawal in the last three years. My patients have had the most success with it, though the side effects, which include sleeplessness and agitation, resemble withdrawal symptoms. Some doctors use both Zyban and nicotine patches, but the dosing can be a little tricky.

In any event, if you are still smoking, work with your doctor to devise a plan to get over your addiction — and follow up with him or her if you're having problems with the program. Recently, with these newer approaches, I've achieved a 50 percent success rate.

REMEMBER THIS

- Smoking is the single greatest cause of preventable death in the United States — almost a half million people die every single year from smoking-related illnesses.
- Cigarette smoking is a chemical addiction because of the effect of nicotine on the brain.
- Smoking puts you at greatly increased risk for heart attacks, strokes, chronic bronchitis, emphysema, and several types of cancer. Smokers are eighteen times more likely to get lung cancer than nonsmokers.
- Stopping smoking, even past age sixty, markedly reduces your risk of getting diseases associated with smoking. Within a year the vascular risk lessens, and chronic bronchitis improves in a few weeks.
- Nicotine itself is not harmful, just addicting. There are scores of other toxins in smoke, however, that can damage the body.
- The use of Zyban in particular and of nicotine substitutes in the form of gum, a nasal spray, or a patch has improved the success rate for people who want to stop smoking.

CHAPTER 6

CANCER

Cancer is a dreaded word that conjures up images of tumors invading bodily organs and ultimately causing painful and degrading death. Along with Alzheimer's disease and disabling stroke, cancer is the disease most feared by my patients. It accounts for about one-fourth of all deaths in the United States.

A few types of cancer are much more common in younger people, cervical cancer and testicular cancer among them. On the whole, however, cancer becomes much more prevalent as people age. Older cells seem more susceptible to the environmental and hereditary factors that can cause malignancy.

Cancer treatment includes surgical removal, radiation therapy, chemotherapy, and immunological and hormone manipulation to slow the growth of tumors. If you're not diagnosed early enough for surgery, the other treatments won't be nearly as effective, though they may send you into remission for a long time. In this chapter I discuss each of the most common types of cancer, what can be done to prevent them, and a program of surveillance to detect them early enough for optimum therapy.

Men, Women, and Cancer

For men, three types of cancer — prostate, lung, and colorectal — account for more than half of all cases and more than half of cancer deaths. Prostate cancer occurs most frequently, but lung cancer causes the most deaths. Prostate cancer is not as relentlessly progressive and in most men is amenable to therapy. Lung cancer, on the other hand, has an extremely high death rate. Until recently there was no satisfactory method for early detection of lung cancer, and the response to therapy in later stages was poor. Despite the dismal statistics, we have a very good chance of nearly eradicating lung cancer: well over 90 percent of lung cancer cases are caused by smoking, a habit that can be kicked.

For women, the predominant types of cancer, and the most common causes of cancer death, are breast, lung, and colorectal cancer. The statistics for breast cancer in women are the same as those for prostate cancer in men. Breast cancer is by far the most common type of cancer affecting women, but because of good methods for early detection and excellent modes of therapy, it causes far fewer deaths than lung cancer.

Once a diagnosis of cancer is made, treatment options are highly individualized and should be carefully reviewed with your primary care physician and the consulting surgeon or oncologist (cancer specialist). Because prostate and breast cancer are so prevalent, and because many of my patients have received contradictory or perplexing advice concerning them, I'll summarize treatment options for them first.

> **Did You Know?**
> Experts in the field of cancer epidemiology believe we can reduce the number of cancer deaths by more than half through:
> - Primary prevention — doing things that may prevent cancer, and avoiding things that cause cancer. Stopping smoking is an example of primary prevention.
> - Secondary prevention — getting regular screening for early detection of cancer, before it has a chance to spread. Detecting a breast mass on a mammogram, making a surgical cure possible, is an example of secondary prevention.

Lung Cancer

The major cause of cancer death for both men and women is also the most preventable. People who have never smoked rarely get lung cancer. If there were no smokers, the incidence of lung cancer would be way down. Lung cancer is about eighteen times more common in smokers than in nonsmokers.

You can see from the charts that the number of cases of lung cancer and the number of lung cancer deaths are about the same. In other words, the outlook for survival from lung cancer is dismal — testimony to the fact that we don't yet have an effective method for detecting lung cancer in its early, potentially curable stage. Over 85 percent of people diagnosed with lung cancer die within five years of diagnosis.

A WORD TO SMOKERS

Even if you've smoked for many years, if you stop now your chances of getting lung cancer will decline with each year that passes. (You'll also immediately lessen your risk of vascular disease.) Your risk of getting lung cancer will never be as low as for someone who has never smoked, but rather than eighteen times the risk of a nonsmoker, after five to ten years you'll run about twice the risk of a nonsmoker — moving you from high to low risk. If you're smoking, there is nothing more important for your health than to stop (see part 1, chapter 5, "Smoking: A Deadly Addiction").

Detecting Lung Cancer

For years, we've used periodic chest X rays on smokers or former smokers in an effort to detect so-called coin lesions, small tumors the size of a nickel or dime. But X-ray screening has been so ineffective that many cancer epidemiologists question its value. Typically, by the time cancer is detected on an X ray, it has spread too much to be cured by surgery. This is probably because many cases of lung cancer start at the root of the bronchial tree and are obscured on X rays by the heart or other large structures in the middle portion of the chest. Furthermore, one form of lung cancer, small cell, spreads so widely and rapidly that an X ray almost never catches it in time.

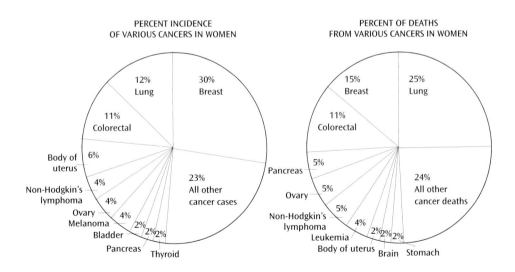

Adopted from estimates from The American Cancer Society for 2000.
Total cases of cancer: 600,400
Number of deaths: 268,100

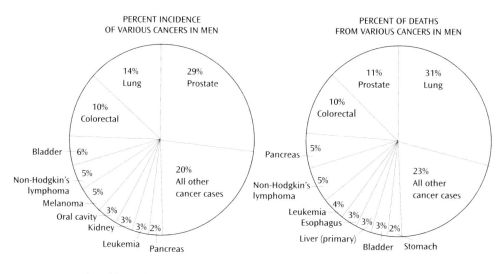

PERCENT INCIDENCE
OF VARIOUS CANCERS IN MEN

PERCENT OF DEATHS
FROM VARIOUS CANCERS IN MEN

Adopted from estimates from The American Cancer Society for 2000.
Total cases of cancer: 619,700
Number of deaths: 284,100

In the last two years, a new method of screening has evolved using spiral CT (computerized tomography) imaging (spiral because of the way the machine moves around the body as the scan is done). So far, the people evaluated by spiral CT scan have been over fifty with at least a ten-year history of smoking. Spiral CTs can detect nodules in the lung as small as two or three millimeters. Some experts are concerned that this method generates so many false positives (small, suspicious nodules that turn out not to be cancer) that a great number of unnecessary and potentially harmful surgical procedures will be performed. Proponents counter that careful evaluation by an expert team specializing in the technique — along with close follow-up on the smallest questionable nodules before biopsy or surgery is attempted — can markedly reduce unnecessary procedures. Spiral CT scanning is in its infancy, but if I'd been a smoker for many years I'd be the first in line to get one.

A WORD OF CAUTION

Don't let the possibility of a technique that can detect early lung cancer serve as a bizarre rationalization to continue smoking. The spiral CT scan will never replace primary prevention, and cigarettes can kill you in a lot of other ways than just by causing lung cancer.

Cancer of the Prostate Gland

Prostate cancer is the most prevalent cancer in men, but because treatment often cures it, and because prostate cancer tends to progress slowly, many men with this type of cancer die of something else; in fact, less than one in five men with prostate cancer dies of it. We don't know much about risk factors for prostate cancer and haven't, as with lung cancer, hit upon a definitive cause. What we do know is that male hormones increase the likelihood of prostate cancer. Men who have a congenital absence of testosterone don't get prostate cancer, and removing or blocking the effect of testosterone can slow progression of the disease. The only practical value of this knowledge in diagnosis and prevention is that any man who is contemplating taking testosterone or a similar androgen drug should have careful prostate cancer screening.

> **Did You Know?**
> African-American men and men who have a father or brother with prostate cancer run a higher risk of this disease and tend to develop it earlier. No major, known reversible risk factors have been identified. Japanese-American men have a higher incidence of prostate cancer than men in Japan, so there may be some dietary connection, such as the amount of fat, or the amount or type of vitamin A or D, consumed. This is one of the few types of cancer where smoking doesn't seem to be a major risk factor.

Because prostate cancer is not preventable, the major strategy for reducing the risk of death is thorough, early diagnosis and definitive treatment. If you wait for the symptoms of prostate cancer — pain in the low back, pelvis or thighs, blood in the urine or semen, or a sudden worsening of urinary symptoms — to linger, the disease will almost always advance beyond the point where it can be eradicated. (These symptoms are nonspecific and much more likely to be caused by something other than prostate cancer.)

Testing for Prostate Cancer

Your doctor has two main ways to detect prostate cancer. One is by feeling a nodule or areas of firmness in the prostate during a digital rectal exam, which should be part of your routine physical. However, by the time the nodule is palpable, the disease may have spread beyond the surrounding capsule of the prostate gland. The second detection method, which has revolutionized the diagnosis of prostate cancer, is the prostatic-specific antigen (PSA) blood test. PSA is a chemical present in low levels in all normal prostate glands. Elevated PSA levels in the bloodstream usually signal that something is awry in your prostate gland.

Significant elevation may point to either cancer or — if the value rises and then plummets quickly — prostatitis, an infection of the gland. If your PSA is over 4 — or if it is under 4 but has gone up over 0.75 units, say from 2.5 to 3.4, in a year — then you may have prostate cancer. Some men with very large, benign prostate glands — a common condition called benign prostatic hyperplasia (BPH) — may have moderately elevated PSA. About 25 percent of men with a PSA level between 4 and 10 have prostate cancer; the number jumps to 65 percent for a sustained PSA level over 10.

A WORD OF CAUTION

Make sure when you're screened for prostate cancer that you get both the PSA test and the digital rectal exam. I have a rare patient with an easily palpable malignancy on the digital rectal exam and absolutely normal PSA levels. And frequently I have patients with high PSA levels whose prostate feels perfectly normal to me and the consulting urologist, but which biopsies prove to be cancerous.

Every man over fifty should have an annual digital rectal exam and an annual PSA test until about age eighty. Although prostate cancer is much more common as men get older — in their eighties and nineties — it's much less likely to spread and cause symptoms or threaten life in that population. Prostate cancer is a much more benign disease in the over-eighty set, and aggressive treatment such as radical removal of the gland isn't done.

How Is the Diagnosis Confirmed?
If a nodule is detected on the digital rectal exam, or if the PSA is elevated, your urologist will do a needle prostate biopsy through the rectum. Usually, an ultrasound probe that shows up "dense" areas in the gland determines the location for the needle sampling. In the absence of a suspicious area, the urologist often takes several needle biopsy samples. Though it sounds harrowing, the ultrasound-guided biopsy is not a particularly painful, difficult, or dangerous procedure.

If the biopsy indicates cancer, several decisions have to be made. To help with these the pathologists who examine the tissue not only report whether it is malignant but also estimate how abnormal the malignant cells are. This is called the Gleason score and is a good predictor, along with the PSA, of how likely the cancer is to spread. Studies such as abdominal CT scans and bone scans are also done to make sure the cancer has not spread out of the prostate bed.

Treatment Decisions

All of this information is important because the choice of treatment options depends on whether the cancer has spread or how likely it is to spread. The facts are weighed against your age, your general state of health, and your life expectancy if you didn't have prostate cancer. If you're over eighty or eighty-five, one possible recommendation is no treatment at all — you would simply have periodic PSAs, and if evidence indicates progression you would start some type of hormone therapy. If you're in your seventies and in poor health from heart or lung disease, this is a reasonable option for you, too. Hormonal treatment can mean surgical removal of the testicles, the source of the testosterone that stimulates prostate cancer to grow, or use of one or both of the drugs Lupron and flutamide, which block the effect of testosterone on the tumor.

The treatment decision for younger, healthy men is even more difficult. First, you have to remember the disease is potentially fatal. If you're under seventy-five and healthy, your life expectancy without the cancer is more than ten years, so definitive treatment should be considered. If the scans show the tumor has spread beyond the prostate area, you're not a candidate for curative surgery and should have radiation therapy, hormones, or both. This gives you an excellent chance of long-term remission.

Surgery or radiation? If the cancer is still contained within the gland, you're a candidate for surgery or radiation therapy. In general, I advise everyone under seventy — and certainly under sixty-five — to strongly consider surgery. For the first few years, perhaps as many as ten, the recurrence rate for radiation-treated men is the same as for those treated surgically, but after that those treated with radiation alone begin to have recurrences, while those treated with surgery have an extremely low — almost zero — rate of recurrence.

Granted, surgery is painful, expensive, and risky — major complications such as blood clots or infection can occur. The operation that used to be done was called a radical prostatectomy, or removal of the gland and surrounding tissue, including the nerves. This procedure left a moderate number of patients with urinary incontinence and a nearly 100 percent incidence of erectile dysfunction (impotence). In the past fifteen years, a "nerve-sparing" radical operation that removes the gland but leaves the surrounding nerves undisturbed has become standard. The incidence of incontinence is much lower than with the old technique — less than 10 percent and somewhat age dependent. About 60 percent of men between sixty and seventy who have this newer operation maintain sexual potency, not a great deal lower than the general male population in that age spread. About 25 percent of men over seventy maintain potency.

EXPERIENCE COUNTS

A word here about choosing a surgeon for the newer, nerve-sparing prostate surgery. As the saying goes, some of my best friends are urologists, and I would feel comfortable having any one of a dozen or so treat most urological problems. However, the nerve-sparing radical prostatectomy is a difficult operation, and if I were the patient I'd want a surgeon who had done a large number of these procedures, preferably in a university-affiliated hospital. If you opt for this surgical technique, choose an experienced veteran.

If you decide on radiation, there are also alternative approaches: external beam radiation, implantation of radioactive "seeds" in the prostate, and recently three-dimensional conformal radiation therapy. This third option offers the best opportunity for a large dose of radiation to be delivered to the malignancy in the gland with minimal damage to surrounding tissue. No treatment for a problem of this magnitude is free of side effects, and some men have incontinence or impotence after radiation, but less than with surgery. With radiation, there is a higher incidence of painful irritation of the bladder or the rectum with bloody urine or bowel movements. The bladder or rectal irritation may last several weeks or a few months but can be relieved.

The important message here is that your treatment options are many and should be individualized. Remember, above all, that you do have to get regular prostate exams and PSA tests if you're going to catch a tumor before it spreads. Get them every year.

Breast Cancer

A woman is more than twice as likely to get breast cancer as lung cancer. In 2000, some 183,000 women had breast cancer compared to 75,000 with lung cancer, according to the National Cancer Institute, though more die of lung cancer. Breast cancer, mainly because of the threat of body disfigurement, is a greater concern among women in my practice.

While being a nonsmoker gives you an excellent chance of avoiding lung cancer, there is nothing you can do to give yourself an equivalent level of protection against breast cancer. Still, more than three-fourths of women with breast cancer survive, a statistic built primarily on early detection. Indeed, a regular program of surveillance for breast cancer offers as much protection against death from this disease as any program, with the possible exception of that for colorectal cancer.

Risk Factors

Although we can't link breast cancer to a single cause such as smoking, we can tie certain characteristics and habits to it, much as we can with vascular disease. We know there are some things in the American way of life that make breast cancer more likely. Americans of Japanese ancestry have an eightfold higher incidence of breast cancer than Japanese women do.

What all these factors are isn't clear, but we have identified certain significant risk factors:

- □ Fibrocystic breasts
- □ Hormone replacement therapy (HRT)
- □ A long menstruating lifetime, with early first menstruation or late menopause
- □ No pregnancy before age thirty
- □ Upper socioeconomic background
- □ Alcohol consumption (two or more drinks a day)
- □ Sedentary lifestyle
- □ Obesity (true obesity increases risk two to four times)
- □ Mother or sister with breast cancer (increases risk two to four times)
- □ Mother and sister with breast cancer (increases risk fivefold)

Keep in mind that large breasts make it difficult for a physician to find a small lump, and dense breasts make mammography less accurate.

You can't change some of the risks, like family history, when you first became pregnant, and how long you menstruated. But others — inactivity, obesity, and heavy alcohol intake — can be changed. The factor that is most controversial is hormone replacement therapy after menopause. There is definitely a slight increase in breast cancer risk, but this is not as significant if there are no other risk factors. For example, one large study suggests if you don't drink, taking hormones doesn't pose a risk. For more information on this complex issue, see part 2, chapter 13, "Hormone Replacement Therapy."

If you're in a very high risk group, there is an alternative to regular hormone replacement therapy: the designer estrogen Evista (raloxifene), which gives the two major health benefits of regular hormone replacement therapy (slows osteoporosis and atherosclerosis) while actually providing some protection against breast cancer. The drug Nolvadex (tamoxifen) gives even more protection against breast cancer but doesn't reduce cardiac risk or prevent osteoporosis.

GENES AND BREAST CANCER

Two clearly delineated genetic patterns have been linked to breast cancer: the BRACA I and BRACA II genes, which can be tested for. About 1 to 2 percent of women with breast cancer have this genetic component, and if you test positive for it, your risk of breast cancer is extremely high. If you have a strong family history of breast cancer or are of Ashkenazi Jewish ancestry, you should speak to your doctor about a BRACA gene analysis.

How Can You Detect Breast Cancer Early?

Even if you can reduce or eliminate some of the risk factors, you still need to be wary. If you're a woman over sixty, you should do three things:

- *Perform a monthly self-breast examination.* The statistics on the benefits of self-breast exam are not as compelling as for mammograms or professional exams. However, I've had several women find a small malignant nodule four or five months after a negative mammogram and a negative breast exam by their gynecologist or me. Finding a cancerous growth seven or eight months before the next scheduled exam may save your life. Self-exams are easy and cost nothing.
- *Get an annual mammogram.* Medicare only pays for a mammogram every two years, except in women with a lump or high risk. Your age, however, is a risk factor, and I think the risk is too high not to get an annual evaluation.
- *Have your gynecologist or primary care physician examine you annually.* A certain number of breast malignancies are missed on mammograms, but they may be caught during an annual physical. Neither a mammogram nor an annual physical is 100 percent accurate in detecting breast tumors, but together these tests are very accurate.

What Happens If a Lump Is Found?

If a breast mass or lump is found, the radiologist or breast specialist may first order a sonogram to determine if the area is solid or cystic. If it's cystic, a needle aspiration may provide a diagnosis without requiring a biopsy. If it's solid or indeterminate, a biopsy is probably indicated. Nowadays, many biopsies are being done with mammographic or sonographic needle localization. That is, a sonogram or mammogram image helps guide the surgeon's biopsy needle into the nodule.

If the biopsy is negative, you still need to be monitored; on very rare occasions a lesion can be missed. If the biopsy is positive, meaning the lesion is malignant, for most women the treatment is local removal of the lump — perhaps with removal of nearby lymph nodes, where the cancer sometimes spreads — followed by radiation therapy.

What Will Treatment Involve?

A new technique that may prevent the need for major surgery to remove lymph nodes in the underarm area is called sentinel node localization and sampling. Rather than removing and examining all the lymph nodes, a blue dye or radioactive material is injected into the breast tumor site, and only the first node that collects the dye or material is biopsied. If this biopsy turns out negative, you have a better than 90 percent chance that the underarm lymph nodes are clear of cancer. This procedure saves a women from the painful arm swelling frequently experienced after wholesale lymph node sampling.

Depending on the estrogen-receptor evaluation of your tumor — most are estrogen-receptor positive — you'll be started on a five-year course of Nolvadex (tamoxifen) to block hormone stimulation of any residual cells. If the sentinel node shows positive results, chemotherapy should be added to your treatment; it substantially reduces the likelihood of a recurring tumor.

If the initial tumor in the breast is large or very close to the chest wall, a full mastectomy — removal of the breast — may need to be done. Recently, several of my patients undergoing mastectomy have had simultaneous plastic surgery to establish a breast contour approaching normal. This procedure has alleviated some of the anguish for some women.

Colorectal Cancer

As with prostate and breast cancer, we don't have an effective strategy for substantially reducing the risk factors for colon and rectal (colorectal) cancer, though certain dietary changes may help slightly. It is, however, the cancer we can detect earliest, even in its premalignant stage, and the cancer with a death rate we can probably make the most progress in reducing. The incidence of death from colon cancer is falling among white Americans but increasing in the African-American population. (This is almost certainly because of discrepancies in the healthcare system and public health information. We need to institute reform and make sure everyone has the same access to the best preventive medicine.)

COLORECTAL RISK: LIFESTYLE AND FAMILY

We know that certain lifestyle factors can affect your risk of colorectal cancer. Aspirin, vegetables in the cabbage family, exercise, and reduced dietary fat seem to lower the likelihood of colon and rectal cancer. This is one cancer for which we also have a few clearly defined genetic risks. Some individuals have a severe genetic disorder that causes them to develop hundreds of colon polyps starting in their teens; almost all these people get colon cancer by age forty if the colon is not preventively removed. Other predisposing disorders are not as clearly defined, but family history is very important in planning the type of screening you should have. If you have a parent or sibling with colon cancer, you are clearly at a much higher risk.

The symptoms of colon cancer are rectal bleeding, abdominal pain, or a change in bowel movements. Bleeding can be an early symptom, even before the polyp has become malignant. Pain or bowel movement changes are late symptoms, which you may never have if you follow the proper screening program.

How Should You Be Screened?

Colon cancer starts as a benign polyp or growth on the wall of the colon. Polyps usually don't become malignant for several years. They may be slightly raised platelike growths on the bowel wall, or they may be "pedunculated," growing like a mushroom or flower bud from the wall of the colon. They often cause a tiny amount of bleeding that's not visible but that can easily be detected by a chemical test. This hidden or occult blood testing is usually done by collecting a small amount of stool on special cards for three days in a row, and returning the card promptly to the doctor for chemical analysis.

The stool examination for occult blood should be done by every person in the United States over fifty years old once each year.

In addition, everyone past sixty should certainly have an examination or scoping procedure of the rectum and colon every three to five years. Experts differ over which examination you should have. One is a flexible sigmoidoscopy, which can be done in the doctor's office after enema preparation but only shows the sigmoid and descending colon. The other, a colonoscopy, visualizes the entire colon. The colonoscopic exam requires more demanding preparation, including a liquid diet and laxatives, and has to be done on an outpatient basis at a hospital or special surgical center under light sedation. I advise colonoscopies for people with a positive stool test for blood (an absolute indication), a family history of colon cancer, or a previous polyp. For people at lower risk, I recommend the easier flexible sigmoidoscopic examination.

Female Genital Cancer

Two types of cancer occur in the uterus. One is cancer of the cervix, the part of the uterus that protrudes into the vagina. It's caused by the human papilloma virus, which is sexually transmitted. Early detection of cervical cancer is the reason pap smears are done. This type of cancer is extremely rare in women over sixty, and if you've had three negative pap smears and the same sexual partner, there's usually no need for further pap smears. But you should continue to have your routine annual pelvic exam for other reasons.

The second type is cancer of the lining of the uterus, or endometrium, and it certainly does occur in women past sixty. Taking estrogen replacement without progesterone is a strong risk; unless you've had a hysterectomy, you shouldn't be on estrogen alone.

A WORD OF CAUTION

Any abnormal vaginal bleeding should be reported to your doctor right away. For women past sixty, this includes all vaginal bleeding except for expected periods produced by cyclical hormonal replacement therapy. If you do experience abnormal bleeding, you'll probably have a sonogram to examine the uterine lining and possibly an endometrial (uterine lining) biopsy. In addition to reporting any abnormal bleeding immediately, you should have an annual pelvic exam.

Cancer of the ovary is a type of cancer that is both hard to prevent and in many cases hard to detect before it has spread. An enlarged or irregular ovary may be detected on your annual routine pelvic exam, but often abdominal pain or swelling is the presenting symptom. Any persistent abdominal pain should be reported to your doctor, who will investigate for a possible ovarian mass or malignancy.

There is a tumor marker for ovarian cancer called CA 125 that can be detected by blood tests. It's helpful in following the course of treatment in a woman with known ovarian cancer, but the test produces too many false positives and false negatives to be a reliable screening tool.

Cancer of the Kidney and Bladder

Cancer of the bladder and kidney, taken together, account for about 7 to 8 percent of cancer cases. These two types of cancer are about twice as frequent in men and more than twice as common in smokers.

Any gross bleeding visible in the urine should be reported immediately. There are many possible causes, including a kidney stone or bladder infection, but cancer of the bladder or kidney should be ruled out. Sometimes gross bleeding doesn't occur, only blood cells in the urine that show up with urine test. I strongly urge everyone over sixty to make sure this test is included in their annual physical exam.

Non-Hodgkin's Lymphoma

This is a group of primary malignancies of the lymph nodes and other lymphoid tissue such as the spleen. Non-Hodgkin's lymphoma is similar in behavior to Hodgkin's disease but has a different appearance under the microscope.

Non-Hodgkin's malignancies, which used to be called lymphosarcomas, now have a very complicated nomenclature based on the malignant cell type and arrangement under the microscope. Some malignancies are very aggressive while others are indolent, often not requiring treatment for months or years.

Some, if detected early, can possibly be cured with radiation; others are treated with chemotherapy. Non-Hodgkin's malignancies usually start with a painless enlargement of lymph nodes in the neck, armpits, or groin. Any swollen lymph gland that doesn't go away in three or four days should be reported to your doctor.

Esophageal Cancer

Cancer of the esophagus is much more frequent in smokers and heavy drinkers. About five years ago, I reviewed the charts of every patient I had who had developed esophageal cancer over the previous twenty-five years. There were fourteen cases, and all but one had been a heavy drinker and a smoker.

One type of esophageal cancer, adenocarcinoma, is related to gastro-esophageal reflux disorder (GERD), which affects the lower portion of the esophagus. This is where the acidic contents of the stomach can back up into the lower esophagus, irritating it and causing a condition called Barrett's esophagus. If the Barrett's membrane continues to be irritated, this condition may progress to cancer of the lower esophagus. Any persistent heartburn or indigestion requires thorough investigation. (See part 2, chapter 19, "Intestinal Problems.")

Cancer can narrow the esophageal opening and cause difficulty swallowing food, particularly bread and meat. The strategy for preventing esophageal cancer is to stop smoking, limit alcohol intake, and work with your doctor to treat GERD and be monitored for deterioration. If you have difficulty swallowing, report it promptly.

Melanoma

There are three common cancers of the skin: basal cell carcinoma, squamous cell carcinoma, and malignant melanoma. The first two are quite common, but because they seldom spread (basal cell never, squamous cell rarely), they are discussed in part 2, chapter 20, "Skin Problems."

Melanoma is a different matter — often lethal. In my first year of practice, a young woman from Brazil came to the office complaining of severe headaches. On examination, I was certain she had a brain tumor; an X ray confirmed that she had several such tumors. The woman reported that she'd had a "mole" removed from her back a few months earlier. The removal area wasn't wide and nothing had been said about it being malignant. She also had an enlarged lymph node in her neck, which was biopsied and showed melanoma. She was referred to the National Institutes for Health for treatment, but despite having the best experts in the world, she died in less than a month.

Melanoma can spread rapidly through the lymph system or bloodstream and go to what we call the regional lymph nodes or to many other organs, including the brain, lungs, or liver. Even now treatment is only palliative; prevention and early detection are crucial.

Most melanoma is caused by excessive sun exposure. Even if you did your sunbathing long before age sixty, you should still be very cautious. Burns seem to be more harmful than gradual tanning, but even with tanning you need to be careful. Use sunblock, a wide-brimmed hat, and keep your shirt on when you're around the pool, on the beach, gardening, or doing anything else for long stretches outside.

What Should You Look For?

Early detection of melanoma is critically important for people over sixty. The signs that distinguish melanoma growths from ordinary moles are color, irregular edges, changing size, and irritation. Melanomas are often very dark or almost black, but a frequent sign is variation of color in the same growth. Any combination of brown, white, black, or a bluish or reddish color may signal melanoma. Also, melanomas often have irregular edges that seem to grow into the skin; moles and keratoses usually have regular edges. Another characteristic is change — the appearance of a new "mole" (true moles don't usually appear after age sixty) or one that gets larger or darker and changes color.

The lesions most often confused with melanoma in older people are seborrheic keratoses. Fairly common, they're brown to tan and look as if they've been pasted on the skin. If you're concerned, have your doctor or a dermatologist check.

If you have a family history of melanoma or have had it yourself, you should have a thorough skin check by a dermatologist each year. Everybody should get in front of a full-length mirror and check everywhere — front, back, buttocks, legs, and soles of the feet — every three or four months.

Thyroid Cancer

Thyroid cancer starts as a nodule in the neck. If you notice an enlargement or asymmetry just below or to the side of your Adam's apple, check with the doctor right away. A family history of thyroid cancer or a history of having X-ray therapy to your face or neck puts you at higher risk for thyroid cancer, and you should let your doctor know about this. Some physicians order thyroid scans for people who have had X-ray exposure, but I simply advise a careful periodic manual evaluation of the gland. An examination of the thyroid should be part of everyone's annual physical evaluation.

Stomach Cancer

A century ago, stomach cancer was one of the most common cancers in the United States, but its incidence has declined dramatically. It's still very prevalent in developing countries. The decline in the United States is attributed to a decrease in the incidence of the bacterium *Helicobacter pylori* in the stomach. Helicobacter causes most stomach and duodenal ulcers and a great deal of gastritis. If you have recurrent indigestion, you should be evaluated for an ulcer or gastritis and have one of several tests performed to find out if you harbor the bacterium (see part 2, chapter 19, "Intestinal Problems"). If you test positive for helicobacter, you should receive antibiotic therapy to eradicate it and follow this up with a Helicobacter breath test to make sure it's gone.

Pancreatic Cancer

Unfortunately, in the early stages pancreatic cancer is not easily detected. Unless it starts as a small tumor in just the right area to block off the biliary tract and cause jaundice, it usually won't be found in time to be eliminated with surgery. Chemotherapy, which won't cure the cancer but may send it into remission, is more effective in earlier, smaller tumors. Any vague pain in the upper abdomen or middle of the back that's worse on lying down should be reported to your doctor. Of course, dark urine and jaundice (yellowing of the whites of the eyes) are emergencies requiring immediate evaluation.

REMEMBER THIS

When it comes to cancer, by far the most important things to remember are what you can do to prevent it, if anything, and what you can do to detect it early, which will give you the best chance for successful treatment. This chart summarizes prevention and early detection strategies for the major forms of cancer:

CANCER PREVENTION AND EARLY DETECTION

Cancer Type	Primary Prevention	Early Detection
Lung	Stop smoking	Annual spiral CT scan of chest
Prostate	Caution with testosterone replacement	Annual digital rectal exam and PSA test
Breast	Lose weight; increase exercise; reduce alcohol intake; caution with HRT	Monthly self-exam; annual physical; mammogram
Colorectal	Low-fat diet, regular aspirin, cabbage-family vegetables	Annual stool exam for hidden blood; flexible sigmoidoscopy or colonoscopy every 3 to 5 years
Uterine	Take progesterone if on estrogen replacement	Report bleeding; annual pelvic exam
Ovarian		Annual pelvic exam; prompt reporting of abdominal pain or swelling
Pancreatic	Quit smoking;limit alcohol intake; treat biliary disease	Not easily detected in early stage
Thyroid	Avoid radiation to gland	Annual checkup for nodules
Melanoma	Limit sun exposure	Annual physician skin exam; periodic self-exam with mirror
Kidney or bladder	Stop smoking	Annual urinalysis; report bleeding promptly
Esophageal	Stop smoking; limit alcohol intake	Careful follow-up of GERD and Barrett's tests
Non-Hodgkin's lymphoma		Report enlarged lymph nodes
Stomach	Stop smoking; Helico-bacter eradication	Periodic test for Helicobacter recurrence; report indigestion

CHAPTER 7

STROKE

Stroke is the third most common cause of death in the United States and a source of fear among many older people, who worry about the helpless dependency that a stroke can introduce into their life. Stroke is second only to Alzheimer's disease as the cause of severe neurological disability in the United States. Fortunately, the incidence of strokes and death from strokes has declined since the beginning of the century, particularly since 1970. Better control of high blood pressure accounts for much of this shift; other preventive and early intervention measures are responsible for the most recent gains.

What Is a Stroke?

A stroke is an abrupt loss or impairment of brain function resulting from an interruption of circulation to that part of the brain. About 80 percent of strokes are due to clots blocking an artery. A blood clot can form in vessels within the brain, in which case it is called a thrombus, or it can travel through the bloodstream from some other place, usually the heart or a larger blood vessel, and lodge in the brain, in which case it is called an embolus.

The other 20 percent of strokes are hemorrhagic — that is, a blood vessel in the brain ruptures. About half of these occur within the brain tissue itself, while the other half occur just at the surface of the brain, with bleeding into the cerebrospinal fluid surrounding it. Any stroke is a serious problem, but hemorrhagic strokes are the most likely to kill.

Maryanne
Maryanne was eighty-seven years old, widowed, and lived alone but had a nurse companion who came each morning and stayed until dinner. Maryanne had a history of high blood pressure that had been difficult to

control, fluctuating greatly even on medication. She had also had an occasional episode of slurred speech. Evaluation had shown no correctable problem in her large arteries, so she was treated only with daily aspirin in addition to her blood pressure medication. One morning Maryanne awoke, complained to her companion that she didn't "feel right," and soon grew unconscious. In the emergency room she was still unresponsive, with abnormal reflexes pointing to damage on both sides of the brain. The optic disks in the back of her eyes were swollen, indicating increased pressure inside her skull.

> **Did You Know?**
> Stroke affects men and women about equally. African-Americans have a higher incidence of and a higher death rate from stroke primarily because of their greater incidence of high blood pressure. The incidence of stroke accelerates rapidly for people over seventy-five: It is about twenty times greater for this population than for younger people.

A CT (computerized tomography) scan showed a large hemorrhage in the right side of her brain that was leaking into the spinal fluid. The right side of the brain was swollen, and the mid-portion of the brain had shifted to the left side of Maryanne's skull.

A neurologist and consulting neurosurgeon advised that any attempt to drain the blood in the hemorrhagic areas would be futile. She had a living will, her only daughter was contacted, and the decision was made to do nothing other than provide for the patient's comfort. She was given oxygen, but about two hours after she arrived in the emergency room, Maryanne stopped breathing and died.

This is a dramatic but not unusual story. Hemorrhagic strokes are often fatal. They're usually associated with high blood pressure, which can be difficult to control in some people no matter how dedicated the effort (Maryanne had seen a university-affiliated specialist in blood pressure). The past treatment of her transient brain circulation symptoms — the slurred speech — had been necessary, but it may actually have increased the possibility of hemorrhage. Often a thin line exists between preventing clot strokes and making a hemorrhage more likely.

The Causes of Stroke

Strokes can be triggered by a wide variety of conditions:

- □ Atherosclerosis
- □ Heart arrhythmia

□ Clots on the wall of the heart (mural thrombi)
□ Valvular heart disease
□ Vasculitis (temporal arteritis)
□ A sudden fall in blood pressure
□ Congenital abnormality in a cerebral blood vessel

Over two-thirds of the strokes in people over sixty are caused by ather-osclerosis, the same type of clogging of the arteries that causes heart attacks. The major risk factors for stroke are the same as those for heart attack: high LDL cholesterol, high blood pressure, diabetes, and smoking. High blood pressure is an even more serious risk factor for strokes than it is for coronary disease. Atherosclerosis can also cause emboli; the clots form on rough, atherosclerotic, or calcified areas at the beginning of the aorta or in the larger arteries leading to the brain. They break off and flow upward until they lodge in a small artery, causing damage to the brain tis-sue beyond it. Finally, a condition called temporal or giant cell arteritis, which is an inflammation of the blood vessels in the scalp, brain, or eyes, can cause strokes or loss of vision.

What Causes Hemorrhagic Strokes?

Most hemorrhagic strokes, particularly those that occur within the sub-stance of the brain, are associated with high blood pressure. In people over seventy years old, an accumulation of a substance called amyloid in the walls of the brain vessels may worsen this condition. Another cause of hemorrhage is a congenital weakness or aneurysm in the wall of the vessels at the base of the brain. Another condition, called arteriovenous fistulae, involves arteries running directly into veins, bypassing the usual capillary networks; this condition weakens the vessels and increases the possibility of hemorrhage.

What Are the Symptoms of a Stroke?

Because the brain performs a wide variety of functions, damage to it can cause many different symptoms, including:

Cognitive symptoms
□ Not making sense when you talk
□ Inability to come up with words (dysphasia or aphasia)
□ Sudden disorientation or confusion
□ Amnesia

Coordination problems
- ☐ Sudden, severe dizziness
- ☐ Falling to one side
- ☐ Loss of coordination in legs or arms

Motor problems
- ☐ Loss of strength or paralysis in an arm, a leg, or facial muscles
- ☐ Sudden inability to walk or stand up
- ☐ Slurred speech

Sensory problems
- ☐ Sudden numbness
- ☐ Peculiar feeling or sensation on one side of the body

Damage to cranial nerves
- ☐ Double vision
- ☐ Sudden loss of vision in any part of the visual field
- ☐ Facial numbness
- ☐ Weakness of facial muscles
- ☐ Difficulty swallowing

Other
- ☐ Headache (for certain hemorrhagic strokes but not usually the more common strokes caused by clots; may also be associated with temporal arteritis)
- ☐ Fainting
- ☐ Coma

The most important thing to remember is this: Any symptom pointing to something wrong with the brain, if it comes on suddenly, is probably a stroke and needs immediate attention.

What Can You Do to Prevent a Stroke?

The first thing everyone should do is address the four major vascular risk factors associated with strokes: high cholesterol, high blood pressure, diabetes, and smoking. The second (we'll discuss this later) is to treat heart conditions that may cause emboli. The third is to recognize and treat transient deficiencies in the circulation to the brain, and to recognize and treat early strokes as quickly as possible. In general, regular exercise is a measure that can help prevent strokes.

Emily

Emily, a seventy-four-year-old retired library assistant who likes to play the piano, had reasonably controlled high blood pressure for many years. One morning she awoke with slurred speech, moderate weakness in her left arm, and a left foot that dragged slightly when she walked. Her weakness seemed to increase during the first hour, then stabilized. She called me at about 4:30 in the afternoon and I sent her to the emergency room immediately.

A neurologist on the stroke reaction team saw Emily right away. An examination confirmed that she had slurred speech, some mild difficulty swallowing, and limb weakness. Her heart tests proved normal. A CT scan showed no abnormality, but a repeat scan two days later revealed that she had had a stroke in the motor (movement-stimulating) portion of the right side of her brain. (CT scans usually don't show brain damage the first day but are done to rule out a hemorrhage.) Emily was given aspirin only on the first day. Stronger medication to help dissolve the blood clot in the right side of the brain would not have been helpful because about nine hours had elapsed between the stroke and her evaluation in the emergency room — the clot had already done its damage.

Emily stabilized and began intensive physical therapy. Her speech improved significantly, but her arm and leg only improved partially. Now she walks with a brace on her left leg and uses a sling on her left arm. She plays the piano but can only use her left hand to keep the beat.

George

George was an eighty-four-year-old retired advertising executive. His wife called one morning at about 7:30 to report that George could not come up with words and was favoring his right side. He had moderately high blood pressure and had had a very mild stroke about three years before, and was taking aspirin regularly. I had him brought immediately to the emergency room, where I saw him in conjunction with a neurologist. George had marked dysphasia, could only come up with a few words, and appeared bewildered. His right arm and leg were minimally weak but had significantly abnormal reflexes.

A CT scan showed evidence of a small old stroke on the right, but nothing new and no hemorrhage. His heart examination showed only previous murmurs. Under the direction of the neurologist, George was given tissue plasminogen activator (TPA), which helps to dissolve clots. He became stable in the intensive care unit overnight, and by the next morning had almost totally regained his speech. The abnormal reflexes became normal in two days, and he was up and walking by the third day. At that point, he started on an anticlot drug called Plavix instead of aspirin. He has had no further stroke symptoms since this episode.

A SPECIAL WORD OF CAUTION

The cases of Emily and George illustrate one of the main points of this chapter: If you have symptoms suggesting a stroke, get immediate emergency treatment. If it's confirmed that you're having a stroke, an emergency CT scan shows no evidence of bleeding, and the stroke isn't more than three hours old, then TPA, the clot dissolver, may turn things around. If the stroke is still progressing, or if symptoms are waxing and waning, TPA or heparin (another anticoagulant) may head off a disaster.

Transient Ischemic Attacks (TIAs) and Strokes in Progress

Frequently, people will have the symptoms of a stroke — decreased vision, facial weakness, slurred speech, difficulty finding words, or any of the other stroke symptoms I mentioned — but the symptoms clear up in a matter of minutes or hours, without apparent damage to the brain. We call these transient ischemic attacks, or TIAs. Ischemia means deficiency of blood supply to a tissue. Any such attack lasting less than twenty-four hours (most last just a few hours) is considered a TIA.

TIAs may be caused by a slight drop in blood pressure, resulting in diminished circulation to the part of the brain served by a narrowed blood vessel. Currently, most doctors believe they are due to tiny blood clots that form on roughened, narrowed arteries, break off, and flow to a smaller vessel, where they temporarily interrupt circulation.

Frederick

Frederick was seventy-four years old and had no significant health problems other than moderate cholesterol elevation and mild high blood pressure, which had been controlled with medication for about five years. He took aspirin occasionally for his circulation. Though he'd taken a statin-family medication to lower his cholesterol in the past, he stopped because it was too expensive.

Frederick called to tell me that his speech had been garbled and he'd felt some weakness in his right arm; the symptoms had lasted about twenty minutes, then cleared. He thought he'd experienced a similar brief episode about three weeks before. I asked him about his vision and, on reflection, he said he had temporarily lost some vision on the right side, but the exact pattern was hard to remember.

I saw Frederick at the hospital. His neurological exam was normal, but I heard a soft swishing sound over his left carotid artery. His blood pressure was 135/85 (a near optimal level), and his heart was fine. A Doppler study — a sound wave test of the carotid arteries in the front of the neck — showed some atherosclerotic narrowing of both the left and the right arteries, less than 50 percent. I diagnosed TIAs and had him start Plavix, an anticoagulant pill. I re-emphasized the importance of taking cholesterol medication and started him on Lipitor 20 mg a day. Subsequent LDL readings remained under 100, and follow-up blood pressure remained under 125/80.

On the Plavix, Frederick has had no TIAs for two years. A repeat Doppler study of his carotid arteries showed no change from the approximate 50 percent narrowing, but no noticeable improvement either, despite aggressive lowering of his cholesterol. We remain hopeful.

Kathy

Several years ago, at age eighty-six, Kathy came to the emergency room about three hours after developing garbled speech and weakness in her right arm and hand. She had thought the symptoms would go away, but they continued to get worse after she arrived at the hospital. A CT scan showed no hemorrhage, but she was having a great deal of trouble coming up with words, the arm weakness was significant, and she had some abnormal reflexes in the right leg. I believed she was having a severe TIA or more likely a "stroke in progress." Kathy was started on heparin intravenously and by the next morning, about twenty-four hours after her hospital arrival, her symptoms disappeared.

Kathy was in the arbitrary gray zone between a prolonged TIA and a stroke in progress. Because a CT scan three days later showed no infarct (stroke damage), I called the episode a prolonged TIA, but we had probably aborted a stroke.

She was discharged and advised to take two aspirin a day as well as to keep her fluid intake above two quarts a day (dehydration can make you prone to a stroke). I followed her closely. In the years after this incident Kathy had a gallbladder attack, and her gallbladder and a stone blocking the bile duct were removed via laparoscopy. She tolerated the procedure without a problem.

Two years ago, Kathy began noticing new episodes of garbled speech. They were brief — less than fifteen minutes — but began to be frequent. After having several in one day, she was hospitalized and given heparin again as well as IV rehydration, whereupon she stabilized promptly and had no more TIAs. I could hear harsh sounds over both carotid arteries; a Doppler study of the left carotid artery showed about 60 percent closure. Because of her age, this was not considered serious enough to warrant surgery to remove the debris from the lining of the artery. Kathy was discharged on Plavix and has done well since.

Frederick and Kathy are good examples of people who have transient ischemic attacks. TIAs signal vascular disease, but they are also frequently harbingers of an impending stroke. A simple TIA may be followed by a stroke at a later time, but when TIAs become very frequent or prolonged, it often means that a stroke, with permanent brain damage, is imminent. Kathy is a perfect example of this.

Any neurological symptom, even if transient, should be investigated. Recent imaging techniques make it possible to study circulation to the brain in detail. If cerebral vascular disease is confirmed, you should be on an anticoagulant. Aspirin was once the drug of choice, but more recently we have used either Ticlid (ticlopidine) or Plavix (clopidogrel), which are a little stronger. I prefer Plavix because it's taken only once a day, and there are fewer side effects than with Ticlid, which can interfere with blood platelets. Both Frederick and Kathy benefited from Plavix.

Surgery to Prevent Strokes

There are four arteries that supply blood to the brain. The two in the front, the common carotid arteries, run up the sides of the neck and divide at the angle of the lower jawbone; one branch, the internal carotid, goes inside the skull to supply the bulk of the brain, while the other, the external carotid, supplies the face and scalp on that side. In the back, two smaller vertebral arteries run alongside the spine. They enter the skull and at the base of the brain come together to form the basilar artery. The basilar artery supplies the cerebellum, the base of the brain, the nerves going to the ears, the balance apparatus, and the muscles that animate the face and move the eyes. This artery also supplies many of the brain centers that control such functions as breathing and heart rate.

Strokes in the parts of the brain supplied by the carotid arteries damage speech, intelligence, emotion, orientation, voluntary movement, sensation, and vision. Strokes in the parts of the brain supplied by the vertebral arteries and basilar artery damage coordination and balance and cause double vision. They may also cause paralysis or sensory loss because nerves from the higher part of the brain run through the brainstem. A very small stroke in the brainstem can cause devastating symptoms, whereas a much larger area of damage in the larger, forward part of the brain, served by the carotid arteries, may result in very few symptoms.

The vertebral arteries are small, not readily accessible, and almost never treated surgically. However, the larger carotid arteries are easily accessible in the neck. In certain situations surgery is performed on these arteries, averting a major or fatal stroke.

The most common operation is called an endarterectomy, in which cholesterol plaques are virtually stripped from the artery's inner lining. Even in the most experienced hands, carotid artery surgery is very high risk. The major concern is that a plaque or a piece of the lining of the artery will break loose during the procedure, travel up to the brain, and cause a stroke. This is not an operation to take lightly.

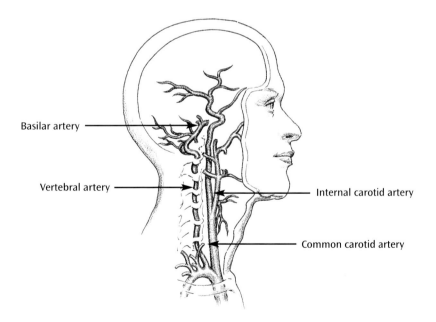

Blood circulation to the brain: the carotid and vertebral-basilar systems.

Who Should Have Surgery?

Determining who should have a carotid endarterectomy has been one of the more controversial questions in medicine over the past thirty years, but we've settled on some recommendations for now.

One of the crucial factors is how much narrowing has occurred in the targeted artery. We can determine this in three ways: with a carotid Doppler or ultrasound test, with an MRA (magnetic resonance evaluation of the artery), or with an arteriogram, in which dye that shows up on an X ray is injected into the bloodstream. The arteriogram is more accurate but riskier because it can loosen a plaque. The Doppler, though not as accurate, is totally painless and risk free. In recent years I've had almost no patients receive carotid arteriograms. The few who have had them were being strongly considered for surgery, and the surgeon needed a more precise understanding of the pattern of damage.

KNOW YOUR SURGEON'S STATS

I know several vascular surgeons who are excellent technicians and through the years have performed many successful procedures on my patients. As good as they are, however, I wouldn't use them for carotid surgery. I've referred the few patients who were candidates to a special-ist who has done a number of the operations and has a low rate of com-plications. If you're a candidate for carotid artery surgery, make sure the vascular surgeon has a great deal of experience with the procedure and a rate of serious complications that doesn't exceed 5 to 10 percent.

In cases where the artery is between 70 and 99 percent closed and the patient has no other major cardiac risks, surgery is probably justified. A narrow-ing of 50 to 69 percent can be enough, particularly if the patient has TIA symp-toms and is in good general condition, or hasn't responded to aspirin or Plavix.

Frederick's was a borderline case, but he did so well on the medication he wasn't considered a candidate for this operation. Kathy might have been considered were it not for her age, which increased the operative risk — we opted instead for treatment with Plavix.

Blood Clots from the Heart to the Brain

As I noted, a certain number of strokes are caused by blood clots forming in the heart and traveling to the brain. These can result in repeated, small, almost imperceptible strokes, or in massive strokes that cause paralysis or death. Anything that interferes with the lining of the heart increases the chance of clots forming — a rare tumor in the heart, infection on the heart valves, a heart attack that leaves the heart wall soft or rough, or certain types of congestive heart failure where the heart muscle is dilated and flaccid. Far and away the greatest cause of embolic clots, however, is a heart rhythm disturbance called atrial fibrillation.

In atrial fibrillation, rather than initiating a slow and regular heart rhythm, the atria start an extremely rapid beat, causing a sort of undulating, boiling muscle activity with no rhythmic contraction. The ventricles beat irregularly as well, and medication is often needed to slow the overall heart rate. In some people, medicine can make the heart return to a normal rhythm, and in some an electrical shock to the heart through the chest wall might restore normal rhythm. Either way, all such patients must first be treated with anticoagulation drugs such as Coumadin (warfarin). Hundreds of thousands of Americans take Coumadin, and it's now considered standard practice for atrial fibrillation. Once the rate of the heartbeat in fibrillation is controlled, the main danger is blood clots and strokes. Because Coumadin prevents clots, people can live symptom free for decades even with an atrial fibrillation heart rhythm that can't be controlled, as is sometimes the case with older patients.

A WORD OF CAUTION

Coumadin is a tricky drug, and the dose varies considerably from person to person. If you have to start Coumadin, you need frequent monitoring of the timing of your blood clotting to be sure it is effectively slowed, but not so much that hemorrhage is a danger. After the dose is established, you should get a blood test about every four weeks.

Numerous drugs such as aspirin, nonsteroidal anti-inflammatory drugs (NSAIDs), and antibiotics interact with Coumadin. Some of these should not be taken at all, while others require more frequent checks of blood clotting. Most drugs that interact with Coumadin make bleeding more likely. Vitamin K, however, negates this effect and may mean you need more Coumadin to keep your clotting in a safe range.

Temporal Arteritis

Temporal arteritis is an inflammation of the larger or medium-sized arteries supplying the scalp, brain, and eyes. We don't know what causes it, but the general consensus is that it's an autoimmune disease, one in which a person's own antibodies begin to attack body tissue. About half the people who have temporal arteritis also have polymyalgia rheumatica — a condition of very sore muscles, particularly in the neck and hip area, accompanied by severe fatigue and a flulike feeling or fever. In polymyalgia the tiny arteries in the muscles, rather than the larger ones in the scalp and brain, are inflamed.

Patty

Patty was eighty-nine years old, although she said she was seventy-nine and looked it. She called to tell me she'd had several episodes of almost total loss of vision in one eye. The vision was "very gray," but the episodes were brief, lasting only a few minutes. She also had a continuing headache and said she felt as if she'd had "the flu" for about two weeks. Immediately, I arranged for a hospital evaluation.

By the time Patty got to the hospital, she'd had one more brief episode of blurred vision, but it cleared. Her neurological and heart exams proved normal, and the retinal exam showed no major vascular clot. The blood vessels in the left temple and left side of her forehead were slightly prominent, with several areas of tenderness. Her sedimentation rate, a test for inflammation, was 95 — very elevated. The diagnosis was temporal, or giant cell, arteritis.

Patty was started on heparin anticoagulants and a moderately large dose of prednisone. She had no eye symptoms after the first three hours, and in two days her headache, the tender areas in her left temple, and the aching or flulike symptoms had subsided. In four days she went off the heparin.

Temporal arteritis is not uncommon and is more frequently seen in women. Almost everyone who has it is over sixty. The vessels to the eyes are among the most frequently involved. I've had two patients lose the sight in one eye with temporal arteritis. As Patty's case suggests, any unusually persistent headache — particularly a headache associated with significant vision change, any neurological change, or flulike symptoms — should be reported immediately.

REMEMBER THIS

- Thrombotic strokes, which account for over 80 percent of strokes, may be caused by blood clots forming in the brain or coming through the arteries from other places in the body.
- The disease that leads to most thrombotic strokes is atherosclerosis.
- Primary prevention of strokes is the same as primary prevention of heart attacks: regular exercise, not smoking, and careful control of blood pressure, cholesterol, and diabetes.
- You can prevent damage from stroke by getting immediate medical attention in an emergency room within three hours of the onset of stroke symptoms.
- Transient ischemic attacks (TIAs) are often harbingers of strokes and should be evaluated immediately. Very frequent TIAs usually signal an imminent stroke and should be treated in the hospital with anticoagulants.
- Narrowing of the carotid arteries in the neck can be treated surgically, but this should only be done in cases of significant obstruction. The patient should be in overall good health, and the surgeon should be very experienced with the procedure.
- Atrial fibrillation, a common type of heart arrhythmia, is the cause of many strokes. Blood clots flow from the heart to the brain (embolic strokes). Almost everyone over sixty who has atrial fibrillation should be on the anticoagulant Coumadin to prevent embolic strokes.
- Temporal arteritis is an inflammatory condition of the arteries to the scalp, brain, and eyes. It causes headaches and fatigue and can result in permanent loss of vision or a stroke. Temporal arteritis responds dramatically to prednisone.

CHAPTER 8

WEIGHT PROBLEMS

Two problems with weight affect a large number of Americans over sixty: excess weight, and too little weight. The first is a much greater problem for those in their sixties and early seventies and is a major mortality risk. After age seventy-five, being underweight is more common. Weight loss in advanced age, a complicated interaction of disease, depression, economic issues, and other factors, will be addressed in part 3. This chapter is for those of you in your sixties and seventies who are carrying around too many pounds.

What's Wrong with Excess Weight?

It's simple: packing extra pounds can impair your quality of life as well as shorten it. The statistics relating excess weight to mortality are sobering. Consider the increased likelihood of dying earlier than a normal-weight person of the same age:

Excess pounds	Percent
20	27
30	43
40	61
50	111
60	227

Source: The Society of Actuaries and Association of Life Insurance Medical Directors of America

The list of medical conditions caused by or exacerbated by excess weight is a long one:

□ *Heart disease and stroke*. By contributing to elevated cholesterol and triglycerides, diabetes, and high blood pressure, obesity can lead to early heart disease and stroke.

□ *Blood clots.* Obesity can cause swelling of the legs and blood clots in the leg veins.

□ *Cancer.* Heavy people have a higher incidence of several types of cancer: uterine (two to three times the incidence), breast (almost double), gallbladder, colon, and prostate. Malignant growths are more difficult for you or the doctor to detect if you're too heavy.

□ *Liver disease.* Liver disease is more prevalent in heavy people.

□ *Gallbladder problems.* Gallstones and inflamed gallbladders are more common in heavy people.

□ *Osteoarthritis and gout.* Osteoarthritis (the wearing out of joints) and gout are more prevalent and more severe in heavy people.

□ *Breathing problems.* Obesity can make breathing more difficult if you have lung problems such as emphysema or asthma, and it can cause breathing problems such as sleep apnea and snoring.

□ *Skin problems.* Heavy people have more of a tendency to develop yeast or fungal infections in the groin or under the breasts.

In addition to medical problems, heavy people may develop low self-esteem and suffer disappointments in social relationships, often contributing to depression or anxiety.

Your Body Mass Index

Most statistics on health problems associated with excess weight use the so-called body mass index (BMI) to define normal weight, overweight, and obesity. Your BMI is your:

$$\frac{\text{weight in pounds}}{\text{height in inches}^2} \times 703.1$$

This means that if your BMI is:

20 to 25	You're in the healthy range
25 to 29	You're overweight
Over 29	You're obese

How Can You Lose Weight?

Few health topics are discussed more than weight control. Last year, three of the top nonfiction bestsellers dealt with weight-reducing diets.

BODY MASS INDEX

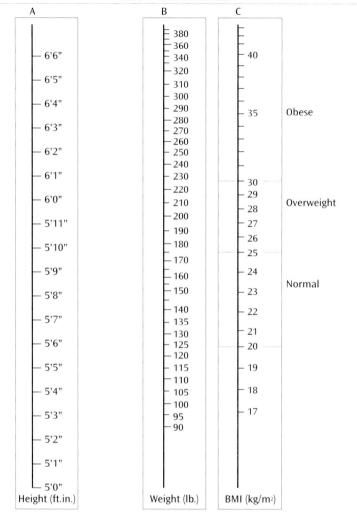

Instructions: place a straight edge on your height in column A and across your weight in column B. Where it crosses column C is your Body Mass Index.

Magazines are brimming with diet hints, many of them useful, others bizarre or even dangerous for your health. Here I present in condensed form an approach to weight loss derived from years of watching patients struggle to lose weight.

If you're overweight or obese and determined to shed pounds, you need to do three things: set a weight goal, exercise, and diet.

To see how the process works, let's follow a hypothetical overweight man — we'll call him David — who stands 5 feet 11 inches (71 inches) and weighs 210 pounds.

Set a Weight Goal

David's BMI is 29.29, which puts him in the lower end of the obese range. His goal should be to lose around 15 percent of his weight, which would put him in the upper end of the healthy range.

To get to a BMI of under 25, David has to lose 30 pounds. At 3,500 calories per pound, he has to run a deficit of 105,000 calories.

Exercise

There are three ways David can reach his deficit: by burning off calories with exercise, by reducing his calorie intake, or by doing both. Exercise should be part of David's program, not only for the calories it burns but also for the multiple health benefits it brings (see introduction to part 2, "Staying on Top of Your Health"). If he relies on increased exercise alone, however, achieving his goal is going to be difficult and take a long time. Why?

To answer that question, let's see how many calories a person burns doing a half hour of various types of activity. Larger people do more work with each activity and thus expend more calories than smaller people, so the following figures merely represent an average:

CALORIES EXPENDED PER HALF HOUR OF ACTIVITY

Activity	Weight (pounds)		
	110	160	210
Lying or sitting quietly	35	50	65
Standing quietly	40	55	75
Gardening	150	220	285
Walking 3 mph (20-minute miles)	100	135	165
Walking 4 mph (15-minute miles)	120	175	230
Golf	130	180	245
Mopping or sweeping	95	130	170
Swimming	225	320	425
Nordic Track or cross-country skiing	215	310	410
Cycling (7.5 mph)	125	180	235
Tennis	165	235	310
Dance aerobics (slow)	100	140	155
Dance aerobics (fast)	205	295	390
Running (11-minute miles)	202	275	370
Climbing stairs	180	245	330

Let's say David walks 15-minute miles, which is the pace I advise for those under seventy-five or eighty. He'll expend 165 more calories per half hour than he would sitting still (that is, 230 minus the 65 he would expend sitting still). For each hour walked, then, he'll run a deficit of 330 calories, and for each mile walked, a deficit of 83 calories. If David's food intake remains the same, he'll have to walk 318 hours or 1,265 miles (about the distance from Washington, D.C., to Houston, Texas) to lose his 30 pounds.

> **Did You Know?**
> The three most important things to remember about weight control are: calories, calories, calories. Did you know that every time you consume 3,500 more calories than you burn, you gain a pound? If you're carrying around excess weight and not dieting, you'll have to walk for roughly thirteen hours just to lose a single pound. All approaches to weight loss and weight maintenance must be based on this simple fact: 3,500 calories equals 1 pound.

Diet

Obviously, David will have to reduce his calorie intake if he wants to lose weight in a reasonable time. And the only way he'll shed pounds and keep them off is by going on a reasonable diet, one he's comfortable with and can stick to. He shouldn't opt for a fad diet or a crash diet — gimmicks don't work for long. He should try to adopt healthy eating habits even while dieting, thus setting the stage for post-diet weight maintenance.

During the weight-maintenance stage, a well-balanced daily diet with all the major food groups would include:

- □ Six to eleven servings of grain foods such as bread, cereal, and pasta
- □ Three to five servings of vegetables
- □ Two to four servings of fruit
- □ Two to three servings of milk, yogurt, or cheese
- □ Two to three servings of meat, poultry, fish, eggs, or beans

These are the recommendations put out by the U.S. Department of Agriculture in its Food Guide Pyramid, and while they may sound like a lot of food for weight maintenance, the servings aren't large. A serving of bread, for example, is a single slice, and a serving of eggs is a single egg.

A reasonable if stringent approach for David would be to adopt a diet of about 1,200 to 1,400 calories until he reaches his weight goal. It would be easier to do this with very little fat in the diet, because one gram of fat equals nine calories, whereas one gram of carbohydrate or protein is four calories. The goal, however, is not low fat, for fat performs certain beneficial functions in your body, including helping you absorb certain minerals

---

A WORD OF CAUTION

Why should you avoid fad diets? Because in general, they're not healthy. Only three nutrients contain calories: carbohydrate, fat, and protein. If you cut out one, chances are you'll be eating an excess of the other two. The current rage for low-carbohydrate diets, based on dubious scientific claims, has created a nation of dieters who are eating lots of protein and fat and in the process inviting the risk of high cholesterol and heart disease. If you opt instead for a near-starvation crash diet — 800 calories or less per day — you can end up dehydrated and develop kidney damage, and your body can become starved for nutrients and fuel. Very-low-calorie diets, moreover, can lower the metabolic rate (the rate at which you burn calories), so that when you stop dieting your sluggish body piles the pounds back on. In short, you're better off avoiding gimmicks and opting for a calorie-reduced diet that feeds your body a healthy balance of nutrients.

---

and vitamins, and it also helps keep hunger at bay. Low-fat diets, more-over, are so boring that they can end up turning the dieter off to dieting altogether. The goal, rather, is low calories. The diet should include a lim-ited intake of fat (olive oil is healthier for your heart than butter), com-plex carbohydrates such as beans and whole grains, plenty of fruits and vegetables, and a moderate amount of protein in the form of lean meat, fish, and chicken.

The Connally Diet

A diet I have advised for several years with good results is low calorie enough for you to lose weight steadily but well balanced enough that you can build on it and add calories once you have attained your goal and you want to maintain your weight. The rate of weight loss will depend, of course, on your size and activity. It's difficult to tell how many calories a given person burns in a day. I recommend that you stay on a reasonably low-calorie diet and weigh yourself daily. After two or three weeks you can get an idea of your daily caloric deficit by dividing the total amount of weight lost by the number of days you've dieted and multiplying by 3,500.

Remember, the first few days you diet you'll lose three or four pounds of water (which will come back rapidly if you overeat again). After this period of quick shedding, weight loss will proceed much more slowly, a pound or two a week. At this reasonable pace, David can expect to lose his unwanted weight within four or five months.

The following is what I advise as a template starter diet. Remember, the entries are just suggestions. My hope is that you'll shape a healthy diet for yourself around your own taste buds, because there's nothing that will turn a person off to dieting more quickly than a prescribed menu. I want to give you the freedom to eat what you want within reason. Build on this diet as you see fit, keeping in mind the fact that 3,500 calories equals one pound, and following the general principle of balance mentioned above. (If you have health problems such as high cholesterol, heart disease, or kidney disease, check with your doctor before proceeding with this or any other diet.)

BREAKFAST:

Dry cereal such as Special K, Total, or Cheerios with high protein content, skim milk, half a banana or another piece of fruit, a small glass of juice, and coffee or tea (no sugar and no cream)

or,

One egg and one piece of dry whole-wheat toast, half a banana or another piece of fruit, a small glass of juice, and coffee or tea (no sugar and no cream)

LUNCH:

Vegetable or fruit salad with low-calorie dressing and a clear soup (not a cream soup), whole-wheat toast or low-calorie crackers (hold the butter)

or,

Nonfat yogurt and fruit, whole-wheat toast or low-calorie crackers (hold the butter)

DINNER:

A small portion of lean meat, salad with low-calorie dressing, and a green or yellow vegetable; add a small portion of complex carbohydrate (rice, potato, pasta, peas, or beans) after one week

If you're hungry between meals, try eating an apple or orange or low-calorie crackers.

How Can You Make Your Diet Work?

The sort of plan I've just sketched for you will work a lot better if you keep these points in mind:

☐ It's important to know the approximate caloric content of all foods and drinks. For many people, alcohol makes weight loss nearly impossible. It's high in calories, and it stimulates your appetite.

Moreover, if you have three drinks or more a day it can interfere with liver metabolism and make you crave high-calorie sweets the next day.

☐ Sweets should be avoided. Like alcohol, they supply only empty calories. Glucose is rapidly absorbed by the body, and it may cause a "rebound" effect, lowering blood sugar three or four hours after ingestion and leaving you ravenously hungry. Try to keep sweets out of your house when you're dieting. Once you reach your goal, you can add a moderate portion of dessert back into your diet.

☐ You should eat breakfast, lunch, and dinner. Almost all my obese patients rarely eat breakfast, and some of the fattest eat no lunch. They come home in the evening and graze until bedtime. Missing a meal makes you eat much more later.

☐ Discuss your weight situation with your spouse or the person who eats with you and enlist his or her help. An uncooperative spouse makes dieting next to impossible.

☐ Stay out of fast-food restaurants that serve high-fat foods. Avoid chips, fries, and fatty meats. If the food chain is called Buddy's or Bubba's, cross the street and don't look back.

☐ When you do go to restaurants, you don't have to eat everything on your plate. Over the past ten years restaurant portions have ballooned in the United States, which is one reason waistlines have. Don't give in to the trend — ask for a doggy bag.

☐ At receptions or parties, look the offering over and choose vegetables and lean meats. Better yet, keep your back to the food table.

☐ When you reach your weight goal, you're entering the second stage of the battle. Get regular exercise, weigh yourself frequently, and as soon as you start inching back up, return to your diet until you're back on track.

☐ While exercise helps in losing weight, it's even more important in keeping weight off.

☐ Take a multiple vitamin and drink lots of water while you're on any weight-reducing program.

What about Drugs for Losing Weight?

There are two general categories of medication for weight reduction: newer drugs that interfere with fat absorption, and old-fashioned appetite suppressants or "diet pills." One of the drugs that blocks fat absorption is Xenical (orlistat). When a person takes this, about 30 percent of the fat he

What Vitamins Should You Take?

Americans buy vitamins and mineral supplements to the tune of $5 billion a year. There's no need to take expensive supplements by the handful. If you're eating a balanced diet with all the major food groups included, and you're limiting your intake of alcohol and sweets, you probably need only three or four supplements:

- ☐ *Vitamin E.* Studies suggest that vitamin E protects against heart disease, helps prevent Alzheimer's, and improves memory. I recommend 400 I.U. of vitamin E a day.
- ☐ *Calcium.* People at risk for osteoporosis need 1,000 to 1,500 mg of calcium a day, and possibly vitamin D to help the body absorb calcium. Most calcium supplements come with vitamin D.
- ☐ *Vitamin B_{12} and folic acid (folate).* Both vitamin B_{12} and folic acid play an important role in the formation of red blood cells. Folic acid protects against atherosclerosis in some people, and vitamin B_{12} helps maintain the integrity of nerve cells. I recommend 400 mg of folic acid and at least 6 mg of vitamin B_{12}.

Few Americans, however, follow a balanced diet. If you belong to the majority, you should be taking a daily vitamin and mineral supplement, preferably one of the brands labeled for seniors. Make sure the supplement you choose contains the above recommended amounts of calcium, vitamins E and B_{12}, and folic acid, along with the minimum daily requirements of zinc, magnesium, and selenium. To save your wallet a beating, stick with house-brand vitamins, and don't worry about taking "natural" vitamins — they offer no additional benefits. The multiple vitamin is a safety valve if you slip off your nutritional diet.

or she eats passes out in the stool. Almost every patient of mine who has tried Xenical has had to stop because of diarrhea, so I'll limit my remarks to appetite suppressants.

Appetite Suppressants

The classic appetite suppressants are amphetamines, which work by raising levels of certain brain chemicals that make a person alert. In addition to suppressing the appetite, however, amphetamines can also cause excitation, sleeplessness, and an inappropriate psychological high. Their effect on the appetite comes at a price. Amphetamines are addicting and should not be taken. Another group of appetite suppressants, still used, acts similarly to the classic amphetamine group. This group includes Ionamin (phentermine) and Bontril PDM (phendimetrazine). Their side effects are so similar to those of the amphetamines that I've stopped prescribing them.

One slightly different appetite suppressant is Meridia (sibutramine). This works on different chemicals in the brain. Its action is more like that of the antidepressants than the amphetamines. In controlled studies over a six-month period, people on Meridia lost about eight pounds more than subjects on a placebo. The side effects were agitation, poor sleep, high blood pressure, and rapid heartbeat. You should be extremely cautious with this medication if you are over sixty.

People who take appetite suppressants tend to regain some or most of the weight lost after the diet has stopped. There's an important lesson here: if you go on a diet, whether you take a drug to help you or not, you have to learn lifetime rules about sensible calorie intake, healthy eating, and exercise, or you'll promptly regain the weight.

REMEMBER THIS

- Being overweight or obese increases the risk of mortality and disabling diseases.
- One pound equals 3,500 calories.
- To lose weight and keep it off, you need a combination of calorie reduction and increased exercise.
- Burning more calories with exercise helps you lose weight, but it's seldom enough. An average-size person has to walk five miles to make up for the calories in one cheeseburger.
- All dieters should avoid alcohol and sweets until the goal is reached.
- Serious side effects and the lack of proven long-term effectiveness limit the usefulness of appetite suppressants and drugs that block food absorption.

CHAPTER 9

PULMONARY DISEASE AND ASTHMA

Several disorders, known collectively as chronic obstructive pulmonary disease (COPD), make it difficult to move air through the bronchial tree into the lungs. The most serious conditions in this category are chronic bronchitis and emphysema. I'll also discuss in this chapter a condition called bronchial asthma, because it may complicate the other problems.

A MAJOR KILLER

The diseases categorized as COPD account for more than 100,000 deaths annually in Americans over sixty years of age. If we count atherosclerosis, which causes most cases of heart disease and most strokes, as one disorder, and all cancer as another, then COPD is the third most common cause of death in the United States. People who die of COPD often have years of restricted activity, invalidism, and discomfort behind them. More COPD patients than cancer patients choose death over a miserable existence made possible by further medical treatment.

I'll describe chronic bronchitis and emphysema separately, but in reality they often occur together. Almost all cases of chronic bronchitis and a majority of emphysema cases are caused by smoking (see part 1, chapter 5, "Smoking: A Deadly Addiction"). A heavy smoker often gets both diseases.

Chronic Bronchitis

A diagnosis of chronic bronchitis is based on the history the patient gives. If you've had a sputum-producing cough for at least three months a year for two consecutive years, by definition you have chronic bronchitis. Chances are you're a smoker.

Smoking and Bronchitis

We have a good understanding of the relationship between smoking and chronic bronchitis. Our bronchial tubes include two types of cells. The predominant cells are cubical and have fine microscopic hairs, or cilia, that line the bronchial tubes. These cilia catch dirt, germs, and mucus and propel them back up, out of the bronchial tree. In a normal person, ciliated cells make up about 90 percent of the lining. Another type of cell, shaped like the bowl of a wineglass and thus called goblet cells, make up the other 10 percent. Goblet cells produce mucus that helps catch germs and dirt particles so they can be propelled outward.

Prolonged heavy smoking increases the number of goblet cells, which results in the production of much more mucus. Now, rather than being a necessary help in clearing the lungs, the mucus becomes a blocking agent itself. It can grow more viscous and lodge in the tiniest bronchial passages or tubules, stopping them up. When this happens the walls of the bronchial tubes get irritated and scarred, which narrows the bronchial tubes and makes the lung less pliable. The extra mucus produces coughing and, in concert with the narrowed bronchial passages, causes shortness of breath (see below).

Most sedentary people don't use their full lung capacity anyway, so the lung damage often progresses significantly before most people notice shortness of breath. The "smoker's cough," a concomitant of long-term smoking, is really the tipoff that chronic bronchitis has developed. Careful measurement of breathing capacity would reveal a compromised ability to move air in and out of the lungs.

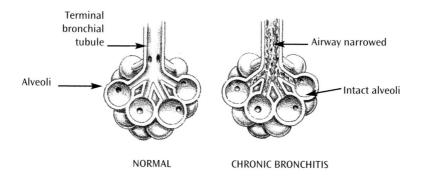

NORMAL   CHRONIC BRONCHITIS

The terminal bronchioles and alveoli of the lungs. In chronic bronchitis, the airways are narrowed but the alveoli are preserved. In emphysema, the alveoli are damaged or destroyed, making oxygen transfer to the blood vessels difficult.

Emphysema

While the definition of chronic bronchitis is based on symptoms, the definition of emphysema is based on a description of the damage done to the lungs. The bronchial tree branches into progressively smaller tubules that end in microscopic sacs called alveoli. A microscopic network of blood vessels surrounds the alveoli. It is here that the oxygen in inhaled air enters your bloodstream, and here that the carbon dioxide transfers from your blood to your alveoli and is breathed out. Emphysema refers to a condition in which the alveoli are destroyed (*see below*).

The Causes of Emphysema

Smoking is the cause of this destruction in most people with emphysema. However, a small percentage of people with emphysema have an inherited disorder called alpha 1 antitrypsin deficiency; even if they don't smoke, their alveoli will be destroyed. Individuals who have this inherited deficiency and also smoke often develop severe emphysema in their thirties or forties.

People with pure emphysema — that is, uncomplicated by other pulmonary disorders — don't cough. Shortness of breath is often the first symptom, and when it appears considerable damage may have already been done.

If you're a smoker, you should talk with your doctor about having a simple breathing test each year. The test, called the one-second forced expiratory volume (FEV 1), measures how much air you can exhale in one second after a maximal inhalation. It's enormously beneficial even beyond its role in diagnosis. For many people, the result of an FEV 1 is the impetus that gets them to quit smoking.

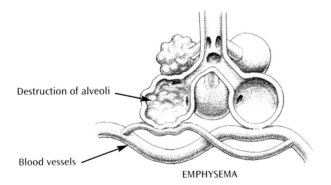

Destruction of alveoli

Blood vessels

EMPHYSEMA

The terminal bronchioles and alveoli of the lungs. In chronic bronchitis, the airways are narrowed but the alveoli are preserved. In emphysema, the alveoli are damaged or destroyed, making oxygen transfer to the blood vessels difficult.

How Are Chronic Bronchitis and Emphysema Treated?

Almost everybody with COPD derives some benefit from stopping smoking. Those with chronic bronchitis reap the most benefit; those with pure emphysema may not improve, but at least lung destruction slows down or stops. If you have smoking-related COPD, you should:

- Stop smoking
- Prevent secondary infections
- Get annual flu shots
- Get a pneumonia vaccine every five years
- Get prompt treatment of secondary bronchial infection with antibiotics

You may also have to use a bronchial dilator. In very rare cases of emphysema with "blebs," or large areas of local destruction, surgery to remove them may improve breathing.

A WORD OF CAUTION

Any change in sputum from white to yellow or green and any sudden worsening of shortness of breath should be reported to your doctor immediately. Most sudden worsening is due to a secondary infection, and prompt use of antibiotics may prevent hospitalization.

Bronchial Dilators

Bronchial-dilating medication is used primarily for asthma, but in most people with COPD bronchial spasms exacerbate the symptoms. If spasms can be relieved with a dilator, breathing may improve.

Dilating medication is best delivered by inhalation. There are three categories of drugs, used in various combinations and doses:

- *Beta agonists.* Albuterol (Ventolin and Proventil) is the most common.
- *Anticholinergics.* Ipratropium and Alupent are the most common.
- *Inhaled corticosteroids.* There are several different types that achieve similar results. Brand names include Beclovent, Vanceril, Pulmonaire, AeroBid, Flovent, and Azmacort. If these don't improve breathing, oral corticosteroids (prednisone) should be considered.

When a Patient Has to Go on a Ventilator

A severe worsening of COPD — often precipitated by bronchial infection or pneumonia — may require hospitalization and temporary reliance on a ventilator in intensive care. The decision whether to use a ventilator has both a technical and an ethical component. Doctors can tell who will not survive without the use of a ventilator. The decision the family, the patient, and the doctor have to make is whether it's really in the patient's best interest to go on a ventilator.

I deal with these issues at length in part 3, chapter 30, "Dealing with Dying." Suffice it to say here, I've counseled patients and their families against a ventilator if lung damage has clearly progressed so far that the patient won't live after coming off the ventilator. On the other hand, if there's a reversible infection or fluid buildup in the lungs from congestive heart failure, and the odds are favorable for surviving off the ventilator once the correctable problem improves, then I advise going ahead with it. Ultimately, patients or their families make the final decision.

Asthma

Vera was eighty-eight years old, very active, and in reasonably good health. She had an occasional mild asthma attack and used inhalers for that. She spent her summers in Maine, returning to Washington in mid-September. One year when she and her husband reopened their house in Washington, it seemed "dank and mildewy." She called me and said she was having an asthma attack that was worse than usual, and her inhalers weren't helping. I advised her to go to the emergency room at once, and she and her daughter promptly departed. On the way to the hospital Vera experienced more shortness of breath. When she got to the emergency room she was fighting for breath, and within minutes she became unconscious.

Vera had an emergency intubation of her trachea — insertion of a breathing tube into the airway through the mouth. She was given massive amounts of medication: beta agonists, anticholinergics, and cortico-steroids both intravenously and through a ventilator. Within an hour she was responsive, and over the next few days she returned to normal. She was discharged with advice to use her albuterol every day. Initially she was on oral prednisone, but eventually she switched to Flovent, an inhaled corticosteroid.

Vera is now ninety-two and has not had another significant asthma attack. But if she and her daughter hadn't acted promptly and gotten her to the hospital, she would have died within a matter of minutes.

What Is Asthma?

Asthma is a disorder characterized by recurring episodes of bronchial airway obstruction, the result of excessive constriction of the muscles in the bronchial walls, inflammation around the tiny bronchial tubules, and increased and thickened mucus in the airway. Wheezing and shortness of breath are the most common symptoms, but sometimes a cough may be present with only minimal wheezing. One hallmark of asthma is the episodic nature of the attacks. Some people have mild wheezing much of the time, with severe episodes periodically, while others are absolutely free of symptoms much of the time with only occasional flareups.

Asthma isn't one of those diseases that become more prevalent in the older age groups; the number of cases in people over sixty has remained stable over the years (it's risen among younger people). Some people with asthma early in life get better or become totally asymptomatic as they grow older. Others may continue to be afflicted with asthma, and the condition may worsen in later years.

Asthma Triggers and Treatment

An asthma attack can be brought on by several things: a viral or bacterial bronchial infection, inhaled chemical irritants, inhaled allergen pollens or dusts, an allergic reaction to food or sulfites in wine, or a worsening of congestive heart failure. Most attacks can be headed off by inhaling albuterol, ipratropium, or a corticosteroid, or by taking oral prednisone.

A WORD OF CAUTION

Sometimes, in spite of treatment, an asthma attack may continue or worsen, in which case emergency treatment is called for. If you have an attack that gets worse after treatment or that lasts longer than usual, or if you feel extremely short of breath, get to the emergency room immediately.

In addition to the inhaled medications and oral prednisone, there are three oral agents that have been shown to reduce the frequency and severity of attacks: Zyflo, Singulair, and Accolate. My experience with these medications in older patients is limited, but I've seen excellent results when my asthmatic patients make regular use of a corticosteroid inhaler. Large studies show that regular use reduces recurring attacks, emergency room visits, and deaths from asthma. Vera uses her Flovent regularly and has had no further attacks.

REMEMBER THIS

- COPD (chronic bronchitis and emphysema) is a major cause of disability and death in older people.
- Smoking is the cause of almost all cases of chronic bronchitis and contributes to over 80 percent of emphysema cases.
- If you smoke and are looking for a reason to quit, talk to your doctor about doing a simple breathing test, FEV 1.
- Flu and pneumonia shots, prompt treatment of secondary infection, bronchial dilators, and carefully supervised physical therapy help patients with COPD.
- Asthma can occur in older people and may be severe. If you have a severe asthma attack, prompt attention in an emergency room may save your life.
- Inhaled corticosteroids are effective in reducing the number of asthma attacks, hospital visits, and deaths from asthma.

CHAPTER 10

PNEUMONIA AND INFLUENZA

Roughly 75,000 older Americans die every year from influenza and pneumonia. Most such deaths occur in frail individuals who may have other major illnesses; pneumonia may simply be the terminal event, the so-called "old man's friend." In very frail or disabled patients — for example, those who have had a stroke or who have Alzheimer's disease — pneumonia comes as no great surprise, and with the patient's or the family's concurrence aggressive treatment is often avoided. Some deaths from pneumonia, however, are unforeseen and occur in reasonably healthy people. This chapter is devoted primarily to the subject of pneumonia in people not yet ready to die.

> **Did You Know?**
> The incidence of influenza cases and the number of fatal cases vary from year to year, depending on international health factors and the virulence of particular strains of influenza reaching the United States. The influenza epidemic of 1918-19 caused the deaths of more Americans than the total of those killed by HIV/AIDS since that disease was discovered in the early 1980s.

Pneumonia can be caused by a virus, bacteria, or even fungi. Influenza, or the flu, is a viral illness; a secondary bacterial pneumonia often complicates influenza. A severe case of influenza can kill anyone, no matter how old, but people in the third third of life are particularly vulnerable because they often have other health problems that can make it harder for their immune system to combat the virus or the secondary bacterial pneumonia.

Pneumonia

Pneumonia is an infection of lung tissue — the tiny air sacs called alveoli as well as the smaller bronchial tubes. The lungs can be infected by any of a large number of organisms. The most common severe form of pneumonia in older Americans is caused by the bacterium *Streptococcus pneumoniae*, or in doctor's jargon, pneumococcal pneumonia.

Most forms of pneumonia, including pneumococcal pneumonia, come with a variety of symptoms, which in older people may not necessarily be the classic chest symptoms associated with this illness. In a typical case of pneumococcal pneumonia, the first symptoms may be a cough, shaking chills, high fever, muscle aches, rapid shallow breathing, and severe weakness. If the part of the lung affected irritates the pleura — where the lung and chest wall meet — the prominent symptom may be a sharp chest pain brought on by deep breathing or coughing.

In people over seventy-five or eighty, particularly those with other illnesses, pneumonia may cause confusion, shortness of breath, abdominal pain, or nausea, without significant fever or a cough. It's only when the doctor listens to the lungs or looks at a chest X ray that the diagnosis is made.

Rudy

Rudy was sixty years old and had a thriving career as a consultant in the international telecommunications business. He was in excellent health, didn't smoke, and exercised regularly, but occasionally he got tired from a heavy travel schedule. He called one morning early, having arrived back in Washington the night before from a trip to Turkey. He said he had had a "cold" for about a week but thought it had "turned into a flu or something worse." He had run a fever and had two episodes of shaking chills during the early morning hours. I saw him right away.

Rudy looked gray. His breathing was rapid and his temperature was 104.6 degrees Fahrenheit. His chest exam was typical for a form of pneumonia that affects the lungs' lobes, and I decided he should go to the hospital. An X ray confirmed that most of his right lower lobe was affected with pneumonia. Blood and sputum cultures were taken, and Rudy was started on two types of antibiotics to cover not only a probable pneumococcal pneumonia but other possible infecting organisms as well.

The next day Rudy, now on nasal oxygen, still had shaking chills; his neck was stiff and he had developed a headache. Fortunately, a spinal tap showed no evidence of meningitis, which I had begun to suspect, but the blood culture drawn the previous day did show infection with a strain of *Streptococcus pneumoniae* that is resistant to penicillin and several other antibiotics commonly used for pneumonia. I had an infectious disease consultant see him, and he was switched to two different antibiotics, vancomycin and cefotaxime. The next day Rudy showed some improvement, and by the third day he was much better. On the fifth day he was discharged, and though in much better health, he tired easily for over a month after leaving the hospital.

Phyllis

Phyllis was sixty-six years old and had smoked for many years. Although she had cut down, she still smoked about fifteen cigarettes a day. She had the morning cough that is the hallmark of chronic bronchitis — it produced sputum. On a trip Phyllis felt she had "a mild case of the flu" and noticed that her sputum had turned a yellowish brown color. She called my office complaining of back pain, which had become progressively worse. Phyllis was also experiencing weakness in her left leg.

An examination revealed marked tenderness over her lower spine, and her temperature was 101 degrees Fahrenheit. An X ray revealed pneumonia in her right lung, and blood cultures grew *Streptococcus pneumoniae* bacteria. MRI (magnetic resonance imaging) scans of the spine showed a mass pressing up against the wrapping of the spinal cord, which was diagnosed as an epidural abscess. Phyllis had pneumococcal pneumonia that had gotten into her bloodstream (a common scenario) and caused an abscess near her spinal cord. A neurosurgeon operated and drained the abscess. After ten days of aggressive antibiotic therapy, she was able to leave the hospital and has done well since. Fortunately, Phyllis quit smoking, and her chronic bronchial cough has disappeared.

These two cases highlight some significant points about pneumonia. Rudy, who was quite healthy otherwise, had a cold and was fatigued from a demanding travel schedule — probably factors in his becoming ill. His shaking chills, high fever, cough, and rapid breathing were classic symptoms of pneumonia. In addition, the organism infecting him was resistant to the usual antibiotics — a scenario that has become increasingly frequent in recent years. Just ten years ago almost all pneumococcal pneumonia was sensitive to old-fashioned penicillin. Now up to a third of the bacteria are resistant, making the disease much more lethal. It's felt that the overuse of antibiotics for minor viral respiratory infections — which antibiotics cannot cure — is the reason for the development of resistant germs.

Phyllis's case illustrates the fact that people with chronic lung problems are more likely to get pneumonia and should report any change in their cough or sputum. Also, it's typical for the streptococcal bacteria, which can spread through the bloodstream, to cause problems elsewhere, causing conditions such as meningitis, heart valve infection, or in this case, an abscess near the spine.

Who Is More Likely to Get Pneumonia?

Developing a strategy to prevent pneumonia or treat it early starts with a list of those most at risk. They include:

- People over eighty years old
- Anyone with a medical condition that makes deep breathing or swallowing difficult, including chronic bronchitis, emphysema, asthma, congestive heart failure, a lung tumor, a neurological disease such as stroke, a chest-wall injury such as a broken rib, alcoholism, or any illness requiring prolonged bed rest
- Smokers
- Anyone with an illness or condition that interferes with the immune system, including people who are undergoing chemotherapy, have had their spleen removed, or have an HIV infection, leukemia, or lymphoma
- Anyone with a viral infection, such as a cold or the flu, that affects the bronchial tree
- People with swallowing difficulties, particularly those that increase the likelihood of aspirating food or drink into the lungs
- Anyone with a seizure disorder

Over eighty. Pneumonia is a much greater risk for people over eighty than for younger people. Typically, people in this age group are less active and more likely to have immobilizing conditions or lung diseases that make them more prone to chest infection. Beyond that, being over eighty means the immune system — and the protective mechanism in the bronchial tree that clears germs or mucus — is less efficient. Any cough or fever should suggest pneumonia, but so should any unexplained weakness or confusion. Rarely, nausea or unexplained upper abdominal pain may be due to pneumonia. In older people the typical pneumonia symptoms of cough and fever may be absent or very minimal.

Other lung problems. People with lung problems such as chronic bronchitis or emphysema are much more prone to pneumonia, and they often get sicker with it than people with normal lungs. If they get pneumonia, people with lung problems often need assisted-breathing devices in intensive care, and pneumonia is frequently the cause of their death. Any worsening of your cough or shortness of breath should be evaluated promptly, and if the usual whitish sputum brought up with a morning cough turns yellow, green, or brown, a secondary infectious bronchitis is probably superimposed on the chronic irritative bronchitis. Prompt, vigorous treatment with antibiotics may prevent pneumonia and hospitalization, but this is a decision your doctor has to make and weigh against overtreatment with antibiotics that can cause resistant bacteria to build up.

Smoking. Smoking is a risk factor for respiratory infections and pneumonia, even in those who don't have chronic lung disease. Smokers get more colds, more acute episodes of bronchitis, and more episodes of pneumonia.

Alcohol. Alcohol is a risk for pneumonia in several respects. In people who drink, the bronchial defenses may be dulled, immunity may be suppressed, and there is increased risk of aspiration.

Injury to the chest wall. People with injury to the chest wall — particularly rib fractures — frequently get pneumonia. When you avoid deep breathing because it's painful, your lungs aren't fully expanding — a perfect setup for the development of an infection. When I prescribe an elastic rib binder as a support for broken ribs, I strongly urge patients not to let the binder inhibit deep breathing to clear the lungs.

> **Did You Know?**
> Anything that keeps you bed bound is a risk for pneumonia because it can prevent you from adequately ventilating your lungs. Doctors are anxious to repair broken hips promptly so that patients will get out of bed and ventilate. Plastic breathing devices called incentive spirometers encourage all postoperative patients to breathe deeply and clear their lungs.

Viral infections. Pneumonia occurs in the lower respiratory tract. Colds or viral infections of the bronchial tree are upper respiratory infections, but they are risks for pneumonia because one, they interfere with the intricate defense mechanism in the bronchial tree, and two, they can lead to bacterial sinusitis, in which infected mucus drains into the lungs. For people with some of the other risk factors for pneumonia, such as chronic lung disease or immobility, a cold or bronchitis may be the factor that tips them over.

Don't Let a Cold Get Worse

The most common medical complaint in the United States is the cold, an upper respiratory infection that doctors call viral rhinitis. Most colds can and should be treated with symptomatic measures. Aspirin, acetaminophen, or ibuprofen is usually adequate for aching and low-grade fever. If sneezing or nasal drainage bothers you, I advise taking pseudoephedrine, available over the counter, or one of the prescription nonsedating antihistamines — Claritin, Zyrtec, or Allegra — which come with or without pseudoephedrine. If you have a history of coronary disease or cardiac arrhythmia, you shouldn't take pseudoephedrine, either by itself or with other drugs. I also advise elderly patients not to use the older antihistamines such as Benadryl or Chlor-Trimeton, because they can cause drowsiness and, in older men, urinary retention. Very thick mucus in the nasal passages or sinuses, and a troublesome bronchial cough, can be treated with guaifenesin, which helps thin secretions and bring them up.

KEEP THINGS MOIST!

If you have a cold or upper respiratory infection, it's important to keep yourself hydrated. You should drink plenty of fluids and humidify the air in your bedroom. If your furnace doesn't have a built-in humidifier, then you should have a room humidifier for use in the winter when the heat is on and the windows are closed. Humidifiers can be found in large drugstores and appliance departments, but always listen to one operating before you buy it: If it's too loud, you'll end up turning it off.

Also, if your head is feeling stuffy or you're beginning to have sinus discomfort, taking a hot shower and letting the water run over your face, or simply bathing your face with hot water, may help drain the mucus that's wreaking the havoc.

Although antibiotics are frequently overprescribed, sometimes it's appropriate to speak to your doctor about possibly taking one. For adults, the two most common complications of colds are bacterial sinusitis and secondary bacterial tracheobronchitis. If you develop pain on either side of your nose or just above your eyes, or if you have a fever and your nasal drainage becomes discolored — heavy yellow, yellow-green, or brownish — then you probably have a secondary sinus infection. If the sputum turns from whitish to the same discolored material, you may have developed bacterial bronchitis. In either case, contact your doctor and be evaluated for the possible addition of antibiotics.

Other Forms of Pneumonia

Several other strains of bacteria can cause what we call community-acquired pneumonia, or pneumonia contracted outside a hospital or nursing home. The organisms that cause community-acquired pneumonia tend to differ from those that cause pneumonia in hospitalized patients, or

---

PNEUMONIA VACCINE

I believe everyone over the age of sixty should get a pneumonia vaccine every five years. The U.S. Public Health Service advises this for everyone over sixty-five, but with emerging resistant strains of streptococcal bacteria, sixty makes more sense. The vaccine is effective against about 90 percent of the strains of *Streptococcus pneumoniae*, either preventing or greatly reducing the severity of the pneumococcal infection. It's safe and has very few significant side effects. The brand commonly used is called Pneumovax.

One word of caution: the vaccine is of no benefit against many other forms of pneumonia. So don't say to yourself, "This cough can't be pneumonia because I've had my Pneumovax." You can still get pneumonia, but your chances of getting a teeth-chattering pneumococcal pneumonia will be dramatically reduced.

---

in debilitated or immune-compromised patients such as those with malignant disease or on chemotherapy.

Some common pneumonia-causing organisms other than *Streptococcus pneumoniae* are:

- □ *Hemophilus influenza*
- □ Staphylococcus
- □ Group A Streptococcus
- □ *Branhamella catarrhalis*
- □ Mycoplasma
- □ *Legionella pneumophila* (which causes legionnaires' disease)

If you get a fever that lasts more than two or three days or have a prolonged cough, discolored sputum, chest pain with breathing, or shortness of breath with a chest infection, you should see your doctor right away. If you're in overall good health, mild pneumonia can possibly be treated with vigorous oral antibiotics outside a hospital setting. Postponing treatment, however, makes it more likely you'll end up in the hospital.

A family epidemic of bronchial or chest infection suggests a mycoplasma infection, which if untreated can keep you sick for three or four weeks, but which will respond to aggressive antibiotic therapy.

Influenza

As I mentioned earlier, influenza is a debilitating viral infection that causes high fever, often extreme weakness, and/or severe bronchitis. People with influenza may also get pneumonia from the direct activity of the virus in the lungs; more frequently, they develop secondary bacterial pneumonia from staphylococcus or *Hemophilus influenzae*.

The influenza virus is elusive and undergoes changes periodically, producing new strains every year or so. The U.S. Centers for Disease Control tracks the strains of the virus that emerge worldwide in an effort to anticipate which are likely to cause epidemics in the United States. They rarely miss, and the resulting vaccines are 60 to 90 percent effective in preventing severe influenza.

Preventing and Treating the Flu

Make no mistake: getting vaccinated against the flu significantly reduces the likelihood of death or hospitalization. Because my practice is in Washington, D.C., where people run a high risk of exposure to international travelers, I recommend an annual flu shot for all my patients over sixty years old. Around late October and early November is the best time for the shot, unless an epidemic seems to be starting earlier than usual. One rare but severe side effect is a paralyzing neurological syndrome called Guiltanin-Barre. If you feel unusually weak after your flu shot, talk to your doctor right away.

There is no dramatic treatment for influenza once you get it, but new drugs in the neuraminidase-inhibitor family, if taken the first day or so, may reduce the severity and duration of symptoms. Relenza (zanamivir), which is inhaled, and Flumadine (rimantadine) or Tamiflu (oseltamivir), taken by mouth, can help, but not if you're already three or four days into the infection. I prefer the oral medications because the delivery system for the inhalant is complicated, and the window of opportunity for Relenza may be even shorter than the two days for the oral drugs. They may also be taken as a preventive in family or nursing home situations.

A couple of other comments about influenza. First, if you have a mild or moderate case and suddenly get worse, get a medical evaluation — you may have secondary bacterial pneumonia. Shortness of breath also needs immediate evaluation. Second, if you get influenza, you should expect the acute stage of fever, aches, and severe cough to last five to seven days. You may also experience a second stage that includes symptoms of weakness, easy fatigue, a chilly feeling, vague aches across the back and chest, and often depression. This can last as long as a month or six weeks depending on your age and previous state of health.

REMEMBER THIS

- Pneumonia due to *Streptococcus pneumoniae* (the pneumococcus bacterium) is common in elderly people, particularly those who are debilitated or bedridden, or have chronic heart or lung disease.
- If you're bedridden or debilitated, or have a chest injury, do your best to stay mobile and practice deep breathing to stave off pneumonia.
- Any fever, chest pain with breathing, or severe or persistent cough should be reported to your doctor immediately.
- If you have chronic bronchial or lung problems, any change in your sputum or breathing should be reported.
- Everyone over sixty should get the pneumonia vaccine every five years. Keep in mind, however, that the vaccine is not a panacea: It won't protect you from several nonpneumococcal forms of community-acquired pneumonia.
- Influenza is a severe, debilitating, and potentially fatal viral disease.
- Annual flu vaccines are dramatically successful in reducing your likelihood of getting a debilitating or fatal case of influenza.
- New antiviral agents, if taken in the first two days, may make influenza less severe.

CHAPTER 11

LIVER AND KIDNEY DISEASE

Nonmalignant fatal diseases of the liver and kidneys, though not of the same order of magnitude as heart disease, cancer, or stroke, are common enough to warrant our attention, particularly because many of these conditions can be prevented. In this chapter, I address the three most common forms of liver failure: viral hepatitis, drug-induced liver disease, and alcohol-induced liver disease. I'll also discuss the damaging effects of diabetes and high blood pressure on the kidneys, as well as nephritis and kidney infections.

Viral Hepatitis

Three significant viruses can attack and destroy the liver: hepatitis A, B, and C. Hepatitis A, primarily transmitted from person to person or from food — shellfish being a typical source — is more common in developing countries, and you can catch it even after a brief visit. Hepatitis B and C are much less easily transmitted; sources include blood transfusion, injection, sexual transmission, or prolonged, close contact with urine or feces, such as working in a day care facility or a nursing home, or living for a long time in an undeveloped country with potential for repeated exposure.

People with hepatitis A are more severely jaundiced in the acute stage than people with hepatitis B or C. The vast majority, however — well over 99 percent — recover without

> **Did You Know?**
> Hepatitis C is on the rise in the United States. For many years we weren't able to detect it in blood screening, and it was transmitted invisibly through transfusions. Now all transfused blood is tested for hepatitis C as well as A and B and AIDS, ensuring the safety of the blood supply.

chronic problems, and only one person in several thousand experiences liver failure. People with hepatitis B and C are not as ill initially but may develop chronic hepatitis, which can linger for years, ultimately destroying the liver. People with chronic hepatitis have a tendency to develop primary liver cancer, an otherwise uncommon malignancy.

Gloria was seventy-nine when she slipped on the ice and fractured her hip, resulting in significant bleeding into the tissue around the fracture (people usually lose more than a pint of blood into injured tissue). During a complicated hip replacement, Gloria required three units of transfused blood. Two or three years later, she began feeling unusual fatigue and ached as though she had a viral illness. Chronic hepatitis C was diagnosed. By her mid-eighties Gloria had developed secondary cirrhosis and liver failure. Once a bright, alert woman, she drifted into a delirium, then a constant stupor. About six years after the transfusion Gloria died of liver failure and a secondary urinary infection.

Liver failure from chronic hepatitis C is on the rise in the United States. Like Gloria, most people who contracted hepatitis C did so in the 1980s and early 1990s, before this virus was detectable in the blood supply. Today, with reliable testing available, your chance of getting hepatitis C is less than 1 in 100,000 transfusions. Hepatitis C is also spread by intravenous drug abuse and through sexual contact. The chance of someone over sixty who has not received a transfusion having hepatitis C is very low.

Primary Liver Cancer and Chronic Hepatitis

Primary liver cancer — cancer that originates in the liver rather than spreading there from another part of the body — is unusual in this country. But around the world, it is currently the number one cause of cancer death. The reason for the almost epidemic proportion of liver cancer is the prevalence of chronic hepatitis B in developing countries. Up to 15 percent of the population in some countries have chronic hepatitis B. Three of the four cases of primary liver cancer I diagnosed were people who had contracted hepatitis in their childhood or teenage years in a developing country.

Preventive Steps

If you're traveling to a developing country, you should get the hepatitis A vaccine before going and between six and twelve months after that. This will give you lifelong immunity.

One thing I routinely advise, as a reasonable hepatitis screen, is to include liver function tests in your annual physical exam. (A comprehensive metabolic profile includes this.) If the function tests are normal, you don't need to worry or get more specific hepatitis B or C antibody tests.

A hepatitis B vaccine is now part of the standard immunization for children and adolescents in the United States. Americans over sixty who should have it are:

- ☐ Healthcare workers
- ☐ People who work or volunteer in day care facilities or nursing homes
- ☐ People planning to live for more than six months in a developing country

A brief trip to a developing country (less than several months) has not been associated with increased hepatitis B infection. Currently, no hepatitis C vaccine is available or advised.

If you have chronic hepatitis B or C, you should avoid alcohol altogether. In certain individuals antiviral treatments can slow the progression of hepatitis B or C.

Drug-Induced Liver Failure

Drug-induced hepatitis can be tragic, progressing dramatically and leading to liver failure and death.

Elaine
Elaine was sixty-two and had just retired as a music teacher. She had had diabetes for several years for which she took two oral medications, but her condition was increasingly harder to control. Elaine was started on another oral drug, Rezulin (troglitazone), while continuing with the two other medications. Her diabetes improved, and periodic checks of liver function over the first few months of therapy showed no problems; as a result, they were done less frequently. About ten months after starting Rezulin, however, she felt nausea, fatigue, and muscle aches and developed jaundice. A blood test of liver function now showed massive liver damage, and Elaine died several days later.

Arthur
Arthur was sixty-four and had suffered periodic back pain. One day while he was moving large flowerpots inside from his porch he developed severe,

unrelenting pain. His orthopedist prescribed Tylenol (acetaminophen) and then Tylenol with codeine. Arthur took both types of Tylenol in "moderately large amounts" and continued to have two or three cocktails in the evening. He developed jaundice and severe liver failure and died within a matter of days, as his family was desperately trying to get him on a list for a liver transplant.

Elaine's death was due to Rezulin, a prescribed drug with possible liver toxicity. Although the monitoring had been reasonable, the drug still led to liver failure. The FDA has since removed Rezulin from the market, but there are similar diabetes drugs — and many other types of drugs — deemed low risk by the FDA that can cause potentially irreversible liver damage. Fortunately, most drugs affecting the liver, like cholesterol-lowering statin drugs, do so in a very gradual fashion and are safe so long as periodic blood screens for subtle liver damage are done. If your doctor prescribes something that may have liver toxicity, be sure you follow up with blood test monitoring.

A WORD OF CAUTION

For many years, we thought that Tylenol was about as safe as a medication could be. Aspirin could cause hemorrhages, ibuprofen could cause ulcers or fluid retention. If you were worried about safety, then Tylenol was the mild painkiller or fever reducer of choice. Cases like Arthur's have taught us better. Short-term use of large amounts or chronic use of moderate amounts, particularly if you're also drinking, can be lethal. Unfortunately, we don't know enough about what is a dangerous amount, and the FDA hasn't been able to publish guidelines. At present, I would simply advise not going over six regular Tylenol (325 mg) a day, and not for more than five days. Don't use Tylenol if you have previous liver damage, and don't drink alcohol when you're taking it. For most people, aspirin or ibuprofen may be the better choice.

Alcohol and Liver Disease

Alcohol damages the liver in two different ways. First, it can cause inflammation of the liver cells, or alcohol-induced hepatitis, which may be mild and transient. Alcohol-induced hepatitis may start after a brief binge. Liver function tests done on college students after just a weekend of binging often show evidence of irritation. Prolonged binging on top of an already irritated liver can result in fatal alcohol-induced hepatitis. (See part 2, chapter 17, "Alcoholism and Alcohol Abuse," for a typical case.)

Alcohol excess can also result in fat buildup in the liver cells and significant liver enlargement. The effects are dramatic when viewed under the microscope: the liver cells are filled with large fat droplets, distorting the cell architecture. This condition is totally reversible in its early stages if you stop drinking. If drinking continues, the problem may progress to irreversible cell damage and scarring, a condition that often coexists with alcohol-induced hepatitis.

Cirrhosis of the Liver

Cirrhosis of the liver — cirrhosis comes from the Greek word for scar — involves a buildup of fibrous or scar tissue throughout the liver, which distorts the arrangement of cells and ultimately kills some of them. Cirrhosis can occur in the wake of many forms of liver damage, but particularly after chronic viral or alcohol-induced hepatitis. Unlike a fatty liver or early alcohol liver irritation, severe cirrhosis damage is permanent, chronic, and potentially fatal, though if you stop drinking progression may be slow. Liver biopsies in people who continue to drink often show evidence of cirrhosis, fatty infiltration of the liver cells, and alcohol-induced hepatitis.

In cirrhosis, blood flow through the liver is slowed. The backed-up pressure can cause fluid to build up in the abdomen and may dilate veins in the esophagus that can rupture and bleed. As liver function begins to fail, episodes of confusion may become common.

Everyone should periodically have a liver function test. If you're a moderately heavy drinker and your doctor notes even the most minimal abnormality, you should stop drinking until every test is absolutely normal, then take a long hard look at your drinking pattern with your doctor or a counselor in alcohol abuse. You may be better off stopping permanently. (See part 2, chapter 17, "Alcoholism and Alcohol Abuse.")

Kidney Disease

The two conditions that cause most cases of kidney disease are diabetes and high blood pressure. Diabetes is the most common cause of kidney failure leading to dialysis. High blood pressure doesn't necessarily result in full-blown kidney failure, but it does damage the kidneys, leaving seriously ill older people more vulnerable if they have heart failure or contract pneumonia.

The best preventive for the kidney complications of these two diseases is strict control of blood sugar and blood pressure. The damaging effect of high blood pressure on the kidneys is much greater if you also have diabetes, and even borderline blood pressure elevation can be dangerous. The blood pressure goal for people with diabetes should be below 120/80. Diabetic patients should also have periodic checks for tiny amounts of protein in the urine, which would be an indication to go even lower, to 120/75.

Nephritis

Nephritis is a general term meaning inflammation of the kidneys, a problem with many different causes. One postulated mechanism for several types of kidney inflammation is an autoimmune reaction, that is, when something influences the body's immune system to turn on itself and damage the kidneys, particularly the tiny clusters of blood vessels where blood is initially filtered. Strep throat, heart infections, and a general autoimmune process of unknown causes are examples of diseases that can set off events that damage the kidneys.

Nephritis may begin as an acute illness with fever, aching muscles, and blood in the urine, or it may be very subtle in its onset. Nephritis can cause a great deal of protein to be lost in the urine, which in turn can result in general swelling. (Protein helps keep fluid in the blood vessels, and low protein allows fluid to build up in body tissues instead.) Certainly any swelling or dark urine should be reported immediately, and a severe sore throat should be seen and cultured promptly to prevent a possible streptococcus infection from setting up a kidney-damaging reaction. As mentioned in part 1, chapter 6, "Cancer," everyone should have a urinalysis every year, which among other things looks for protein or red blood cells as a sign of nephritis or early bladder or kidney cancer, and white blood cells suggesting an infection.

The Dangers of Kidney Infection

Recurrent or chronic kidney infection can lead to kidney failure, something that should never be allowed to happen. Urinary tract infections in women are much more frequent than in men and should be treated promptly and thoroughly.

If you have frequent, urgent, or painful urination or blood in the urine, you should report it immediately and have a urinalysis and urine culture (which determines whether a minute amount of urine put on a bacterial culture plate grows germs). If the urinalysis shows white blood cells, your doctor can make an educated guess about the most likely antibiotic to initiate treatment while awaiting the culture result.

Three or four weeks after the acute infection is treated, once the symptoms are gone and you're off antibiotics, you should have a follow-up urine culture to make sure the infection has completely cleared. If infections recur, you'll need to have a test of the urinary tract to be sure there is no blockage.

The urinalysis done during your annual physical exam is a good screen to rule out infection, but if you've had several infections in the past, a urine culture should be done to ensure that the infection hasn't come back.

REMEMBER THIS

- Viral hepatitis B and C can be chronic and fatal. They are spread by transfusions, sexual contact, major contact with body fluids, and medical accidents. Tranfusions are safer today because these two forms of hepatitis can now be screened for.
- Most people past sixty don't need a hepatitis B vaccine unless they're medical professionals, they work in nursing homes or day care centers, or they plan to live abroad.
- Many prescribed drugs can cause liver failure and require monitoring and caution. In large amounts, over-the-counter Tylenol can also cause liver failure.
- Liver function tests should be done as part of your lab blood profile on annual exams.
- Strict control of diabetes and high blood pressure offers the best hope to prevent most types of kidney failure.
- Bloody and dark urine and unexplained swelling are possible signs of nephritis and should be reported immediately.
- Urinary tract infections should be treated promptly. A culture should guide the ultimate choice of antibiotics, and it should be followed up with another culture confirming eradication of the infection.
- A routine urinalysis for protein and red and white blood cells should be part of your annual physical exam.

PART TWO

STAYING ON TOP OF YOUR HEALTH

LEROY "SATCHEL" PAIGE was a legendary pitcher who started out in the Negro leagues and, when racial barriers broke, went on to the major leagues, where he pitched until he was in his fifties. The press perpetuated the myth that Paige didn't know how old he was, and he enjoyed feeding it. When asked his age, he once answered, "You're only as old as you think you are, if you didn't know how old you were."

You're only as old as you think you are. Today, more and more people in their sixties and beyond adhere to this philosophy. And it's a good one, up to a point. If you watch your health and take measures to prevent or control degenerative disease, chances are you'll live a more youthful life than your parents and grandparents did at your age. There are all sorts of things you can do to protect yourself, such as staying out of the noonday sun, learning proper lifting techniques, cutting down on your alcohol consumption, getting enough calcium, and in general, knowing when to call the doctor. In part 2, I'll be covering all these topics and many more, in the hopes of better positioning you to guard your health. But first, let's talk about exercise.

The Importance of Exercise

If I had to make a single recommendation for helping people stay on top of their health, it would be this: exercise. Any number of studies on the aging process show that exercise can prevent disease, boost spirits, and help people maintain their independence, but studies aren't needed to convince me — I've seen this every day in my practice. My eighty-year-old patients who exercise regularly look like sixty-year-olds, and my sixty-year-old couch potatoes grow frail and sick before their time.

How Can Exercise Benefit You?

The benefits of exercise are dramatic. Regular, moderately vigorous activity can extend your youth by a decade or two and enhance your pleasure in life. If you're very old, regular activity can keep you independent longer. Specifically, exercise helps prevent disease, including:

- Heart disease (inactive people have about an 80 percent greater chance of a heart attack than active people)
- Stroke (strokes are much less prevalent in exercisers)
- Osteoporosis (exercise slows bone deterioration and lessens the chance of disabling fractures)
- Arthritis (building muscle helps support the joints)
- Cancer (though the statistics are not as dramatic for cancer as for heart disease, fit people die less from cancer, particularly colon cancer)
- Mild infection (moderate exercise appears to improve the immune system)

In addition to preventing disease, exercise has a striking effect on quality of life. Regular activity can improve your mood, help you sleep, and relieve mild depression. For years patients have been reporting these advantages to me; recent studies have clearly confirmed what they've said.

What Kind of Exercise Should You Do?

There are two basic types of exercise, aerobic and anaerobic. Aerobic exercise includes walking, jogging, swimming, cycling, dancing, racket sports, golfing (if you walk the course), gardening, and certain household activities. Aerobic exercise strengthens your lungs and your heart. It makes you breathe faster and sends your heart rate up. You consume more oxygen and burn calories faster. If you move from a sedentary lifestyle to a lifestyle of regular aerobic activity, you'll notice that while exercising you grow less fatigued and less short of breath. Why? Because over time you're increasing the number of mitochondria, the tiny energy factories in your muscle cells; your muscles become more efficient at producing energy. Aerobic exercise also raises HDL cholesterol (high-density lipoprotein, the good kind) and lowers LDL cholesterol (low-density lipoprotein, the bad kind), which is good news for your heart. And last but not least, aerobic exercise helps you control your weight.

The second type of exercise, anaerobic, builds muscle strength and tone. Weight lifting and strenuous calisthenics like push-ups are typical anaerobic activities. The difference between the two types of exercise is somewhat artificial, because aerobic exercise also builds muscle and anaerobic exercise also increases endurance. And like aerobic exercise, anaerobic activity helps you control weight or lose it. Muscle tissue has a higher metabolism than fat, and as you gain muscle through anaerobic exercise, you burn calories faster.

In general, both types of exercise help turn back the clock. A regular program of aerobic and anaerobic activity builds muscles throughout the body, even the facial and neck muscles that are so important in maintaining a youthful appearance.

MUSCLE WASTING AND EXERCISE

One of the most troublesome signs of aging is what doctors call sarcopenia, a loss of muscle tone and strength. Fortunately, muscle wasting in the elderly can be dramatically reversed with anaerobic exercise. For people in their sixties and seventies, weight training added to an aerobic exercise program dramatically improves strength and athletic performance. Studies on nursing home patients in their eighties and nineties show that properly designed weight training improves quality of life and increases independence, even for people in wheelchairs. This new philosophy about exercise — add weight training to your aerobic program — has been one of the most encouraging trends in geriatric medicine in my professional lifetime.

Starting an Exercise Program

All exercise programs must be launched cautiously. If you push yourself too hard in the beginning, you run the risk of heart attack (with aerobic activity) or muscle or tendon injury (with aerobic or anaerobic activity).

Talk to your doctor about whether you need a stress test. If you're just embarking on a walking program or light calisthenics, you probably don't need a stress test, but if you've been sedentary for a long time and you're considering more ambitious exercise such as cycling or jogging, you probably should have one. A stress test will tell you whether your heart can handle the unaccustomed burden and what level of activity is safe for you.

If I've convinced you that weight training is worth pursuing, make sure you begin with a trainer. If you plan to lift weights at home, ask your doctor to recommend someone. Gyms and fitness centers usually have trainers on staff. A trainer will start you out on low weights and instruct you in proper lifting techniques.

Whatever you end up doing, whether it's walking or running a marathon, lifting two-pound weights or one-hundred pounders, remember: Protect your heart and muscles. Start slowly and build up gradually.

Aerobic Exercise: Strengthening Your Heart

To reap the benefits of any aerobic exercise, you need to work up at least a mild sweat and get your pulse above 100, preferably 120 to 130. To take your pulse, press your inner wrist on the thumb side and count the beats for fifteen seconds, then multiply by four.

The best exercise is convenient and fun, an activity you want to do regularly. Some people enjoy suiting up and going to the gym to walk on a treadmill — it's a social occasion. For others, the prospect of a gym puts up more psychological roadblocks than just stepping out the front door for a brisk walk.

How much aerobic exercise do you need? If you want to strengthen your heart, you should exercise for thirty minutes five or six times a week — at least two and a half hours total. For people who are still working, daily exercise may be difficult to schedule. One alternative is to do an hour of aerobics on Saturday and an hour on Sunday, with thirty minutes on Tuesday and perhaps another thirty minutes on Thursday.

Keep in mind that you don't have to engage in a formal exercise regimen to meet your aerobic goal. You can fulfill part of your goal simply by becoming more active — walking up steps instead of taking the elevator, pushing a lawn mower instead of riding on one, sweeping the porch instead of watching television.

A WORD OF CAUTION

Do you enjoy jogging? Remember, as a runner ages the risk of knee, hip, and ankle injury goes up. If your knees or hips begin to hurt, back off and shape a new, less ambitious aerobic program. Rapid walking or slow jogging is a good substitute for hard running. And don't forget swimming — this non-weight-bearing exercise is great for people with joint aches.

Anaerobic Exercise: Building Your Muscle

To prevent or correct muscle wasting, you should do anaerobic exercises on each group of muscles. Using a universal gym or weight machine is best, if one is available, but free weights in your home and some calisthenics can nearly duplicate the benefits. Sporting goods stores sell dumbbells and weights you can strap on to your ankles and wrists.

In the gym, work on the upper body with presses, pull-down machines, and arm curls. For older people, a cautious workout on leg machines can help prevent falls. In your home, you can use dumbbells for your torso and arms and leg raises with ankle weights for your legs and abdomen. If you're a small woman, you may need to start with three pounds or less, gradually moving up to five or more pounds. Men can usually start with ten pounds and some can work their way up to twenty pounds or more. A good program is to work the upper body three days a week and the legs the other three days, but it may be more convenient for you to combine upper and lower body in single sessions done three times a week.

Staying on Top of Your Health

While it's important that you keep your heart healthy and your muscles from wasting, exercise isn't a cure-all for the diseases of aging. It won't protect you from a hereditary predisposition to certain diseases, and it won't undo damage you may have inflicted on your body in the carefree days of youth, for example, when you overexposed yourself to the sun or listened to too much loud pop music. To live a more active life in the third third, what you need, in addition to exercise, is information — information about everything from osteoporosis and sexual dysfunction to back pain and fatigue. How can you prevent or cope with these problems? Read on.

CHAPTER 12

OSTEOPOROSIS

Osteoporosis is a loss of bone tissue. People with osteoporosis have sparse, porous bones that can easily break. This condition is most commonly seen in women, who as they advance in years lose 30 to 50 percent of the bone mass built in childhood and young adulthood. But while osteoporosis is typically associated with women, it is an affliction that also visits men in extreme old age (*see below*).

A Scourge in the Elderly

Osteoporosis can be devastating. Simple acts such as bending over or sneezing can cause compression fractures in the vertebrae, which, viewed on X rays, appear wedge-shaped rather than square or rectangular (*see opposite top*). Osteoporotic women often shrink and develop the characteristic stooped posture known as dowager's hump; if height loss is severe, the ribcage may come to settle on the pelvis, cramping the abdominal organs and causing the belly to protrude, especially in women with weak abdominal muscles (*see opposite bottom*). In women with dowager's hump, back pain can be severe and last for weeks. Another complication of osteoporosis is severe constipation after a fracture because of swelling around the nerves that supply the intestines.

Normal calcified bone *(left)* and weak, porous, osteoporotic bone *(right)*

Normal vertebrae *(left)* and wedged or partially collapsed osteoporotic vertebrae *(right)*

People with severe osteoporosis are typically as fragile as twigs, and though they may have perfectly normal vascular systems and mental abilities, they can easily become invalids. A patient of mine in her early nineties developed three separate, spontaneous leg fractures simply from walking around her small apartment. Each event resulted in hospitalization, and ultimately she was relegated to a wheelchair, her independence gone.

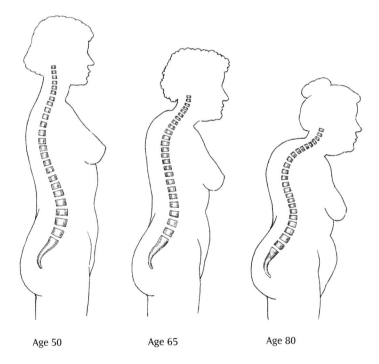

Age 50   Age 65   Age 80

Typical osteoporotic posture. This diagram illustrates an average case of osteo-porosis; many women have more pronounced deformity.

What Causes Osteoporosis?

The easiest way to understand osteoporosis is to picture bone as a living structure, with some cells that build it up and some cells that break it down. One group is the construction crew, the other the demolition crew. The construction crew, made up of osteoblasts, builds a framework of proteinlike material and adds calcium to it. The demolition crew, made up of osteoclasts, breaks the structure down and sends calcium back into the bloodstream. Until you reach the age of about thirty, your bone is in "positive balance." The osteoblasts are harder at work than the osteoclasts. Your skeleton is strong and has enough resilience to withstand heavy weight bearing as well as most falls and blows. Around thirty, however, the balance moves gradually to the negative side. The osteoclasts become a little more active than the osteoblasts, and slightly more bone is broken down than built up.

> **Did You Know?**
> The statistics are sobering. About 20 million Americans have osteoporosis, and among this population 1.3 million fractures occur each year, often resulting in the loss of independent living. About one-third of all postmenopausal white women suffer hip fractures. Only one-fourth of them return to their former lifestyles, and each year about 65,000 women die following such fractures. As for men, one-sixth of those in extreme old age break a hip.

Most men, because the loss of bone is slow enough or the amount of bone at age thirty was great enough, tolerate bone loss without symptoms until extreme old age. In menopausal women, bone loss accelerates, and the potential for osteoporosis in just a few years becomes significant. Some women are at much greater risk than others.

Risk Factors

Both hereditary and environmental factors play a role in osteoporosis. Some of the common predisposing factors are:

☐ *Heredity*
   Female
   Asian, Latin American, and particularly northern European ancestry
   Small stature
   Mother or sister with osteoporosis

☐ *Medical conditions*
  Early menopause
  Postmenopausal
  Surgical removal of ovaries before menopause
  Overactive thyroid gland
  Overactive parathyroid gland
  Overactive adrenal gland
  Excessive thyroid replacement
  History of medication with corticosteroids (prednisone)
  Rheumatoid arthritis
☐ *Lifestyle*
  Physical inactivity
  Excessive alcohol intake
  Smoking

Among women, those of African ancestry run the least risk, those from the Mediterranean are at intermediate risk, and Asians, Latin Americans, and women of northern European ancestry run the greatest risk. No matter what the ancestry, women whose mothers had osteoporosis are at greater risk. Small-boned women tend to develop osteoporosis more frequently, though large-boned women can also suffer from the disease.

Several medical conditions are associated with premature osteoporosis. Early menopause or early surgical removal of the ovaries is a major risk, since they result in loss of estrogen, which accelerates bone loss. An overactive thyroid, parathyroid, or adrenal gland can cause osteoporosis in either sex. Drugs, such as too high a dose of thyroid hormone given for an underactive thyroid gland, and particularly the use of cortisone-like drugs, prednisone being the most common, can be major risks. If you run any of these risks, you should be assessed earlier than most people, and preventive measures should be taken earlier.

While you cannot change hereditary risk factors, there are risk factors over which you have some degree of control. Because alcohol inhibits osteoblasts in their task of building bone, limiting your alcohol intake can help prevent or slow down the development of osteoporosis. If you are a smoker, keep in mind that your habit is associated with an increased incidence of osteoporosis. The reason for this connection is unclear. Does cigarette smoke contain a toxin that causes osteoporosis, or are smokers simply less active than nonsmokers and therefore less able to maintain bone strength? Whatever the answer is, the connection between smoking and osteoporosis is one good reason among many for breaking the habit.

THE SLOUCH FACTOR

For most people — those who aren't predisposed by heredity to osteoporosis — the greatest risk factor in osteoporosis is inactivity. Becoming active is the single most beneficial step you can take to help prevent or slow the course of this disease. It is one of the miracles of biology that the physical signal from weight-bearing exercise can be transmitted into a stimulus for bone building. This sort of exercise turns sluggish osteoblasts into worker bees, moving a person at any point in life to a more positive or at least a less negative bone balance. Extreme inactivity, even short term, has the opposite effect. The astronaut suspended in the weightlessness of space, or the young person suddenly bedridden with an injury or sickness, experiences a dramatic increase in bone breakdown — so dramatic, in fact, that if no preventive steps are taken, the calcium "washout" from bone can cause kidney stones. When I did my residency training, one of the most common complications suffered by paralyzed polio patients was kidney stones.

Testing for Osteoporosis

In the old days, people at risk for osteoporosis were given only X rays to assess bone density. An older woman whose tests showed typical osteoporotic changes and who had experienced fractures would be given what was then aggressive treatment for osteoporosis. But plain X-ray films do not usually detect osteoporosis until it is very advanced. Today the standard method for detecting early osteoporosis is a bone-density evaluation, usually with dual-energy X-ray absorptiometry (DEXA). A DEXA scan compares a person's bone density with that of a person of the same gender at the peak of bone buildup, about age thirty. Usually two tests are performed, one of the lower spine and one of the hip. The tests are evaluated according to the World Health Organization's so-called T-scale:

- Normal bone mass: a T-scale between 0 and minus 1
- Low bone mass: a T-scale between minus 1 and minus 2.5
- Osteoporosis: a T-scale below minus 2.5
- Established or severe osteoporosis: a T-scale below minus 2.5 and one or more osteoporotic fractures

If your densitometry reading or T-score is normal or less than 1 standard deviation below normal, you are at low risk of developing osteoporosis. If your T-score is between 1 and 2.5 standard deviations below that of a thirty-year-old, then you are osteopenic, meaning you have reduced bone mass but are not yet osteoporotic. If you are more than 2.5 standard deviations below, you have osteoporosis.

Researchers in osteoporosis have not reached a unanimous opinion about when and how frequently women should have bone-density tests. As with most medical tests, they should only be performed when they are likely to influence decisions on more vigorous treatment or prevention. The patient's age, race, and other risk factors determine the timing.

Preventing and Controlling Osteoporosis

If you already have osteoporosis, or if you run the risk of developing it, you would do well to memorize this mantra: exercise, calcium, and vitamin D.

Exercise

To prevent osteoporosis, every person over fifty should engage in some form of regular weight-bearing exercise. The minimal amount is thirty minutes at least four times a week. Walking, step aerobics, light jogging, dancing, tennis, rollerblading — anything that keeps you moving on your feet — will help the bones of the lower spine, pelvis, and hips. I also advise the use of light dumbbells (three to five pounds) four times a week, ten minutes at a stretch. Weight-bearing exercise is the only therapy that stimulates the osteoblasts to build bone; drugs and other therapies simply slow the breakdown.

Calcium

To prevent or slow down bone loss, you must have an adequate intake of calcium. Most Americans do not consume enough calcium in their diet. I'm reluctant to advise patients to make a major dietary shift to include enough calcium, simply because it might complicate the overall health goals of low saturated fat, low cholesterol, and high fiber. Calcium supplements are cheap, easy to take, and have very few side effects. I generally advise women past sixty, who run an increased risk of heart disease and other conditions exacerbated by a high-fat diet, not to worry about calcium in the diet but to rely instead on calcium supplements. Tums, which contain calcium carbonate, are affordable and easy to take — an excellent source of calcium.

The recommended calcium intake for adult men is 1,000 mg a day up to the age of sixty-five, 1,500 mg a day over sixty-five. For women, the recommendations are a little more complicated. Up to age fifty, 1,000 mg a day is sufficient. Postmenopausal women up to age sixty-five should take 1,000 mg a day if they are on hormone replacement therapy and 1,500 mg a day if they are not. Anyone with a T-score below minus 1 should take 1,500 mg per day.

Vitamin D

As you age, your ability to absorb calcium from the intestines lessens. Vitamin D aids in the process of calcium absorption, and while this vitamin is important at any age, it is more important in the elderly because of their need to absorb extra calcium, and because they absorb less vitamin D as they age. People between the ages of fifty and seventy should take 400 I.U. of vitamin D a day, and those over seventy between 600 and 800 I.U. Most multiple vitamins contain 400 I.U. If you're taking multiple vitamins and are over seventy, or if you're under seventy and are not taking multiple vitamins, you can get your extra vitamin D in calcium tablets. I advise patients taking 1,000 mg of calcium to take two plain 500 or 600 mg calcium citrate or calcium carbonate tablets; if they need extra vitamin D, they should take one plain calcium citrate or calcium carbonate, and one calcium citrate or carbonate with 400 I.U. vitamin D. (Calcium citrate is absorbed slightly better than calcium carbonate.)

Weight-bearing exercise, adequate calcium, and vitamin D are risk-free preventive measures for almost everyone. If you have had calcium kidney stones or other rare disorders of calcium metabolism, calcium or vitamin D supplements may not be the right preventive therapy for you. Check with your doctor before starting.

Medication for Osteoporosis?

If you already have osteoporosis, you may need more than just exercise and dietary supplements. The next step is medication. Before prescribing drug therapy, your doctor has to know the degree of bone loss you've experienced as well as any possible contraindicating medical conditions. Medications that have approval from the Food and Drug Administration for osteoporosis are:

☐ *Hormone replacement therapy (HRT).* This is a form of estrogen, either alone or combined with progesterone. Premarin (conjugated estrogen) used alone or with Provera (medroxyprogesterone acetate) is the most commonly prescribed HRT. Prempro, which contains both hormones, is another common brand.

□ *Designer estrogens, or SERMs (selective estrogen receptor modulators)*. They are called designer estrogens because they were "designed" by pharmaceutical companies to perform some of estrogen's roles without the side effects. Evista (raloxifene) is the one used most.

□ *Bisphosphonates*. At present, Fosamax (alendronate) and Actonel (risedronate) are the only bisphosphonates approved by the FDA for osteoporosis.

□ *Calcitonin*. Miacalcin Nasal Spray is the only available form.

Combination therapies of two or more of the above-mentioned medications may be employed, though such treatments are not FDA approved. All four groups of medication work by slowing bone loss. So far, other than exercise, no therapy exists to stimulate bone buildup.

Each of the four medication options carries pluses and minuses. Many considerations must be weighed before a patient decides to go on hormone therapy. Because the issue is a complex one, I have devoted the entire next chapter to this topic and only briefly cover HRT for use in osteoporosis here.

ARE YOU A CANDIDATE FOR OSTEOPOROSIS MEDICATION?

Maybe and maybe not. The Osteoporosis Foundation offers some useful guidelines about who should advance to treatment beyond exercise, calcium, and vitamin D:

□ Menopausal women with T-scores below minus 2
□ Women with T-scores below minus 1.5 who smoke or have other risk factors such as inactivity and small stature
□ Women over seventy with multiple risk factors

Of course, these are only general guidelines, and I have modified them slightly in my own recommendations to patients. As with all medications, whether you take drugs for osteoporosis depends on your unique situation and can only be determined after careful consultation with your physician.

Hormone Replacement Therapy

Estrogen, the principal female hormone, clearly slows bone loss. It is the abrupt reduction or near cessation of estrogen production at menopause that significantly accelerates bone loss. Several well-designed studies comparing large groups of women on estrogen HRT with women not on HRT have shown considerable slowing of bone loss in treated groups. Estrogen replacement, which seems most beneficial for the bones when initiated at menopause, nonetheless appears to be helpful at any age.

Some medical authorities feel that all postmenopausal women, whatever their age, should be on estrogen or an estrogen substitute. Because of the potential for side effects such as breast and uterine cancer, I prefer to base decisions about HRT on a woman's individual situation. In my opinion, if your T-score is below minus 1.5, you should strongly consider starting HRT. In fact, I advise almost all postmenopausal women to consider HRT. I cover the pros and cons for individual cases in the next chapter. For now, let me just point out that HRT clearly and significantly reduces your chance of developing a fracture or symptomatic osteoporosis.

Designer Estrogens

To find a medication with the benefits of estrogen and without unwelcome side effects, medical researchers developed the category of medications called SERMs. Currently, Evista (raloxifene) is the SERM most commonly prescribed in the United States. Like natural estrogen, such as Premarin, Evista appears to have a beneficial effect on the bone, though some large studies suggest that it is not as effective as natural estrogen. Other recent studies suggest the effects are almost equal. The dose is 60 mg a day, taken every day. The good news about Evista is that it does not increase uterine or breast cancer risk, which natural estrogen appears to do. Indeed, Evista may reduce the likelihood of breast cancer in some women. The bad news is that this medication does not have certain minor beneficial effects of natural estrogen, such as reducing hot flashes and preventing vaginal membrane atrophy. Another disadvantage: Evista is considerably more expensive than HRT.

SERMs are a very useful addition to the menu of choices for staving off osteoporosis, and are particularly appropriate for women at high risk for breast cancer.

Bisphosphonates

This category of drugs has been the single most important addition to our ability to slow the development of osteoporosis.

Both Fosamax (alendronate), which has been in general use for several years, and Actonel (risedronate), on the market since early 2000, act to block bone breakdown and increase bone density. More importantly, both have been shown to reduce by about 50 percent the number of vertebral fractures in people with established osteoporosis, and by about 30 to 35 percent the number of other fractures in such patients.

I have more experience with Fosamax. Despite the drug's advantages, two side effects have caused a sizable percentage of my patients to discontinue it. First, Fosamax is not easily absorbed, particularly on a full stomach. You have to take it with a full glass of cool or tepid water thirty minutes before eating breakfast, then sit upright or stand until it's time to eat. (Actonel has this same disadvantage.) Second, Fosamax tends to irritate the lower esophagus, in some cases causing ulcers, scarring, or narrowing. Actonel was developed in part to reduce this problem of esophagitis. One large study suggested that it was less likely to cause esophageal irritation, but in my limited experience several patients experienced the same irritation

---

BISPHOSPHONATES: WHAT'S THE DOSE FOR YOU?

Do you have:

- A *high risk of osteoporosis?* If you're thinking of taking a bisphosphonate as a preventive, the dose should be 5 mg of Fosamax or 5 mg of Actonel a day.
- *Clinical osteoporosis (a vertebral or other symptomatic fracture), or a T-score below minus 2.5?* In either case, whether or not you're on HRT, I would recommend that you take 10 mg of Fosamax or 5 mg of Actonel. Recently, a new dosing regimen was introduced for osteoporotic women in which a full week's dose – 70 mg – is given one time once a week. The medical benefits of this regimen seem the same as those for multiple dosing, and the side effects no worse; single dosing, moreover, is dramatically more convenient.
- A *T-score below minus 1.5?* If you've taken HRT for some time, I would recommend starting Fosamax 5 mg or Actonel 5 mg. If you have not tried HRT, then I would start it or Evista and repeat your densitometry in one to two years; if your condition is not improved, or if it has grown worse, I would definitely add Fosamax or Actonel. If you're opposed to HRT or Evista or cannot take them, you should at least try Fosamax 5 mg or Actonel 5 mg.

on Actonel as on Fosamax. At this point, I think we have to consider them both as potential esophageal irritants, but further comparative studies may clarify the issue.

Calcitonin

Calcitonin or thyrocalcitonin is a hormone produced by your thyroid gland that blocks the breakdown of bone. Because calcitonin is destroyed in the stomach or intestines before it can be absorbed, it cannot be given in pill or capsule form. This medication, absorbed through mucous membranes, is available as a nasal spray called Miacalcin.

Calcitonin has been shown to increase bone density but does not appear to be as potent as Fosamax or Actonel. I have reserved it for osteoporotic patients who cannot tolerate Fosamax or Actonel. The dose of Miacalcin is one nasal inhalation daily, in alternating nostrils.

Combined Treatment

Data on combination treatments is scarce, but I can tell you anecdotally that in my practice, I've had numerous patients on combination Fosamax/HRT with good results. Many physicians with a large osteoporosis practice routinely prescribe this combination. Indeed, some have even added Miacalcin to the regimen.

Common sense, in the absence of data disproving it, would certainly point toward prescribing HRT or Evista, along with Fosamax or Actonel, for patients with a T-score below minus 2.5 where osteoporosis is symptomatic or threatens to become symptomatic.

Osteoporosis in Men

As noted, on average women who live a full life span lose 30 to 50 percent of their bone density, and some lose much more. Men who live a full life span lose only 20 to 30 percent on average, and have heavier skeletons before bone loss sets in. This gender difference shouldn't encourage men to neglect their bone health. Because very elderly men commonly suffer hip and pelvic fractures, all men should follow the universal prevention regimen of regular exercise and an adequate intake of calcium and vitamin D.

A very small number of men will develop symptomatic osteoporosis earlier, in their late sixties or seventies. They may benefit from a medication (Fosamax, Actonel, or even a male hormone) in addition to exercise and calcium.

While it is not practical to perform bone densitometry on all men to detect the minuscule percentage who are osteoporotic, a few factors suggest the need for testing. If you have had a spine fracture or lost height more rapidly than other men of the same age, or if you have taken corticosteroids (prednisone) or been on thyroid replacement medication without close monitoring, you should ask your doctor for a bone-density test. Otherwise, keep your body moving, use those dumbbells, and worry about something else.

Recommendations for Treating Women

The World Health Organization's T-scale and the Osteoporosis Foundation's recommendations are useful in treatment decisions for osteoporosis, but they are just guidelines. There are no hard and fast rules about treatment therapies for osteoporosis, or about who should have bone densitometry when. Your physician will depend on clinical experience to steer the decision about what sort of therapy you require. My own recommendations for women, derived from both official treatment guidelines and years of practice, are as follows:

- Women should have bone-densitometry evaluation at menopause if they are undecided about starting HRT. (An exception could be made for African Americans who have no risk factors.) A low T-score might be reason to decide in favor of HRT.
- If you're in your sixties and you've never had a bone-densitometry test, you should have one now.
- If your T-score is normal or higher than minus 1.5, you could decide on HRT for other reasons and repeat the densitometry in five or six years.
- If your T-score is below minus 1.5, you should strongly consider starting HRT, if you have not decided to start it for other reasons and you have no contraindications.
- If you are on HRT and your T-score is below minus 1.5, you should consider adding Fosamax or Actonel to your medication regimen.
- Regardless of whether you begin HRT, you should repeat the densitometry test in two years. (Changes in bone density occur slowly, and you are probably not going to see a significant shift one way or the other before two years.) If bone deterioration is evident, you should consider starting therapy or switching therapies.

REMEMBER THIS

Osteoporosis is a central health concern for the elderly. It affects a sizable percentage of this population, especially women, and can quickly turn a mobile, independent person into an invalid. To prevent or control the course of osteoporosis, keep the following in mind:

- Regular weight-bearing exercise is the single most important factor in the prevention of osteoporosis.
- Your calcium and vitamin D intake should meet the needs of someone your gender and age.
- Bone densitometry can help you and your doctor decide what further treatment might benefit you.
- All women should consider HRT or SERMs as part of a prevention plan.
- Fosamax and Actonel are each very effective and should be considered when other therapies are inadequate.
- If you cannot tolerate Fosamax or Actonel, calcitonin may be a helpful addition to therapy.

CHAPTER 13

HORMONE REPLACEMENT THERAPY

Hormone replacement therapy (HRT) after menopause is one of the most studied, and most controversial, problems in medicine. The only matter researchers and physicians agree on is that advice to the patient must be individualized. The benefits, risks, and side effects of HRT are different for each woman.

To understand the pros and cons of taking HRT, you have to understand what happens in your body during and after menopause. Menopause, if defined as a woman's last menstrual period, occurs at an average age of about fifty-one, though it may happen as early as forty or as late as fifty-eight. Throughout much of human history women were not expected to live long past menopause. Today, however, women in developed countries can expect to live one-third to one-half of their lives with the biological changes that take place after menopause.

Menopause and the Loss of Estrogen

Once you are past menopause, the most significant change in your body is the virtual disappearance of estrogen, the hormone secreted by your ovaries. For all practical purposes, menopause is the near absence of estrogen.

What roles does estrogen play in the body? This is an important question, because the answer will guide your decision whether or not to take replacement therapy. Especially when given therapeutically, estrogen:

☐ Prevents hot flashes
☐ Tends to stabilize certain interactions between brain cells, possibly relieving depression and improving memory
☐ Slows the breakdown of bone and prevents osteoporosis

- ☐ Restores collagen, one of the supporting tissues for skin, bones, joints, and the pelvis
- ☐ Prevents thinning and dryness of the vaginal membrane
- ☐ Helps build muscle
- ☐ Lowers LDL cholesterol and lowers the risk of cardiac disease and stroke
- ☐ Improves the body's ability to metabolize sugar and possibly lowers the risk of diabetes
- ☐ Improves blood flow
- ☐ Stimulates certain breast cells, possibly increasing the risk of malignancy
- ☐ Stimulates the uterine lining so that menstrual periods may restart, and increases the risk of uterine malignancy
- ☐ Can increase the tendency for blood to clot, thereby raising the risk of thrombophlebitis

Clearly, estrogen is a busy hormone. Each of the above effects can translate into real-life benefits or risks for you. Let's look at each.

Hot Flashes

Hot flashes refer to an uncomfortable, overheated feeling that may be accompanied by sweating. They are caused by a dilation of blood vessels under the skin associated with a rapid fall in estrogen levels. While hot flashes can occur during perimenopause, they are most severe during menopause itself. Typically, they are transient and disappear after a few months or a year, but a few women are visited by hot flashes for five years or longer. If you decide to stop HRT later in life, you may experience hot flashes at that time, but on average the hot flashes experienced by the older woman who abruptly stops estrogen are less troublesome than those noted during natural menopause.

Action on the Brain

In general, estrogen contributes to a sense of well-being and elevates a woman's mood. One serious complication of the postmenopausal state is depression, occasionally serious enough to require hospitalization or to warrant medication. Estrogen deficiency is not the only factor causing depression; some women on HRT become depressed, and most women who do not take estrogen do not have clinical depression. Still, in studies of large groups of women, depression, both mild and severe, is more common in estrogen-deficient women.

In addition to its action as a mood elevator, estrogen improves blood flow to the brain and helps preserve certain brain cells that may otherwise die. Because it seems to preserve some of the neurons associated with memory, estrogen may help stave off the mild memory loss that comes with aging. More importantly, estrogen may play a role in delaying the onset of Alzheimer's disease.

ESTROGEN AND DEMENTIA

One of the most intriguing aspects of estrogen is its possible role in dementia, specifically Alzheimer's disease. Alzheimer's is more common in women than in men, and preliminary studies suggest that estrogen replacement may improve memory in Alzheimer's patients and delay onset of the disease. No large-scale, long-term studies have been completed to prove this, but preliminary studies strongly suggest that if you have a family history of Alzheimer's, you would be well advised to take HRT and continue it indefinitely.

Preserving Collagen

Estrogen's beneficial role in the prevention and treatment of osteoporosis, discussed in the last chapter, is one compelling reason for taking HRT. Another is estrogen's ability to prevent the deterioration of collagen. Collagen is the chemical that makes up most of the microscopic tissue that supports all other body tissue. Collagen strengthens bones and keeps the skin from thinning, helps support and connect muscles and the cartilage that lines joints, and keeps capillaries from breaking. In the laboratory, estrogen has been shown to keep collagen from deteriorating, but more importantly, in large groups of women it has been shown to alleviate several of the conditions associated with collagen deterioration.

Estrogen's role in collagen preservation brings multiple benefits. For example:

- Prolapse of the uterus, a condition in which the uterus sags or protrudes, tends to be less severe or even improves with estrogen therapy.
- Loss of bladder control often improves when the support structures are strengthened by estrogen.
- In preserving collagen, estrogen helps alleviate one of the more troublesome problems of older women: thin, easily bruised skin, especially on the forearms and the backs of hands and shins. In these areas, the skin tears easily, veins are visible beneath the skin, and red

or brown hemorrhagic spots appear near capillaries. Estrogen has been proven to thicken skin and stabilize tiny blood vessels.
□ Although osteoarthritis is caused by factors other than lack of estrogen, deficient collagen in joint cartilage and muscle tendons can put extra wear and tear on already damaged joints.

Preserving the Vaginal Membrane

The most frequent type of vaginal irritation suffered by postmenopausal women is atrophic vaginitis. This is a thinning and drying of the vaginal membrane that leaves it susceptible to irritation, bleeding, and secondary infection. This condition, which develops slowly over two or more years after estrogen levels fall, is the major cause of painful sexual intercourse in older women.

Atrophic vaginitis responds dramatically to oral estrogen therapy or topical estrogen creams. Improvement can be seen within a week or two.

Muscle Building

Both men and women experience a decline in muscle strength as they age. The reduction of estrogen in women, of hormones called androgens in men, and of growth hormone in both sexes plays a role in muscular decline. Careful analysis of grip strength in women shows that those who take estrogen, even if they are inactive, retain muscle power better than those who do not.

Of course, regular exercise helps enormously in building strength. All the "superwomen" I saw in my own practice — remarkably fit, youthful-looking patients in their late seventies, eighties, and even nineties — both exercised and took estrogen.

Preventing Heart Disease and Stroke

Its ability to prevent heart disease and stroke is one of the principal reasons for taking estrogen. From the point of view of years of life added, this effect is clearly the most important.

Among forty- to fifty-year-olds, coronary heart disease is much more common in men, but in people seventy or above the incidence for men and women becomes the same. During their sixties women run an ever-greater risk of heart disease, especially if they don't take estrogen replacement. Heart disease is still the number one cause of death in women. An average woman has about a twelve times greater chance of dying from coronary artery disease than from breast cancer. The incidence of death from stroke and breast cancer is about equal.

How does estrogen protect against heart disease? Most prominently, it:

☐ Raises HDL cholesterol (high-density lipoprotein, the good stuff)
☐ Lowers LDL (low-density lipoprotein, the troublesome stuff)
☐ Dilates the blood vessels and may stabilize their membranous walls

Although a few studies point to no significant reduction in vascular disease with estrogen — one recent study even suggested that in the first two years after a heart attack, repeat attacks actually increase among women on estrogen — most experts in the diseases of older women, including cardiologists, internists, and gynecologists, agree that estrogen greatly lessens the likelihood of heart attacks and strokes.

> **Did You Know?**
> Most studies comparing the incidence of heart disease (heart attacks or angina) in women who take estrogen and in those who don't show a reduction in disease of about 50 percent in the former. Other studies show a stroke reduction of about 40 percent in women on estrogen.

This beneficial effect seems to disappear in about five years if estrogen is stopped — another compelling reason for even the oldest women to continue HRT.

In general, the death rate from all causes is much lower for women on estrogen than for women who have never taken it. Although studies differ, they show that estrogen adds about two years to a woman's life.

Improving Blood Flow

Estrogen improves blood flow throughout the body, which may play a role in many of the beneficial effects already noted, such as improved brain function and reduction in the deterioration of collagen and muscle strength.

Improved blood flow, however, is not necessarily beneficial for women with a history of migraine headaches, which are caused by overactive, abnormally dilated blood vessels in the brain. Many migraine sufferers see an improvement in their condition after menopause, when they have ceased producing estrogen. HRT may cause the migraine attacks to resume. My advice for women who have had migraines but who want to take estrogen is to give it a three- or four-month trial. If the attacks resume, a lower dose of estrogen or an artificial estrogen can be tried.

Stimulating Breast Tissue

The estrogen effects I've discussed so far have been largely beneficial. Now we get to the downside. In women of childbearing years, estrogen works with other hormones to stimulate certain breast cell activity. The stimulation stops at menopause. In postmenopausal women estrogen replacement can have three disadvantages:

□ Breast tenderness
□ Stimulation of breast cysts
□ Increased risk of breast cancer

The first effect, breast tenderness, is usually minor and for most women is not a problem. The second is more troublesome. Many women during childbearing years develop numerous or recurrent cysts. Not only do breast cysts often cause discomfort, but it can be difficult to distinguish between benign cysts and malignant growths. Many women with cysts must have fluid withdrawn (aspiration) or surgical biopsy to test for malignancy. For most women with recurring cysts, the loss of estrogen after menopause brings welcome relief. Severe fibrocystic disease is certainly one contraindication to estrogen therapy — and may be a strong reason to consider the new artificial "designer" estrogens instead.

The third disadvantage of estrogen stimulation — an increase in the incidence of breast cancer — is the main reason many women and their physicians are cautious about HRT. Study results vary. One large study shows no increase in the risk of such cancer in women who take estrogen and who do not drink alcohol. Most studies, however, show an increase in the incidence of breast cancer of anywhere from 10 to 60 percent, with an average increase across studies of 30 percent. All postmenopausal women should have regular breast examinations and mammograms and perform monthly self-examinations; if HRT is elected, these early detection measures become even more important.

The risks of breast cancer, heart disease, and osteoporosis, which are different for each woman, must be carefully weighed by both patient and doctor. If a woman has good bone density, a low-risk profile for heart disease, but a family history of breast cancer, then HRT is probably not a sensible treatment for her. I would advise her not to use estrogen unless she had some significant postmenopausal symptom such as severe atrophic vaginitis, in which case I would prescribe estrogen in the form of a topical cream.

If a woman has a family history or other high risk of breast cancer but also runs considerable risk of osteoporosis or heart disease, she would be an ideal candidate for one of the designer estrogens, or SERMs (selective estrogen receptor modulators). This reasonable alternative to traditional HRT will be discussed later in this chapter.

Stimulation of the Uterus

Throughout a woman's childbearing years, estrogen helps stimulate the buildup of cells and blood vessels lining the uterus that results in the monthly menstrual cycle. One of the few advantages of menopause is the end of a woman's period. Depending on the regimen, HRT may reintroduce uterine bleeding in the form of spotting, breakthrough bleeding, or a monthly or even tri-monthly period.

Much more significant is the fact that HRT with estrogen alone increases the incidence of cancer of the uterine lining, or endometrium. Studies indicate anywhere from a doubling to a tripling of this risk. If, however, a second female hormone, progesterone, is taken along with estrogen, the increased risk of endometrial cancer vanishes — women on both hormones have the same risk as women on no hormone. The addition of progesterone is unnecessary and should be avoided in women who have had a hysterectomy. For women who still have their uterus, the addition of some form of progesterone is standard medical practice.

A WORD OF CAUTION

Estrogen appears to increase the risk of certain types of cancer. Studies show that estrogen increases the incidence of cancer of the uterine lining, or endometrium, although this risk vanishes when progesterone is added to the therapy. Another, very recent study suggests that women on estrogen run a slightly higher risk of ovarian cancer. The increase is modest but statistically significant, and while further studies will have to be done, it is a reason for caution and individualized therapy.

Most women tolerate estrogen and progesterone well, but for some, progesterone has side effects. It may cause fluid retention and is part of a hormone mix that can contribute to tension or depression. One of my patients called it the grumpy hormone; a Jewish colleague of mine called it the kvetcher hormone. In any event, as with all medicines, you should try to take the lowest dose possible to protect the uterus.

Thrombophlebitis

Although estrogen replacement is clearly beneficial in reducing your risk of arterial disease, and thus lessening your chance of heart attack or stroke, it is associated with a small but definite increase in the risk of blood clots in the leg veins and the retina. This risk seems dose related. Women who have already had blood clots in the veins should take estrogen only if there is a very high risk of osteoporosis or cardiovascular disease, and they should take the lowest possible dose. And since retinal vein problems seem to occur in the very old, I favor reducing the dose of estrogen in women over eighty if they are not already on the lowest effective dose.

HORMONE REPLACEMENT PROGRAMS

Premarin is the estrogen most commonly used, and in the following typical doses:

       0.3 mg Probably enough for protection; may become the standard dose for women under seventy-five; I use it as the standard for women over seventy-five

   0.625 mg Usual starting dose, and the most commonly prescribed

    1.25 mg High enough to stop hot flashes, but I rarely prescribe it

Premarin, taken every day with no progesterone, is sufficient if you have had a hysterectomy. If you have not, and need protection against uterine cancer, you can add progesterone to your regimen. Common dosing patterns are:

Monthly cycling, which for most women results in a period

    Day 1 through 25, Premarin 0.625 daily
    Day 16 through 25, Provera 5 or 10 mg daily
    Day 25 through end of month, no pills

Three-month cycling, which results in a period every three months

    Premarin 0.625 mg daily for two months and the first 25 days of the third month
    Provera 5 or 10 mg for the last 10 to 14 days of the cycle

Combined hormones, no period, adequate uterine protection

    Premarin 0.625 mg and Provera 2.5 mg daily in a single pill (Prempro)
    Premarin 0.625 mg and Provera 5 mg daily if there is breakthrough bleeding or spotting with the former regimen

As noted, a lower dose of Premarin, 0.3 mg, should be considered for women over seventy-five.

Designer Hormones

For women at high risk of breast cancer who do not tolerate progesterone, or who are simply worried about the possible increased risk of breast cancer with estrogen, a dramatic new way to gain protection against osteoporosis and heart attack comes in the form of selective estrogen receptor modulators, or SERMs, most notably Evista (raloxifene). Evista has nearly the same ability as estrogen to protect bone and blood vessels, but doesn't increase the risk of breast and uterine cancer. Indeed, Evista may have a protective effect on the breasts. Since Evista carries no risk of uterine cancer, progesterone is not needed.

Why not just put everybody on Evista and forget the worries about breast cancer and the problems with progesterone? Because Evista is no fountain of youth. Unlike estrogen, Evista doesn't alleviate hot flashes (and may make them worse), nor does it prevent vaginal atrophy, skin thinning, muscle and tendon loss, or loss of pelvic support. For all these reasons, I think the first choice for HRT should be an estrogen/progesterone program, with Evista reserved for special cases.

Deciding What's Best for You

At the beginning of this chapter, I stressed that all decisions about HRT should be based on the unique circumstances of each patient. The following cases from my own practice show just how individualized the therapy can be, and may give you some insight into your own situation.

Are you more like Eve?

Eve is sixty-five and has been on HRT since menopause at age fifty-two. Her two major reasons for taking hormones are the vascular risk and her desire to prevent osteoporosis. Two years ago Eve switched from cycling progesterone to a daily dose of Prempro. She has no family history of breast cancer, no breast cysts, no cardiac risk factors other than her age, and no history of blood clots in the legs. She exercises regularly and her last bone density T-score was minus 0.3 (a very good score). Her mother developed Alzheimer's at about age seventy.

Eve's is an in-between case. Her history and her exercise program indicate that even without HRT, she would not likely develop vascular disease or osteoporosis in the near future. Yet there are no undue downside risks to her taking hormones — no family history of breast cancer, no breast cysts or blood clots. She has tolerated the hormones for years without difficulty. I advised Eve to continue HRT in order to preserve her muscle tone and connective tissue, and also — even though her mother's developing Alzheimer's at age seventy is not a great risk factor for Eve — because there is still a chance that HRT will protect her from that disease. Eve agrees with my opinion.

Or Frances?

Frances is sixty-one. She has moderately high cholesterol, and her father died of coronary disease at age seventy-six. Her last bone density T-score was unsettling: minus 2.1, in the osteopenic/near-osteoporotic range. For two years after menopause at age fifty Frances took HRT, but she has not been on hormones since then, and she takes no cholesterol-lowering medication. Though one maternal aunt had breast cancer, which is considered a second-order risk, Frances has no breast cysts and no history of blood clots. I advised her to resume HRT with Prempro because of her risk of vascular disease and her low bone density. The aunt's breast cancer, I told her, did not increase Frances's risk enough to rule out estrogen therapy. If she was concerned about estrogen and breast cancer she could start Evista instead, but Evista wouldn't provide the additional benefits of standard HRT. I gave Frances prescriptions for both and told her to call me. After reading up on the subject, she called to tell me that she would start the estrogen therapy.

Or Gerry?

Gerry is sixty-six and has had one compression fracture of the spine. Her bone density T-score is minus 2.7, in the osteoporotic range. She has never taken HRT, partly because her mother and sister both had breast cancer — her mother died of it. Gerry has no risk of vascular disease. Clearly her concern about breast cancer is justified, but she needs some treatment to keep the osteoporosis from progressing. She was started on a daily regimen of Evista. Because of her T-score and fracture, I also prescribed Fosamax and recommended that she follow a supervised weight-bearing exercise program.

Or Harriet?

Harriet is sixty-eight and began HRT at the time of menopause. After two years she developed a blood clot in the deep veins of her leg and stopped hormone therapy. Harriet had a similar clot during pregnancy thirty-five years before. She has no family history of breast cancer, but her father died of a heart attack at age fifty-eight and had been diagnosed with angina in his early fifties. Her cholesterol readings have been high enough for concern, and her last bone density T-score was minus 2.3 — osteopenic, almost in the osteoporotic range. Though vascular risk and poor bone density are typical reasons favoring HRT, either standard or Evista, Harriet's history of deep-vein thrombosis is a strong strike against it. I advised that she follow a special diet and take a statin drug to lower her cholesterol. To help stave off osteoporosis, Harriet took up weight-bearing exercise and started on Fosamax.

I hope you come away from these four cases a little better informed about your own situation. As you can see, overall I favor hormone therapy for women if there is no medical reason not to take it. How does the scale of its likely benefits and relative risks weigh for you? The answer will determine the direction you take. More important than anything is that, after close consultation with your doctor, you feel comfortable with your decision.

REMEMBER THIS

- Many women today will be living one-third to one-half of their life after menopause. This is a new phenomenon in human history. Living without estrogen — as postmenopausal women do who are not on HRT — is not necessarily a "natural" condition.
- The decision whether to take HRT, and what regimen to follow, should be individualized.
- Estrogen replacement cuts your risk of a heart attack by about 50 percent and your risk of stroke by about 40 percent.
- Because heart disease is so much more common than breast cancer, for most women the overall health gain from HRT far outweighs the risk of breast cancer.
- Estrogen replacement significantly slows the development of osteoporosis.
- Estrogen replacement stops hot flashes and vaginal atrophy, and slows muscle and tendon atrophy, skin thinning, and other physical manifestations of age.
- Estrogen replacement alone increases the risk of cancer of the uterus, but this is totally reversible if progesterone is added.
- Though estrogen replacement modestly increases the risk of breast cancer, the increase appears more often in women with other risk factors for this disease, such as family history.
- Evista is a reasonable alternative for women concerned about breast cancer, but it does not confer the additional benefits of estrogen.

CHAPTER 14

OSTEOARTHRITIS

Arthritis is a condition in which the joints are inflamed. Osteoarthritis is the most common form of arthritis, but strictly speaking it is a misnomer. In osteoarthritis the joints actually wear out, causing mild, secondary inflammation. Some physicians use the term degenerative arthritis instead of osteoarthritis, referring to the several other forms of arthritis as inflammatory arthritis.

Whatever you call it, osteoarthritis is a major problem for the over-sixty set, affecting about half of the people in this age group and causing about 90 percent of their joint problems.

What Is Happening in Osteoarthritis?

A joint is the place where two bones meet and flex over each other. The end of each bone carries a cartilage cushion and a membrane — the synovial membrane — that secretes fluid over the cartilage. The cartilage cushions the joint from stress, and the fluid lubricates the joint. Your bone, your cartilage, and your synovial membrane are all living tissue.

What wears out in osteoarthritis is primarily the cartilage cushion. Osteoarthritis occurs after years of trauma to the joints, and it may also be the result of an inherited tendency toward cartilage degeneration. One type of inherited osteoarthritis occurs primarily in the hands and is much more prevalent in women than in men. The knuckles, particularly those near the fingertips, become knobby and distorted. While this condition can be unsightly, the hands maintain nearly normal function and after the initial stages of the disease are not very painful. As with most arthritis, the affected joints feel stiff in the morning.

The most troublesome form of osteoarthritis attacks the large weight-bearing joints — the knee, hip, and spine. Worn cartilage is a major cause of osteoarthritis in the weight-bearing joints, but a biochemical predisposition in the living cartilage contributes to this condition and probably explains why people with seemingly similar histories of wear and tear have markedly different degrees of osteoarthritis. As the cartilage wears down, it becomes rough and may even break up; this action irritates the membrane and causes pain. Meanwhile the bone underlying the cartilage is damaged, develops cysts, or grows bony spurs called osteophytes. On X rays, spurs characteristically appear as sharp ridges (see below).

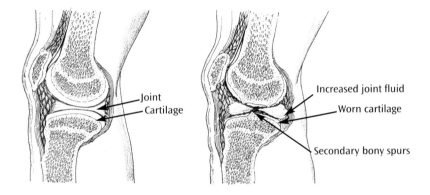

A normal joint (left) and an osteoarthritic joint (right)

When Should You See Your Doctor about Joint Pain?

Anyone over sixty is going to experience a little morning stiffness and some hip and knee stiffness after a long car ride. This usually goes away in a few minutes and is no reason for seeing the doctor or taking medication in large doses. However, you should visit your doctor if:

- ☐ The stiffness, pain, or discomfort lasts beyond the few minutes it takes to get limbered up.
- ☐ Joint pain interferes with activities — for example, if you have a knee that hurts so much you can't exercise.
- ☐ You experience a sudden painful swelling or warmth in a single joint.
- ☐ Joint or muscle aches worsen overall and cause fatigue or fever.

OTHER TYPES OF ARTHRITIS

Rheumatoid arthritis. In rheumatoid arthritis, which can come on at any age, a person's own antibodies somehow attack the joints, causing inflammation and ultimately destruction of the joints. Though any joints can be involved in this disease, it frequently attacks the hands and wrists. Affected joints tend to be painful, warm, and puffy. The condition usually deteriorates much more rapidly than in osteoarthritis. Initially, rheumatoid arthritis is treated with aspirin or nonsteroidal anti-inflammatory drugs (NSAIDs). Severe cases may require medication similar to the chemotherapeutic drugs used in cancer treatment.

Gout. Gout, the result of an abnormal accumulation of uric acid crystals in the joints, starts in a single joint, usually in the foot. Typically the joint is often hot, red, and extremely painful. Gout is often treated with NSAIDs. Attacks, if frequent, can be prevented with the uric acid-lowering drug allopurinol.

Polymyalgia rheumatica. A common joint and muscle problem seen in older people, particularly women, is polymyalgia rheumatica (PMR). This inflammation of the muscles' tiny blood vessels primarily affects the neck, shoulder, and hip muscles. Strictly speaking, PMR is muscle inflammation, but diagnosis can be tricky since it is difficult for patients to distinguish between joint and muscle pain. Symptoms of PMR may include fatigue, lethargy, and occasionally even fever. This condition is treated with prednisone. (For a more thorough discussion of PMR, see part 2, chapter 21, "Fatigue.")

Other types of arthritis include Lyme disease and viral infections that affect the muscles and joints. Like rheumatoid arthritis and PMR, these usually make a dramatic debut, involve several joints, and may cause general symptoms such as fatigue or fever. In rare cases a single joint becomes infected with a bacterium like staph or strep. This life-threatening situation requires extensive antibiotic treatment. If a single joint is very swollen, fluid may have to be withdrawn and analyzed to diagnose the cause of infection.

Physical Therapy for Osteoarthritis

Some people find that heat applied to a joint, either with an electric pad or in a hot bath or shower, helps control osteoarthritis. Paradoxically, ice or some other cold application after exercise may alleviate local pain. But the real front-line treatment for osteoarthritis is cautious exercise. A moderate exercise program under proper supervision limbers up the joints and, more importantly, strengthens the muscles and tendons that support the joints. Strengthening a knee with exercise is like giving yourself a permanent, comfortable brace.

You should avoid the undue stress of exercises such as high-impact running on asphalt or vigorous hiking over rough terrain. Studies suggest that if you are running sensibly — jogging on a soft surface — and your knees don't hurt, you need not stop; just be careful and wear well-padded running shoes. Exercise that hurts, however, may be causing damage. If you are over eighty and have advanced arthritis, use a cane or walker for long strolls.

A WORD OF CAUTION

Before hitting the treadmill or hoisting weights — or even before walking around the block if you've been sedentary for a while — you should consult with a physical therapist. This person will design an exercise program that will maximize the benefits to your body while preventing injury. Once you get started, you can continue the program on your own.

Medication for Osteoarthritis

The second component of osteoarthritis therapy is medication, primarily for pain and inflammation. Pain medications and anti-inflammatory drugs do not restore damaged cartilage, but they can alleviate symptoms. With so many elderly Americans afflicted with osteoarthritis, these medications are big sellers.

Pure Analgesics

Acetaminophen (Tylenol). This is an over-the-counter drug for pain only and has no anti-inflammatory action. Unlike aspirin it doesn't cause stomach upset, and it used to be thought quite safe. Recent reports of fatal liver damage with high doses, particularly when taken with alcohol, have made doctors much more cautious in advising it. You should take acetaminophen only in small amounts — probably no more than six 325 mg tablets a day and not for longer than five days. The FDA has not established guidelines for use.

Tramadol (Ultram). In the spectrum of pain control medication, this prescription drug lies somewhere between acetaminophen and narcotics. It should only be used if acetaminophen and anti-inflammatory drugs have not managed to control disabling pain. Tramadol can cause dizziness, somnolence, confusion, and intestinal problems. People who go off this drug abruptly may experience withdrawal symptoms such as anxiety, sweating, and insomnia.

Combination Analgesic/Anti-Inflammatory Medications

Over-the-counter salicylates. This class of drugs, which includes aspirin, is an old standby, around since the nineteenth century. Salicylates may help prevent heart attacks and strokes in some people and are a common treatment for arthritis and other painful conditions. To achieve relief, arthritis sufferers need to take moderately high doses — six to eight 325 mg tablets per day.

The main side effect is serious intestinal irritation and bleeding. To mitigate gastric irritation, some brands are coated and others are mixed with antacids.

Nonsteroidal Anti-Inflammatory Drugs (NSAIDs)

Over-the-counter NSAIDs. These include ibuprofen (Advil, Nuprin, Motrin) and naproxen (Aleve). Like the prescription NSAIDs, these can cause ulcers, gastritis, intestinal bleeding, and fluid retention and thus should be taken in the lowest dose that gives relief. You can take four 220 mg Aleve tablets a day. You should not take more than 800 mg of ibuprofen a day without your doctor's consent. If you experience mild joint pain or stiffness after exercise, taking one or two Aleve or one or two 200 mg ibuprofen tablets before vigorous activity may help.

Prescription NSAIDs. Prescription NSAIDs come in many forms, as follows:

Naproxen (Anaprox, Naprosyn, Naprelan)
Diclofenac (Arthrotec, Cataflam, Voltaren)
Sulindac (Clinoril)
Oxaprozin (Daypro)
Diflunisal (Dolobid)
Piroxicam (Feldene)
Etodolac (Lodine)
Indomethacin (Indocin)
Fenoprofen (Nalfon)
Ketoprofen (Orudis)

Mefenamic acid (Ponstel)
Tolmetin (Tolectin)
Ketorolac (Toradol)

Other than a few variations in their duration of action, these drugs are similar. All of them pose the risk of stomach or duodenal ulcers and intestinal bleeding, which may result in the patient's hospitalization. These drugs can also cause fluid retention and elevated blood pressure. Kidney and liver function tests need to be conducted periodically if you are on prescription NSAIDs for more than three months.

Cox 2 inhibitor NSAIDs (Celebrex and Vioxx). These two anti-inflammatory drugs, which have been on the market for about two years, are widely prescribed. They were designed like earlier-generation NSAIDs to control pain and inflammation, but also to reduce the side effect of ulcer or intestinal bleeding. I prescribe them almost exclusively because they are safer and equally effective. Of course, no drugs are entirely safe, and Cox 2 inhibitors occasionally cause the same intestinal symptoms, fluid retention, and elevated blood pressure associated with older NSAIDs. Insurers don't like Vioxx or Celebrex because they are expensive. Despite the occasional side effects and the expense, this latest generation of NSAIDs has a superior track record, and I predict that in the near future Cox 2 inhibitors will become standard.

WHAT'S THE SCOOP ON GLUCOSAMINE?

Glucosamine/chondroitin is an alternative over-the-counter medication containing some of the chemicals that make up cartilage. Anecdotal evidence suggests that glucosamine repairs cartilage, and recently a well-designed study in Europe offered partial confirmation of this observation. Furthermore, some rheumatologists and orthopedists report very good results when they inject glucosamine/chondroitin into larger joints. I've started recommending glucosamine, particularly as it doesn't appear to have significant side effects, but until further studies prove its effectiveness I won't swear by it.

Corticosteroids

Some corticosteroids such as oral prednisone are useful in treating the inflammation associated with certain arthritis conditions, but they should almost never be used in osteoarthritis. The amount of inflammation seldom warrants it, and the side effects, particularly in people over seventy-five, can be severe: confusion, ulcers, intestinal bleeding, muscle atrophy, easy bruising, and dramatic worsening of osteoporosis. I only use a corticosteroid if an osteoarthritis patient is crying out with pain or unable to get out of bed, and then only for a short term. Injecting a corticosteroid into a very painful joint can sometimes bring welcome relief, but the use is limited, and a single joint should never be injected more than three times a year.

What If Medications Aren't Working?

You've protected your joints, done physical therapy, and taken medication either orally or by injection — but your joint's still killing you. What to do?

Minor Surgery

If your problem is in the knee, a surgeon may be able to repair the damaged cartilage through a fiber-optic tube called an arthroscope. This can be helpful if there is minor or moderate damage to the cartilage, or if a piece of cartilage is loose in the joint. Arthroscopic surgery is not beneficial if the cartilage is destroyed, nor is it useful for joints other than the knee.

Joint Replacement

For a joint with substantial damage, the treatment of last resort is replacement. Hip replacements are the most common, with knee replacements a close second. Few other joints are replaced for osteoarthritis. The decision whether to get a new hip or knee should be based on two general considerations: How much pain or disability are you experiencing with favorite or necessary activities, and how much joint damage shows up on an X ray?

Remember, joint replacement is a major operation and you may have a long recovery time. If, because of other health problems, your only exercise is walking and you can do that without difficulty, then you should put off a replacement. If you're intent on playing golf, or hiking, gardening, or dancing, and you're frustrated by a painful, destroyed joint, then you should consider a replacement. Don't get the operation for minor reasons, though. Why? First, you might experience complications such as blood clotting or infection. Second, replaced joints themselves loosen or wear out over time. If a joint is replaced too early in life, you may need a repeat replacement in later years. When considering joint replacement, press your orthopedist until you are sure that the joint cannot be salvaged by other means. If you have so-called bone-on-bone damage, replacement may well be liberating. Be sure to seek out an orthopedist who has performed a large number of joint replacements. It's your body — put it in the hands of an expert.

REMEMBER THIS

- Osteoarthritis, the most common form of arthritis, affects about half of people over sixty.
- Osteoarthritis is primarily a degeneration of the cartilage cushion in the joints, with secondary inflammation and alteration of the adjacent bone.
- Osteoarthritis is treated with physical therapy, and analgesic and anti-inflammatory drugs.
- Ulcers and intestinal bleeding are serious side effects of the older NSAIDs. The newer Cox 2 inhibitor NSAIDs are much safer and just as beneficial in treating pain and inflammation.
- Glucosamine/chondroitin may help preserve cartilage, but the jury is still out.
- If your doctors have done everything possible short of a hip or a knee replacement and you're still disabled or have pain, surgery may be indicated. This decision should not be taken lightly. Make sure X-ray tests show positive evidence of joint destruction — and put yourself in the hands of an expert.

CHAPTER 15

BACK AND NECK PAIN

In older patients, problems of chronic back or neck pain with spine or nerve involvement are common reasons people withdraw from vigorous, active lives. Most back or neck pain is muscular, minor, and short-lived, but as patients get older they are more likely to develop chronic or serious problems.

If I were to visualize a single scene in my office, it would be an older patient with a cane and a swaying gait, favoring one side as he or she tottered through the door from the waiting room. Back and neck problems tend to sap all an elderly person's vigor, resulting in a sense of resignation despite valiant attempts at stoicism. Often trouble in or around the spine causes pain elsewhere, such as in the legs or arms, depending on which nerve roots are involved.

What Causes Back and Neck Problems?

Back and neck pain stem from a variety of conditions, including:

- Muscle strain or injury
- Herniated disk
- Osteoarthritis
- Osteoporosis with compression fractures
- Cancer
- Spinal stenosis (usually a result of herniated disk and osteoarthritis combined)
- Kidney disease

UNDERSTANDING THE ANATOMY OF YOUR BACK

One of the first steps toward preventing back and neck pain, or coping with it, is to understand the complicated anatomy of your back. You have thirty-one vertebrae in your spine. Each vertebra is a bony cylinder with extensions, or wings, called processes. The processes meet to form the spine. The spinal cord runs down through a canal formed by the processes. Fibrous disks of softer material similar to washers separate the cylinders from each other. These are the intervertebral disks.

Muscle Strain or Injury

The most common cause of back or neck pain in elderly patients is muscle strain from inappropriate bending or lifting or sitting in an awkward position. Simple actions such as putting luggage in a car trunk, carrying out the trash, or moving large potted plants have laid many of my patients low. A soft or sagging bed can be a problem, too. Most neck pain is caused by using a pillow that is too high or too low, which strains the neck.

When you have a strain in the low back or neck, it might indicate that the muscle is irritated or has tiny tears. The muscle may go into spasm, making one side of your back or neck feel harder than the other.

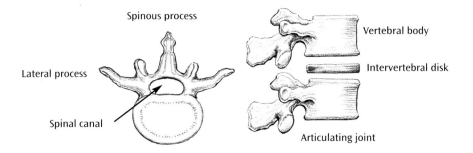

Vertebra seen from the end *(left)* **and vertebrae seen from the side** *(right)*. **Arthritis of the spine occurs in small joints where the protruding portions of vertebrae interlock.**

A WORD OF CAUTION

People who are out of shape are especially at risk for back pain. Your abdominal muscles help the muscles along your spine maintain your posture. If you have back pain and your doctor gives you the okay, you should begin a program of exercises to strengthen your abs. Many exercises designed to help the back are directed at these critical muscles.

Herniated Disk

Your back's intervertebral disks (see box, "Understanding the Anatomy of Your Back") are rings of tissue with pulpy material on the inner side. When someone has a herniated disk — what most people call a slipped disk, and doctors may call a ruptured disk — it doesn't actually slip; rather, a portion of the fibrous ring is injured or wears out and the pulpy center protrudes *(see below)*. The medical term for this is herniated nucleus pulposus (HNP).

The protruding pulpy material can press a nerve against a bony process, causing pain, numbness, or weakness. The pain may be in the back but is usually felt over that part of the body the nerve serves. For example, if the ruptured disk is in the low back, the pain will be felt in the buttocks, groin, or down the leg. Ruptured disks in the neck cause pain in the arms. Depending on the location of the pain, numbness, or weakness, your doctor or consulting neurosurgeon will probably be able to pinpoint which spinal nerves are involved.

Pain from a disk can be acute, coming on suddenly, often after an injury, or it can be chronic, building up over several weeks. If you have back pain radiating to the buttock, groin, or leg, or neck pain radiating to the arm, you should see your doctor right away. A ruptured disk or something else could be pressing on the nerve root.

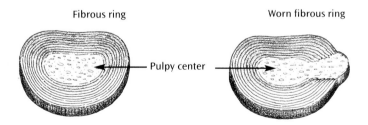

A normal disk *(left)* and a herniated disk *(right)*. In the herniated disk, the worn fibrous ring allows the pulpy center to protrude.

Osteoarthritis

Many forms of arthritis can involve the spine, but in people over sixty most arthritic back pain can be attributed to osteoarthritis (see part 2, chapter 14, "Osteoarthritis"). The pain comes not from the disk area, but from the small joints where the processes rest on each other. The same wear and tear that occurs in the hip or the knee occurs in these small joints, causing an aching pain that grows worse with activity and better with rest, although your back may be stiff and painful when you first get out of bed. The bony part of the joints can build up as joint cartilage is worn, resulting in spurs that press on the nerves.

Osteoporosis

Osteoporosis is a common cause of back pain, predominantly in older women (see part 2, chapter 12, "Osteoporosis"). The pain stems from subtle or severe fractures of the vertebrae called compression fractures. Over the years the vertebrae collapse or crunch down. The pain can build up gradually and involve several areas in a chronic ache, or it can be sudden, severe, and localized. A fall or injury can cause a compression fracture, or it may happen spontaneously; in a woman with severe osteoporosis, the simple act of walking a few steps can result in fracture.

A WORD OF CAUTION

X rays often indicate that a woman has both osteoporosis and osteoarthritis of the spine. It is difficult to separate the pain caused by one from the pain caused by the other. If you suffer from both conditions, you should be treated for osteoarthritis (nonsteroidal anti-inflammatory drugs are helpful) and seek maximum therapy for osteoporosis — not just medications, but also physical therapy.

Cancer

Secondary or metastatic cancer — cancer that spreads from some other organ — and a condition called multiple myeloma, a primary malignancy involving bone cells, are the most serious causes of back pain. Prostate cancer in men and breast cancer in women are common causes of secondary spine cancer. The pain tends to be constant and may worsen in a reclining position. If your back pain is not relieved by rest, or certainly if you have any history of malignancy, you should see your doctor right away.

Spinal Stenosis

Though the spinal cord ends before the spine does, nerves from the cord trail down and out of the spinal canal into the pelvis and legs. These nerves form the corda equina, or horse's tail. They are the most susceptible to compression or stenosis because they take up more room, and because disease is more prevalent in the lower than in the upper part of the spine. A herniated disk, arthritis with bone spurs, even a vertebra that juts forward can press on these lower nerves, causing pain and weakness (*see below*). The symptoms are usually slow in developing and have to be differentiated from leg pain caused by narrowed arteries to the legs. Pain in both conditions can come on with walking.

Compression that occurs higher on the spinal cord can cause leg pain or numbness, or loss of bowel and bladder control. If you experience any of these symptoms, see your doctor immediately.

Kidney Disease

Frequently older patients complain of a "kidney problem" because they're experiencing low back pain. Kidney infections, though they are common in older people, particularly women, don't typically cause back pain. In the rare case where there is back pain from a kidney infection, it occurs not in the low back but under the lower ribcage and on one side only. The symptoms of kidney infection are much more likely to be frequent or uncomfortable urination, fever, or delirium.

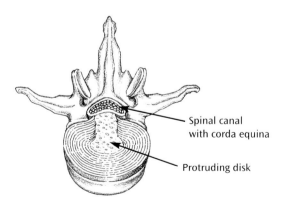

Spinal canal with corda equina

Protruding disk

A herniated disk protrudes back into the spinal canal, narrowing it and compressing the nerves.

Treating Back and Neck Pain

As with so many physical problems that plague the elderly, the first line of therapy consists of noninvasive measures such as rest and exercise. If this frontal attack brings no relief, then it is time to resort to medication. And if medication has no effect — in cases of ruptured disk or spinal stenosis — surgery may be required.

Techniques for Muscular Back Pain

Most back pain responds to rest, heat, massage, physical therapy, or avoiding what has brought on the problem. Heat can be applied at home with an electric pad, moist packs, or hot showers or baths. If that doesn't work, deep heat with ultrasound or diathermy (heat induced by electrical currents), or in a whirlpool under the supervision of a physical therapist, may help. If an acute, easily defined injury has caused the pain, ice may be appropriate for the first two days, followed by heat on the third day.

A WORD OF CAUTION

Does your back pain result from strain? Then you absolutely have to avoid the activity that caused it. Heavy lifting is out — nothing over ten pounds for two or three weeks. Learning safe lifting techniques will help protect you in the future. Keep your back straight and bend your knees, even if you're just picking up a shoe. And be careful getting out of bed — face the edge of the bed, bring your knees up until your thighs are perpendicular to your back, then roll up to a sitting position with your legs over the side.

Start an exercise routine. Over the years I've recommended several exercises that many of my patients who had recurrent problems with acute muscle strain swear by. These exercises strengthen the abdominal and back muscles without straining the back:

- ☐ KNEE LIFTS. Lie on your back on the floor or a firm bed. Bring each knee up alternately to the chest and then back down. Start with about ten repetitions for each knee, then over the days gradually work your way up to thirty. Once you're comfortable bringing your knees up separately, you may start very gradually bringing both up together.
- ☐ PELVIC TILT. Lie on your back, tighten your abdominal muscles, and lift your buttocks a few inches off the bed or floor. Hold for

eight to ten seconds and relax. Do ten or twenty repetitions daily. Most people feel relief in the lower back immediately.

☐ LEG CROSSOVERS. Lie on your back and with your knee bent, bring one leg over the other until the knee nearly touches the floor. Let the hip above your bent leg swivel up to prevent discomfort. Hold the leg in this position about twenty seconds, then do the same with the other leg. Start with five repetitions and gradually work up to twenty.

☐ BENT KNEE SIT-UP. Lie on the floor with knees bent. Bring the upper part of your body as far forward as you can without straining. Hold the position for about five seconds, then relax. Start with five repetitions; over time you can build up to thirty.

If you suffer from severe, recurrent muscular pain, you should see a physical therapist recommended by your doctor and follow a more extensive program of back-strengthening exercises.

Swimming is an excellent exercise for people with muscle problems in the back. Because swimming is non-weight-bearing, you can avoid strain while stretching, relaxing, and strengthening your muscles. Swimming is often helpful for other types of back pain such as that caused by arthritis.

For many kinds of back pain (but not always arthritis), regular walking is excellent exercise. Start at a moderate pace and travel a short distance the first time, gradually increasing it as the days go by. Interestingly, walking seems to be much easier on the back than standing — museum guards and bird watchers often experience mild low back pain.

Check your sleeping arrangements. If your back pain visits you at night or when you wake up in the morning, check your bed and mattress. Are they giving you proper support? Pain that occurs during the day and continues into the night may be caused by arthritis or something more serious such as cancer, but pain associated only with your bed is most likely due to muscle strain.

Far and away the most common cause of neck pain in my practice is patients sleeping with pillows that are too high or too low. Most of these patients have acute muscle pain on one side of the neck or the other and respond well to heat and massage therapy. If you do experience this sort of pain, you should invest in an orthopedic pillow that gives you proper head and neck support.

Correct your posture at the computer. Prolonged sitting, particularly at a computer, can cause both low back and neck pain. Neck pain from slouching at the computer tends to occur on both sides, unlike neck pain from an improper pillow. Buying a chair that seats you comfortably and provides lower back support, and getting up to stretch and move around every thirty minutes, can greatly improve your condition.

Medication

Four types of medication are commonly taken for back or neck pain: aspirin, acetaminophen, muscle relaxants, and nonsteroidal anti-inflammatory drugs (NSAIDs). For mild pain, I generally recommend aspirin or acetaminophen and emphasize the benefits of heat therapy, rest, and avoidance of further strain. If the pain is clearly muscular, acute, and disabling, I may use muscle relaxants such as Flexeril, Robaxin, and Parafon, but these often cause grogginess, confusion, dizziness, constipation, and urinary difficulties in elderly people. If I suspect that the pain arises from both arthritis and muscle spasm, I may recommend NSAIDs such as Motrin, Aleve, or Celebrex. Again, however, the side effects in the elderly — intestinal bleeding and ulcer and fluid retention — are reason for caution.

When Exercise and Drugs Don't Help

Some of my patients, finding no relief from exercise or drugs, have benefited from alternative treatments such as acupuncture, chiropractic manipulation, and transcutaneous electric nerve stimulation (TENS). I tend to regard these as third-line therapies, to be resorted to only if regular, proper exercise and medication don't bring results. In any event, before you try one of these treatments make sure you discuss it with your doctor. Depending on your diagnosis, alternative therapy, especially chiropractic manipulation, may do you more harm than good. And if you do go alternative, find an able, experienced practitioner.

How Should You Treat a Herniated Disk?

If your neck or back pain radiates to the arms or legs, or if it lasts more than two or three weeks, you should see your doctor. To find out if you have a herniated disk, you'll have to have a neurological exam, regular X rays, and possibly an MRI scan. If indeed this is the diagnosis, then the question is whether you should have surgery. I tend to be very conservative with herniated disks. Unless a patient has flagrant, progressive nerve damage that the neurosurgeon feels is extremely unlikely to heal without surgery, I advise medical therapy first — bed rest, very cautious resumption

of activity, heat applications, NSAIDs (here they may work), and cortisone injections at the inflamed site. Injections should be given by an anesthesiologist or a pain expert experienced with the procedure.

To Do or Not to Do Surgery?

I once had a patient who worked as a ranger for the U.S. National Park
Service. Thirty years ago David had a disabling herniated disk in his
lower back. He couldn't work because of severe pain and leg weakness.
When he walked, his leg dragged slightly. The neurosurgeon advised
surgery, but this was in the days before MRIs, and he couldn't be sure
exactly what sort of damage the ranger had sustained. David was intent
on not getting surgery. He rested in bed for about ten days, cautiously
resumed his activities, protected his back by observing proper bending
and lifting movements, did some muscle-strengthening exercises, and as
I recall took a little Indocin, which was about the only NSAID available then. Gradually he got better and returned to work. Today he is
still careful with his back and does muscle-strengthening exercises regularly. Thirty years after his disk ruptured, he is ending a successful career
that included lots of outdoor activity without any more back pain.

I mention this case because some people with severe symptoms and
nerve deficits may respond to nonsurgical treatment. Today, with the
advantage of MRIs, neurosurgeons can tell whether damage is so severe
that it is not likely to respond to noninvasive measures; they can operate
early, before the problem grows worse. More and more, however, physicians are successfully using nonsurgical treatment for herniated disks.

Pain or weakness radiating from the neck can be caused by a herniated
disk or an arthritic spur. In most cases, I have found, neck traction helps
relieve the symptom. Home traction devices, which fit on the chin and
back of the head and come equipped with a water bag weight and a pulley
device that is affixed to the top of a door, are easy to use. They should be
used only under the direction of a physician or physical therapist.

In most cases, neck surgery for herniated disks can be avoided — a good
thing, since this type of surgery is complicated and can damage nerves and
blood vessels. For those patients who do elect to have surgery for herniated disks in the neck or low back, I generally recommend tried and true
techniques, which usually remove the spinal process against which the
nerve is pressed. In my opinion, more recent techniques — microsurgery
disk repair, and enzyme injections into the disk to dissolve the protruding
portion — are too new to be recommended with confidence.

Spinal Stenosis

Many older patients suffering from the pain and disability of spinal stenosis lose the ability to take care of themselves. Pain occurs in the back, buttocks, and legs and worsens with walking. Unfortunately, NSAIDs, cortisone injections, and physical therapy often don't bring relief.

An operation may be the only alternative to progressive invalidism. Surgery for spinal stenosis tends to be much more complicated than surgery for a single disk and may involve spinal fusion, where transplanted bone or metal plates are used to hold the vertebrae in place. Only people who are in good physical condition otherwise — free from significant heart, lung, or other neurological disease — can be considered for surgical correction.

REMEMBER THIS

- The most common cause of back pain in people over sixty is muscle strain in the neck or lower back. Muscle strain is commonly caused by improper lifting or prolonged strain from sitting or lying in a cramped position. Most people recover with rest, heat, and protective exercise.
- Muscle relaxants have a high incidence of unwelcome side effects in older people.
- If any back pain lasts for more than three weeks, see your doctor.
- If you have pain radiating into an arm, a leg, a buttock, or the groin, you may have a herniated disk. See your doctor right away. Rest, back protection, and corticosteroid injections are appropriate early interventions and may prevent the need for surgery.
- Diffuse back pain is often caused by a combination of osteoporosis and osteoarthritis. This condition can be managed with NSAIDs and aggressive treatment of the osteoporosis.
- In rare cases, back pain results from cancer. Relentless, progressive pain that grows worse when you lie down should be evaluated right away.
- If you have a history of cancer, report any back pain to your doctor immediately.
- Spinal stenosis, which is frequently disabling, doesn't usually respond well to conservative therapy. While surgery may be the only true remedy, it is complicated and usually reserved for people who are otherwise in good health.

CHAPTER 16

DEPRESSION

Depression should be approached as a medical illness and never a character flaw. It is a common illness in older people — up to 60 percent who have significant medical problems may suffer from concomitant clinical depression. I'm not referring only to the blues, that mild down feeling all of us get from time to time. While the term depression refers to that condition, it also covers more severe forms of depression, including those that can lead to suicide. The incidence of suicide is higher in men over sixty-five than in any other group — one of many reasons depression in the elderly must be taken seriously.

Depression's Different Faces

The following four cases, which cover the spectrum from mild to severe depression, may enlighten you about various aspects of depression in older patients.

Al

Al was eighty-two years old and had several health problems, including pernicious anemia and an irregular heartbeat. He had had a small stroke with no significant impairment but was taking anticoagulants. Al had retired about twelve years earlier, following a distinguished career as a lawyer with the federal government. He had written the regulations for his department and had been praised in Congress and the press. His younger colleagues regarded him as the conscience of his department — a patrician patriot who had the rare ability to rise above partisan politics.

To my surprise, Al appeared one day and confessed that he felt very low, that his life had been a failure, and that he didn't think he could go on.

Though he still enjoyed bridge and a few other hobbies, he was getting less and less pleasure out of life. He felt he was becoming a burden on his family and society.

My heart went out to him. "Do you feel suicidal?" I asked. "I would never do that," he replied. Like most people his age, I told Al, he had some health problems that would sap some of his vigor, but these were not debilitating and could be controlled. "You're one of the most admired men in Washington," I said sincerely, reinforcing the point by saying that one of his younger colleagues felt he should get a Presidential Medal of Freedom. I advised Al not to focus overly much on his health. I would work with him in this area, but in the meantime he should try to develop a new interest. "A feeling of failure is a common part of mild depression," I reassured him. We discussed the possibility of antidepression medication, but he said he would rather wait and see how he felt.

Al returned in a week and announced that he felt much better. During lunch with two former colleagues, he had decided to write an article about the departmental regulations he had developed and what they had accomplished. On subsequent visits he continued to sound upbeat.

Ruth

Ruth was eighty-seven. Her husband had died the previous year, and though he'd been in his nineties, his death was sudden and something of a shock. Ruth had several health concerns, including a nagging worry about the possibility that breast cancer would recur — she'd been treated surgically several years before — and a vascular problem in her legs that resulted in pain on prolonged walking. Her major symptoms were lethargy, fatigue, a loss of interest in almost everything, and what her live-in nurse called "constant snippiness," uncharacteristic for this once lively, gregarious personality. Ruth had lost her appetite and was beginning to shed pounds. A thorough physical exam, blood tests, and X ray showed no evidence of a new health problem.

Obviously, Ruth was depressed. After discussing this, we decided to try an antidepressant. I chose Zoloft, a selective serotonin re-uptake inhibitor, starting her on a quarter of the usual dose prescribed for younger people and later increasing it to one-half. In about a week Ruth's enthusiasm for life began to return. Three weeks later, her companion reported that she was snapping less and eating more.

Jack

Jack was a sixty-four-year-old architect working for a small, highly regarded firm who had been very active in a national professional organization as well as community activities. Jack, by nature an energetic, upbeat person, was well known for his work in historic preservation. His physical health was good, although he was moderately overweight and only exercised sporadically.

One day Jack's wife called, alarmed about a personality change in her husband. He was "moping around," she said, and couldn't sleep at night. His usual self-confidence had been replaced by an unrealistic fear of failure. He was working on an unusually ambitious project for a demanding client, who he worried might sue for shoddy work. Jack had had a flu-like virus with secondary bronchitis about six weeks before this change in mood. He told his wife he was thinking of jumping under a subway train. He had no family history of treated depression, but his father had become moody and withdrawn at about age sixty.

Without delay, I referred Jack to a psychiatrist, who diagnosed major depression, started him on antidepressants, and saw him or talked with him daily. In about three or four weeks Jack was better; within two months he was back at work and functioning normally. Six months after the medication was started, Jack stopped taking it. That was five years ago, and since then he has not had another episode of depression. Jack is now retired and remains extraordinarily active in volunteer historic preservation work.

Bill

Bill, a retired businessman, was referred to me by a neurologist who wanted a general medical evaluation. Over the short course of several weeks, Bill had experienced a marked loss of memory in certain areas, and his family feared he had Alzheimer's. He could recall details of a baseball game watched the day before and some current events, but not personal business, social obligations, or names of family members. He said he felt he had failed his family and that the IRS might be after him for massive tax evasion (this was totally imagined). I found no evidence of physical problems. The neurologist and I referred Bill to a psychiatrist, who confirmed our diagnosis: he was experiencing the pseudo-dementia of depression, that is, depression with forgetfulness mimicking Alzheimer's or vascular dementia. The rapidity of onset, the feelings of worthlessness and guilt, and the preservation of memory in certain areas pointed to something other than typical dementia.

Bill was hospitalized and started on medication but continued to deteriorate and stopped eating. His brother had had a similar problem that had been successfully treated with electroconvulsive therapy (ECT). Faced with a life-threatening illness, Bill and his wife agreed to ECT. During the course of the therapy, as expected, Bill's memory grew worse, but by the end of six weeks he had regained most of the mental function he had had before the onset of illness — overall, a significant improvement.

WHAT CAUSES DEPRESSION?

While the causes of depression are not clearly understood, we do know that in depressed people certain chemicals called neurotransmitters that influence moods fall to lower than normal levels. The two most important neurotransmitters associated with mood are serotonin and norepinephrine . Factors that predispose to depression include:

- *Heredity*. This factor is most notable in cases of severe depression such as Bill's, though evidence points to a link between heredity and milder forms of depression as well. Levels of brain serotonin have recently been shown to vary from person to person, even in childhood, and are considered an inherited trait.
- *A loss or perceived loss*. This can be a precipitating factor, as the case of Ruth, who lost her husband prior to the onset of depression, suggests.
- *Disappointment*. This includes the failure or perceived failure to meet unreasonable expectations. Fear of failure certainly played a role in the depression that plagued Jack, who was working on a high-profile project for a demanding client.
- *Constant stress in work or personal life*. Recent research shows that chemical changes in the brain seen with severe anxiety can lead to the somewhat different chemical changes associated with depression.
- *Loneliness or lack of contact with people*. The loneliness Ruth experienced in the wake of her husband's death contributed to her depression.
- *Physical illness*. Depression is often seen in patients like Jack who have recently had influenza or other infections. Physical illness can cause chemical changes in the brain that contribute to depression.

Other common precipitating factors in depression are excessive use of alcohol (even a brief binge can bring on depression) and medication, particularly beta blockers and certain tranquilizers.

Symptoms of Depression

☐ A pervasive feeling of sadness, attended by hopelessness
☐ Lack of energy
☐ Loss of pleasure in life
☐ Loss of confidence or self-esteem
☐ A feeling of guilt or remorse
☐ Anger or irritability
☐ A sense of helplessness
☐ Thoughts of suicide
☐ Slowed speech or physical movement
☐ Inability to concentrate
☐ Changes in appetite, weight loss
☐ Insomnia, particularly in the early morning
☐ Loss of sexual desire or sexual dysfunction

The most pervasive symptom of depression is feeling low and lacking in energy. You don't see how you can accomplish goals, and the future looks bleak. You may lose the pleasure you once took in life and begin withdrawing from activities. When all pleasure in life vanishes — a condition doctors call anhedonia — you have clinical depression and become a candidate for medication. Al had not quite reached this point, but Ruth, Jack, and Bill had.

Another hallmark of depression is loss of confidence or self-esteem, often to the extent that you begin to feel guilty, reproaching yourself for not living up to some standard that may have been set years before. All three of my male patients suffered from loss of self-esteem.

A personality change, particularly increased or inappropriate anger, is a common symptom of depression in the elderly. Many older people exhibit a chronic ill temper. Ruth did, before treatment.

Severe Depression

As symptoms worsen you may begin feeling helpless, harboring the thought that nothing can be done to turn your situation around. Suicide may seem the only way out of your hopeless existence. If physical illness saps your strength, it can exacerbate this sense of hopelessness.

You may become so self-involved that you can't concentrate or pay attention to what's going on around you. Your speech may falter, and you may lose part of your memory. Bill had this problem, as did Jack, who though he was brilliant began functioning far below his usual capacity once depression set in.

Physical Symptoms

The classic somatic or physical symptoms of depression are loss of appetite and weight loss (some people go on an eating binge and gain weight), loss of sexual desire or sexual dysfunction, and insomnia, usually early morning wakefulness. Bill's loss of appetite was so severe that he required intravenous feeding.

Interestingly, of these somatic symptoms, appetite and weight loss are much more common in older patients than loss of self-esteem and feelings of worthlessness or guilt. In this sense Ruth's case was typical of my older patients — though the blues had set in, she still felt good about herself.

Should You See a Doctor?

Overall, Al's case was probably the most typical of my elderly patients — a short-lived bout with depression that thankfully disappeared. Even though Al recovered and never required medication, he made the right decision in consulting a doctor about his condition. When should you see a doctor? If you answer yes to any of these questions, it may be time to pick up the phone and schedule an appointment:

- ☐ Do you feel sad or down much more than you used to, or more than you think you should?
- ☐ Has the pleasure you used to take in certain activities ebbed?
- ☐ Have you been feeling less good about yourself for some time?

A WORD OF CAUTION

If your doctor has diagnosed you as mildly depressed and you aren't taking medication, keep close tabs on your condition. Do you exhibit any symptoms of a worsening condition, such as further withdrawal, continued weight loss, or suicidal thoughts? Don't wait — contact your doctor immediately. With depression, it is critical to battle the feeling of hopelessness that can prevent you from seeking professional help.

General Plan of Treatment

If a patient comes in to my office and answers yes to two of the above questions, then I seriously consider medication. Drug therapy becomes even more likely if a patient answers yes to any of the following:

☐ Do you feel sad all the time?

☐ Do you take no pleasure in anything you do?

☐ Does your situation seem hopeless?

☐ Have you thought of yourself as a worthless or bad person, or a burden on people?

☐ Are you experiencing insomnia? Loss of appetite or sexual desire?

Of course, any patient who reports thoughts of suicide is immediately referred to a psychiatrist or sent to a psychiatric hospital.

How Is Depression Treated?

As with any medical illness, the treatment for depression should be tailored to the severity of the problem. The two major treatments for depression are psychotherapy — a fancy word for simply talking with the doctor, who may help you change or avoid a precipitating factor — and medication. More and more today, clinically depressed people are being prescribed medication with good results. The occasional patient like Al responds to sympathetic advice and a verbal pat on the back, but doctors should follow patients who appear even mildly depressed closely. If they do not recover promptly, they should receive medication and thereafter be seen every three or four weeks for signs of progress or decline.

A WORD OF CAUTION

Most medications for depression take three or four weeks to work. If you're given medication and don't get better in that time, hold on a little longer. If you grow worse in the interim, get in touch with your doctor. In any case, let your doctor know how you're doing about a month after the pills start.

When you go for a follow-up, be sure to tell your doctor about anything bothering you — and be sure your doctor's listening. He or she should be available for brief directive therapy. If your personal problems are becoming complicated, you might ask to see a psychiatrist or clinical psychologist. Depressed people who get regular professional counseling on top of medication do better as a group than depressives on pills alone.

What Medications Are Used for Depression?

Today the most commonly used antidepressant drugs are selective serotonin re-uptake inhibitors (SSRIs), of which Prozac was the first to be marketed. SSRIs work by preventing serotonin from re-entering the cells and thereby making it available at the synapse, or cell junction (*see below*). In addition to Prozac, the SSRIs include Zoloft, Paxil, and Celexa. Despite different duration profiles and perhaps different sedation and stimulation properties, the SSRIs have similar side effects: somnolence or confusion in people over seventy-five, delayed or absent orgasm (at any age), and nausea or abdominal discomfort. It takes about one to four weeks for SSRIs to take effect.

Tricyclic antidepressants — most notably Elavil (amitriptyline) but also Sinequan, Triavil, Norpramin, and Surmontil — have been used for over thirty years. Tricyclics also raise serotonin levels, but I have found them less effective, slower acting, and more likely to result in side effects than SSRIs.

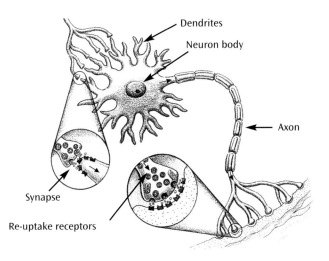

The axon of one neuron produces serotonin, which transmits impulses across the synapse to the adjacent cell. SSRIs block re-uptake of serotonin, making more available to transmit nerve impulses.

I usually start mildly depressed patients on one of the SSRI drugs. Patients over seventy-five should be started on a lower dose. Ruth, who was small and frail, was started on one-fourth the usual dose and then raised to one-half. If a patient is not doing well on the SSRIs, I try a drug from another family, usually Wellbutrin, although sleeplessness, agitation, and confusion have been reported in older patients, or I send them to a psychiatrist. If they don't tolerate or benefit from a second drug, I definitely send them to a psychiatrist.

If your primary-care doctor starts you on antidepressant medication and you aren't doing well after two different drugs, or if you've contemplated suicide, you should see a psychiatrist. Remember, there should be no stigma attached to seeing a psychiatrist. Like a cardiologist or a gastroenterologist, a psychiatrist is a specialist in a certain group of diseases — which happen to be diseases of the brain.

St. John's Wort

St. John's wort may be one alternative if, like Al, you're mildly depressed. European studies showed this herbal medicine, made from a common wildflower, to be better than a placebo in mild depression. St. John's wort is used extensively in Europe. However, one recent U.S. study comparing this herb with a placebo indicated no difference in response. Another study comparing St. John's wort with an SSRI is now under way. Are you and your doctor uncertain about whether you should begin antidepressant therapy? St. John's wort may be worth a try. But if your condition doesn't improve within a matter of weeks, ask your doctor for one of the more mainstream medications.

What to Do When Medication Doesn't Work

I included Bill's case because he was so ill we took the rather severe measure of using electroconvulsive therapy. He was deteriorating under our eyes, being fed intravenously on account of severe appetite loss, and the highest tolerable dose of medication was not working. So-called shock therapy is alarming, especially if you observe a treatment, and many people outside medicine think it's barbaric, but I have had four patients whose lives I am sure were saved by it. In the severe depression of the elderly, it may be the only therapy that works.

Can You Prevent or Stop Depression?

Some people like Jack and Bill have such an inherited, metabolic tendency to depression; they need only the mildest nudge to push them into clinical depression. Most cases of depression in older people, however, resemble Al's or Ruth's — they are mild, the kind that can possibly be prevented or made much less severe. Prevention and mitigation strategies involve coming to terms with getting older. Some people see getting older as an unfortunate series of losses — loss of abilities, loss of respect, loss of friends and loved ones. Others anticipate losses and regard them as an integral part of the cycle of life. Older patients who prepare psychologically for loss tend to tolerate it best. Other coping strategies include making sensible living and social arrangements, keeping busy, engaging in regular exercise, taking care of your health, and moderating your intake of alcohol and medications with depressant effects.

You cannot avoid grief after loss, but eventually you do have to move on, and you can. People who have a fallback position do better than those who don't. If you lose a spouse — often the greatest blow — try to build on your relationship with your children or your closest friends. For a single person, the loss of a close friend can be wrenching. Nurture other friendships so that you have people to fall back on in case of loss. Don't try to tough out grief alone. Being alone itself can be a cause of depression and certainly is no way to cope with grief.

Activity and socializing are vitally important. Join a book club, a bridge group, a garden club, or a bowling league; church or fraternal lodge activities are wonderful. My father became a Shriner when he was about sixty. Schedule time with remaining family members or valued friends. Remember that you are very important to your children and siblings. You are very important to your friends. Many of them need you more than you need them. Don't let your social chatter focus on medical problems or grief. Talk about the news, politics, books you have read, a TV program, a movie, funny things or odd characters you have known in the past. For your children and grandchildren, your stories are a firsthand window on the past; they value your special wisdom.

REMEMBER THIS

- Depression should be looked on as a physical illness, not a character flaw, which has both physical and psychological causes.
- The major physical cause is heredity, but other illnesses, excessive alcohol intake, and some drugs can contribute to depression.
- Loss and disappointment are major psychological triggers of depression.
- Sadness and loss of pleasure are almost universal symptoms of depression. Loss of self-esteem, though less common in the elderly than in younger patients, can be a symptom.
- Common physical symptoms of depression are loss of appetite and weight, early morning wakefulness, and sexual dysfunction or lack of interest in sex.
- You should see your doctor if you experience symptoms of depression for more than a brief period.
- Medication, especially with one of the SSRI drugs, is indicated for significant, persistent, or recurrent depression. Doses should be lower for all persons over seventy-five. All antidepressants have potential side effects, most commonly sleep disturbance, confusion, dizziness, nausea, and bowel problems.
- In the very rare case of severe depression that persists in spite of medication, electroconvulsive therapy may be appropriate.

CHAPTER 17

ALCOHOLISM AND ALCOHOL ABUSE

Alcoholism and alcohol abuse make up the third most serious health problem in the United States, just behind tobacco addiction and obesity. Most of the severe alcoholics I see over the age of sixty are women. Some die of their disease after a long decline. However, the vast majority of heavy drinkers I see in this age group — the alcohol abusers — are men. Though some die of alcohol abuse, most just suffer alcohol-related health problems and experience a markedly diminished quality of life.

Two or three times a week, someone comes into my office with a complaint stemming from alcohol abuse, although they don't always realize it or they don't want to acknowledge it. It might be the senior businessman who can't sleep and feels wiped out every afternoon, the retired government secretary who doesn't always make sense to her friends, or the daughter worried about her father falling at night.

Alcohol can damage both your physical and your mental health. What is alcoholism? What is alcohol abuse? How can you tell if a loved one suffers from alcoholism or just drinks too much, and what can you do about it?

Physical Effects of Alcohol in Excess

The alcohol-related medical problems I see are wide-ranging. Some problems are major and life threatening; others are more subtle but erode quality of life and accelerate aging. In addition to the common symptoms of hangover — headache, nausea, gastritis, and irritable bowel — alcohol can cause erectile difficulties, potentially fatal pancreatitis, and a host of other problems, including:

☐ Hepatitis and cirrhosis of the liver
☐ Cardiomyopathy

☐ Cardiac arrhythmia
☐ Transient memory loss
☐ Dementia and Korsakoff's psychosis
☐ Cerebellar degeneration
☐ Myopathy
☐ Withdrawal symptoms
☐ Psychiatric problems

Hepatitis and Cirrhosis of the Liver

These two conditions, one fairly acute, the other chronic, are life threatening. Hepatitis or inflammation of the liver has a number of triggers, usually viral, but a heavy binge on top of prolonged drinking can result in severe inflammation. A few years ago at a college reunion, I noticed that the wife of a classmate had jaundice — I could

> **Did You Know?**
> Alcoholics have a life expectancy of fifteen years less than average.

tell from the deep yellow color of the whites of her eyes. She was not a patient of mine but I knew she drank heavily, and I urged her to see her own doctor right away. She reluctantly said she would, following a trip to New York. In New York she continued to drink heavily, was hospitalized on her return, had irreversible liver failure, and died within a few days.

Cirrhosis, a scarring of the liver, is a chronic condition that may follow alcohol-related hepatitis. Though not immediately fatal, cirrhosis is debilitating and usually not reversible. People with cirrhosis have wasted arms and legs and often fluid-filled abdomens. They may experience episodes of mental confusion and can die of massive intestinal hemorrhage from ruptured esophageal veins.

Cardiomyopathy

Alcohol can have a direct toxic effect on the heart muscle, causing it to enlarge and lose its pumping power. People who are moderately heavy drinkers and have some form of heart disease increase their risk of congestive heart failure. In my experience, alcohol is the fourth most common cause of heart failure behind coronary heart disease, high blood pressure, and valvular heart disease.

Cardiac Arrhythmia or Holiday Heart

Heavy drinking, particularly binge drinking, often precipitates prolonged bouts of heart arrhythmia, or disturbance in the heart's rhythm. If the arrhythmia originates in the atria of the heart, it gives the drinker enough time to get to an emergency room, where he or she can be treated and observed in a monitored unit until the danger has passed. If the arrhythmia originates in the ventricles and lasts more than a few seconds, it is almost immediately fatal. I have had several patients treated for rapid arrhythmia during the Christmas holidays. They were the lucky ones. Over the years three other patients, all heavy drinkers, none with known heart disease, died suddenly at home on December 27! Presumably they all suffered from alcohol-induced arrhythmia.

Transient Memory Loss

Moderately heavy drinkers may experience a number of transient symptoms owing to altered brain chemistry, including blackouts and memory loss. Transient symptoms are the most common effects of alcohol I see in my practice.

After just two or three drinks, most older people have less recall. They often confabulate — talk around the point — so as not to reveal memory lapses. After a night of heavy drinking, lapses may carry over into the next day. For most people who return to limited alcohol use, this condition seems reversible, but there is reason for caution.

A WORD OF CAUTION

The parts of the brain responsible for recall — the mamillary bodies, the hippocampus, the amygdala, and sections of the cerebral cortex — are affected by alcohol and are more vulnerable to injury than other parts of the brain. If you find your memory lapses, which are normal with aging, become much worse after two or three drinks, be very careful: drink by drink, you may be slowly and permanently damaging these sensitive parts of your brain.

Dementia and Korsakoff's Psychosis

Though all of us lose brain cells as we grow older, nature usually gives us enough to get by on. Heavy drinking accelerates cell loss and may push a person into dementia. People who have neurological problems such as early Alzheimer's or multi-infarct dementia (a series of small strokes) should drink no alcohol — period.

Alcoholics or prolonged heavy drinkers may also suffer from Korsakoff's psychosis, an almost total loss of short-term memory but remarkable preservation of distant memory. A retired patient with Korsakoff's related a long and remarkably accurate history of events leading up to the Korean War — he had been a diplomat — but did not remember that his wife had died the previous month or whether he had had breakfast that day.

Cerebellar Degeneration

Alcohol damages more than just the memory portion of the nervous system. The cerebellum, which controls coordination and the long nerve fibers in the peripheral nerves, can be damaged irreparably by alcohol. Some of my most pathetic patients are alcohol abusers who have lost the ability to get around on their own. They stumble into my office and often complain of burning or painful feet.

Myopathy

Excessive drinking reduces muscle mass, sometimes dramatically but often slowly and subtly. One nearly dead giveaway for women alcoholics is skinny, birdlike leg muscles. The sign is so obvious I could probably pick these women out of a parade.

Withdrawal Symptoms

Sudden withdrawal from alcohol can cause seizures, delirium tremens (DTs), sweating, nausea, marked anxiety, tremors, and vivid nightmares. A person with full-blown DTs is pale, tremulous, and often dizzy or faint, has a rapid heartbeat and high blood pressure, and may be visited by wildly vivid hallucinations. One of the first patients I saw in my days as an intern at the University of Rochester had DTs. Frightened by "grizzly bear," he escaped from an aide who was trying to secure him to his bed, jumped out of a second-floor window and ruptured his spleen. The alarming sight of this man beset by hallucinations is indelibly etched in my memory.

Psychiatric Problems

Both anxiety and depression are clearly precipitated or made worse by heavy drinking. Because of this, and alcohol's possible interference with medications for anxiety or depression, I strongly urge all my patients who have clinical anxiety or depression to be extremely careful about drinking. A one-drink limit seems sensible.

Even mild depression can be exacerbated by alcohol. One unusually jovial and successful seventy-year-old once said that only three things depressed him: the "trash" on television, the darkness of winter, and three glasses of wine, in ascending order.

Why Differentiate between Alcoholism and Alcohol Abuse?

Medical textbooks give the impression that alcoholism and alcohol abuse are two distinct syndromes. They define alcoholism as increased alcohol tolerance and a physical dependence on alcohol, with severe withdrawal symptoms if the alcoholic stops drinking. Alcohol abuse is characterized as less severe, simply drinking so much that it can cause health problems and interfere with social functioning. From years of medical practice, I have to say that the difference is not so clear-cut.

However, full-blown alcoholics may have a hereditary predisposition to alcohol addiction that heavy drinkers don't share. Certainly heredity plays a significant role in alcoholism. If one identical twin is an alcoholic, the other has a much higher likelihood of being an alcoholic than the fraternal twin of an alcoholic. Adopted children have the same rate of alcoholism as their natural parents, not their adoptive parents. Whether people who are moderately heavy drinkers have a mild inherited tendency toward drinking is not known.

The distinction between the alcoholic and the alcohol abuser is useful from the perspective of treatment. Clearly true addicts, unlike heavy drinkers, cannot stop drinking and stay sober without help. Alcoholics usually have to be urged to seek treatment through intervention from family, friends, or a doctor. And they need a structured system to stay sober. Moreover, the true alcoholic cannot just cut down. Only abstinence prevents lapses. This truth was sadly borne out recently, when one of the national proponents of allowing alcoholics to drink moderately was herself involved in a major auto accident while intoxicated.

How Much Is Too Much?

If you exhibit any of the signs of alcoholism, it is essential that you talk to your doctor, who can help get you into treatment. If you've got some of the more severe symptoms — bottle hiding, falls, or morning drinking — then seeking help may save your life. But if you're like most of my patients who drink too much, you're probably not a full-blown alcoholic. Still, alcohol may be causing health problems. How much can you drink safely?

First, let's define "drink." For our purposes, one drink is a:

- 12-ounce (standard) beer
- 5-ounce glass of wine
- 1.5 ounces of 80 proof (40 percent) spirits (a jigger)

The alcohol content is approximately equal in each of these.

HOW TO SPOT AN ALCOHOLIC

Do you remotely suspect that you, a loved one, a friend, or a colleague is an alcoholic? Here are some signs to look for:

☐ Drinking alone

☐ Drinking three or more drinks every day

☐ Concealed drinking (bottle hiders are almost by definition alcoholics)

☐ Drinking in the morning

☐ Alcohol on the breath (vodka, which has little odor, is a favorite of alcoholics)

☐ Unexplained falls, not reporting falls

☐ Any minor confusion or behavior change

☐ Unexplained shakiness, sweating, or rapid heartbeat

Keep a watch for these signs in yourself; if you see them, seek help. And intervene if you think a friend or loved one is an alcoholic. Remember, older alcoholics are extremely unlikely to seek help on their own.

Reasonable Limits

The guidelines for avoiding alcohol-related health problems are as follows:

	NUMBER OF DRINKS	
	Per week	On a single occasion
Men	14	4
Women over 120 pounds	9	3
Women under 120 pounds	7	2

Note that as you get older, your tolerance for alcohol decreases and the potential for adverse health effects from alcohol increases. At about age seventy-five, these limits should be cut in half for both sexes. And the limits are lower if you're driving. The legal definition of alcohol intoxication is 0.08 or 0.1 in most states. Men can reach this level after just three drinks; women can reach it after just two.

The body metabolizes alcohol, or gets rid of its effects, at the rate of about one drink an hour. If you're going to have a third drink, you should not have it until at least one hour has elapsed since your first drink. If you'll be driving, always wait at least an hour after your last drink. If you stick to these limits, you shouldn't develop alcohol-related health problems.

Staying within the Limits

A heavy social schedule, for example during the holidays, can be an invitation to drink in excess. So can living with a spouse who drinks heavily, or living alone. Here are some tips to help you to stay within the guidelines:

- If you're drinking spirits, always use a 1.5-ounce jigger. If you're drinking a martini, manhattan, or margarita, each drink should count as two.
- If you're at a dinner party and are likely to have wine with dinner, pace yourself during the cocktail hour. Nurse your drink or get something nonalcoholic.
- In terms of alcohol content, beer is safer than wine — beer contains roughly a third the amount of alcohol per ounce.
- If you're living alone and want a drink, never have more than one.
- Having no alcohol two nights a week is good discipline.
- If you and your spouse are drinking heavily together, it's up to you to take the lead and say, "Let's both cut down." Get your spouse to read this chapter.

You have to be honest with yourself. Honest about the drink count, and honest about the effect it's having on your body and your relationships. If you cannot stay within the guidelines, stop all alcohol totally for two weeks and try again. If the guidelines remain an elusive goal, talk with your doctor or seek out a specialist who can evaluate your drinking problem.

Treating Alcoholism

Your doctor can assess the severity of alcohol abuse, but you must be truthful about the amount you're drinking, or as accurate as possible about the amount your relative is drinking. Be honest, too, in describing associated psychological or physical symptoms, no matter how painful the subject may be to talk about. If your doctor thinks you or your relative is suffering from alcoholism, the situation may require a temporary stay in a detoxification unit or a special alcohol inpatient facility. Getting a loved one into treatment often requires group intervention by family members or close friends, perhaps in the presence of a doctor or counselor.

Most specialists in alcoholism strongly recommend that after withdrawal the alcoholic become part of a formal Alcoholics Anonymous

(AA) support group. AA should be continued even when the alcoholic has been sober for some time. In my experience, a significant majority of patients who become active in AA conquer their disease and remain sober. The vast majority of those who do not drift back into alcoholism. Whatever the reason for AA's success, I believe the men and women in AA do a better job than the medical profession in keeping people sober.

One other auxiliary treatment used after detoxification is a medication called Antabuse (disulfiram). The recovering alcoholic takes Antabuse every day and has a severe reaction if he or she resumes drinking while it remains in the body. Common reactions are flushing, headaches, nausea, vomiting, dizziness, and fainting. Because reactions are so dramatic, and because Antabuse raises the risk of heart attack, I do not generally recommend it for recovering alcoholics in the third third of life — certainly not for people in their late sixties or older. Newer, more promising drugs for the treatment of alcoholism are now on the horizon, but their potential for success remains uncertain.

Recovering alcoholics are often treated for depression or other psychiatric problems with a combination of medication and counseling.

> **Did You Know?**
> A given amount of alcohol has a greater effect on women than on men. If a 120-pound woman drinks the same amount as a 180-pound man, she has a 50 percent higher alcohol level. Women also have less of the enzyme that rids the body of alcohol, so alcohol levels build up more quickly and remain high longer in women. This gender difference, which may partially explain the severity of alcoholism in women, lowers the amount of alcohol any woman can drink safely.

Women Alcoholics in My Practice

In the general population, alcoholic men outnumber alcoholic women about two to one. The word alcoholic makes us think of a man, often the bum on skid row. In my experience with patients over sixty, however, women are several times more likely than men to be alcoholics. Alcoholism in postmenopausal women is one of the deadliest diseases I take care of in my practice. I can only recall one postmenopausal female alcoholic who stopped drinking and stayed sober. She had transient mental confusion and cerebellar ataxia, and I think she realized she would die if she didn't stop. Some two dozen others have died from the direct toxic effect of alcohol on one or more of their organ systems. They seemed oblivious to advice from family, friends, doctors, and in some cases legal authorities; their drinking, carried on despite the devastating health effects, was so deliberate it almost seemed like slow, conscious suicide. Most of these women had attended college and were in the upper middle class.

REMEMBER THIS

- Alcoholism is a severe disease that can cause a myriad of health problems, both for the alcoholic and for the alcohol abuser. It is potentially fatal.
- In the over-sixty population, women with alcoholism seem sicker and more resistant to treatment than men.
- True alcoholics in the elderly population do not usually seek help. A family member, friend, or doctor has to get them into therapy.
- For the true alcoholic, only a program that supports full abstinence works.
- One beer, a 5-ounce glass of wine, and 1.5 ounces of liquor contain equal amounts of alcohol.
- Safe limits for consumption are fourteen drinks a week, no more than four at a time for men, and for women nine drinks a week, no more than three at one sitting.
- Past the age of seventy-five, you should reduce your intake to about one-half the guideline amounts.
- Drivers, drink no more than three drinks if you're a man, no more than two if you're a woman, and wait an hour after your last drink before driving.
- If you cannot stay within the drinking guidelines, or if you suspect you have a drinking problem, bring your concern to the attention of your doctor.

CHAPTER 18

SEXUAL DYSFUNCTION

Some people well into their golden years still enjoy sex. Several years ago a ninety-one-year-old man waited near my office door while his eighty-four-year-old wife was getting dressed in the examining room. She had had a very minor stroke about a month before, and he wanted to know when they could safely resume intercourse. "Whenever you feel like it," I replied.

Not all elderly are so lucky. "Without it, I'm Elmer Fudd, with it I'm Warren Beatty," one sixty-five-year-old lawyer once told me. He was talking about Viagra, the medication that has revolutionized the treatment of erectile dysfunction — impotence, as we used to call it — and withal paved the way for more aggressive treatment of women's sexual problems. In the wake of Viagra's success in men, pharmaceutical companies have been busy formulating medications to improve desire and arousal in women. In this chapter, I'll discuss problems with male sexuality at somewhat greater length because erectile dysfunction is the number one cause of loss of sexual intimacy in the elderly.

Sexual Dysfunction in Men

Treating erectile problems in men of any age, particularly older men, was one of the least satisfactory exercises in medical practice until the debut of Viagra in the 1990s. But despite its wild success, Viagra does not hold all the answers. Sexual dysfunction in aging men is a complicated business, one that involves the mind as well as the body.

The Three Stages of Sexual Activity in Men
Most specialists in sexuality divide sexual activity in men (and women) into three stages:

□ Desire
□ Arousal
□ Orgasm

Desire. The first stage, desire or libido, is primarily influenced by the male hormone testosterone, although thyroid hormone also plays a role. As men get older their testosterone levels gradually decline. Before the advent of Viagra, doctors prescribed testosterone much more readily for men with diminished desire and for men with erectile problems, hoping against hope that it would help that also. Recent studies suggest, however, that unless testosterone levels are very low, extra testosterone doesn't increase desire, and in my experience testosterone helped only a minority of men with a flagging libido and very, very few with erectile problems. One problem with testosterone medication is that after a while it inhibits your own testosterone production; when the outside source is stopped, you really do need it. Now with Viagra we are much less likely to dole out the testosterone, and only if blood levels are clearly low.

Arousal. Arousal, or erection, is a much more complicated business. Two spongy chambers lie along the length of the penis, one on each side. Called corpora cavernosa, or cavernous bodies, they are rich with blood vessels that fill up during an erection. The walls of the blood vessels dilate as blood enters, and owing to a compressive effect the blood cannot escape, which causes an erect penis. For an erection to take place, the corpora, certain parts of the brain, the nerves leading to the penis, and the larger vessels carrying blood to the penis all have to be intact and functioning.

Orgasm. In a normally functioning man, penile stimulation results in a peak of sexual pleasure, or orgasm, accompanied by rhythmic contraction in the sexual organs and a faster-beating heart. For many men, this third stage of sex comes too quickly for full enjoyment, is delayed too long, or doesn't occur at all. Orgasm has a psychological as well as a physical component. Prolonged foreplay seems to help lengthen intercourse. The man relaxes and pays attention to his partner's needs, and when his partner is enjoying the act, it enhances his own pleasure.

Causes of Sexual Dysfunction in Men

Almost all men have trouble with sexual performance at one time or another. If this happens, "stage fright" may set in and the fear of not achieving an adequate erection may interfere with performance. Repeated difficulty with erection may ultimately reduce desire. Sometimes stress or an extremely busy schedule can cause loss of libido, an erectile problem, or both. Many a thirty-five-year-old can work hard and still play, but too much work can be sexually draining for a sixty-year-old.

Men over sixty experience an increasing incidence of erectile problems with each passing year. The problems may be psychological, but more frequently they're either physical or a mix of the physical and the psychological. Anything that interferes with the brain mechanism that sparks arousal, with the nerves or arteries supplying the penis, or with the erectile mechanism itself can lead to sexual dysfunction. The causes are many, and include:

- Medication
- Neurological disorders
- Diabetes
- Vascular blockage
- Alcohol abuse

Medication. The list of medications that can interfere with sexual activity is long, and you should ask your doctor about each drug if you're having a problem. The worst culprits are drugs used to treat high blood pressure, especially beta blockers. Almost all tranquilizers or antidepressants can result in sexual dysfunction. SSRI (selective serotonin re-uptake inhibitor) antidepressants, for example, frequently prevent orgasm. Other problem medications that can weaken desire or cause impotence include:

- NSAIDs (nonsteroidal anti-inflammatory drugs), commonly taken for arthritis
- Too much or too little hormone in thyroid replacement treatment
- Female hormones or testosterone-reducing drugs used to treat prostate cancer
- Tagamet, the ulcer drug
- Over-the-counter decongestants and antihistamines

Neurological disorders. Impotence may result from a stroke or a degenerative neurological disease that damages the spinal cord or that affects areas in the brain associated with arousal. A much more common cause of impotence is damage to the nerves leading to the penis following pelvic injury or prostate surgery.

Diabetes. Diabetes interferes with both the vessels carrying blood to the penis and the nerves that help trigger erection. This disease is one of the

---

A WORD OF CAUTION

Unfortunately, even in the best of hands you run a risk of impotence after prostate surgery for cancer. If you've got to have this operation, improve your chances of avoiding risk: choose a surgeon who has experience with nerve-sparing techniques. (See part 1, chapter 6, "Cancer.")

---

more common causes of erectile dysfunction in men in their sixties and seventies.

Vascular blockage. Atherosclerotic blockage of the arteries that supply the penis or pelvic area is a frequent cause of dysfunction. Men with this problem usually have other vascular disorders such as coronary disease or hardening of the arteries to the legs.

Alcohol abuse. The severe alcoholic doesn't have much of a chance at adequate sexual function. Alcohol diminishes the brain activity associated with arousal and interferes with local reaction in the penis. Moreover, the liver disease common in alcoholism throws the body's hormonal mechanism off. Even a moderate drinker may have difficulty achieving an erection. If you are only marginally able to achieve an erection, just one or two drinks may erase even that ability.

Treating Sexual Dysfunction in Men

For the purposes of treatment, we'll approach sexual dysfunction as one of three problems:

☐ Loss of libido but adequate erectile function
☐ Loss of erectile function but adequate libido
☐ Premature, delayed, or nonexistent orgasm

Loss of libido but erectile function. Often in this case the patient doesn't complain. His wife will tell me, or will tell him to talk with me. The first thing I do is check blood testosterone and thyroid levels. If they're normal, I do a general checkup to rule out health problems that can sap energy and result in loss of libido. Psychological or couples counseling may be appropriate. Sometimes sexual dysfunction arises from short-term stress rather than longstanding emotional problems. A sixty-year-old director of a large public interest lobbying group who was under intense pressure to head off some legislation told me he was experiencing sexual problems. After an initial exam revealed no physical cause, I suggested he turn over the legislative problem to someone else and take a vacation. He took a month's leave and his sexual relationship with his wife improved dramatically.

If the testosterone level is low, it should be supplemented. Testosterone can be given in pill form, by skin patch, or by injection every three or four weeks. Before starting this therapy, the man should have a digital prostate exam and a PSA (prostatic-specific antigen) test to rule out prostate cancer, because testosterone can stimulate the growth of malignancies. Testosterone can also enlarge the prostate gland and make urination difficult.

Loss of erectile function but adequate libido. This second problem, impotence, is much more common. There are literally millions of middle-aged and older American men who are impotent, and before Viagra came on the market it was difficult to treat them.

Yocon (yohimbine) has achieved success in some men, but the tradeoff is numerous side effects. Nitroglycerin paste applied to the penis can produce an erection — along with dizziness or a headache in the man and his sexual partner. Prostaglandins or other chemicals delivered by tiny suppositories in the urethra can sometimes cause erections. Some people can self-inject tiny amounts of these chemicals into the penis, though this therapy is no longer common.

Another therapy is to use a vacuum pump that draws blood into the penis. The pump has an elastic ring around the base to keep the blood from flowing out. This treatment seems designed to kill whatever romantic flame the man kindles in his partner.

Surgical techniques include the insertion of an inflatable balloonlike device in the corpora; the patient inflates the device with a tiny pump located in the scrotum. Some men have had semirigid rods surgically implanted, but these have their drawbacks and are now a therapy of last resort.

For years, doctors recommended these inadequate treatments for frustrated men whose only alternative was sexual inactivity. The medical profession needed a more effective therapy to offer patients, and several years ago, partly by chance, one became available. The wild success of Viagra deserves a section all its own (*see opposite,* "*Viagra*").

Premature, delayed, or nonexistent orgasm. SSRI antidepressants have a proven track record in delaying orgasm, and many doctors have used low doses of SSRIs such as Prozac to treat premature ejaculation. But SSRIs are problematic when taken in the high doses necessary for treating depression: occasionally the ejaculation is so delayed it doesn't happen at all. SSRIs can also reduce libido or cause difficulty with erections.

The decision to raise or lower the dose when someone is on an SSRI drug and has sexual problems is not always easy. If sexual dysfunction started because of an SSRI drug, the dose may need to be reduced, but if the dysfunction preceded the medication — depressed men often experience sexual dysfunction — the dose may need to be higher. For patients who need a high dose of an antidepressant, the addition of Viagra, often just temporarily, can be helpful.

Viagra

Without doubt, this medicine has turned out to be far more successful than any previous treatment for erectile dysfunction. Large clinical trials show a success rate of about 80 percent, a figure I can verify from my own practice. But despite Viagra's track record — and despite former Senator Dole's endorsement — many men who could benefit from this drug either are reluctant to talk to their doctor or harbor a false sense of machismo. One of my urologist colleagues dubbed Viagra the "by the way pill." At the end of an office visit for some other disorder, men often say, "By the way, maybe I could use Viagra." This has happened so often I start writing the prescription before my patient has even finished his sentence. If you're having a problem, don't be shy around your doctor. Remember, it's the in thing for guys to ask about Viagra.

THE VIAGRA STORY

Viagra (sildenafil) was first used in drug trials as a possible treatment for heart problems. The drug, a vascular dilator, was expected to improve blood flow through narrowed coronary arteries. Viagra didn't prove effective for heart patients, but men who were enrolled in the trials were reluctant to give back their unused samples. The drug clearly enhanced erections! Subsequent tests showed it to be safe and far more effective than other drugs being used to improve penile function. Pfizer pharmaceutical company, which put Viagra on the market, enjoyed a boost in its stock, and magazine cartoonists got a lot of play out of the new medication.

How does Viagra work? Viagra maintains high levels of a chemical called cyclic GMP in the penis. GMP dilates the blood vessels of the penis and stimulates blood flow in while preserving the mechanism that prevents it from exiting. Viagra is effective about thirty minutes after ingestion and lasts two to three hours, though several patients have told me it can last up to seven hours. The remarkable success of this drug is that, unlike other therapies, it enhances the penis's natural function. Sexual stimulation is still required to produce an erection, and — fortunately for the man's sense of dignity — the erection subsides after orgasm.

Side effects. Viagra's side effects, which include headache, facial flushing, and nausea or abdominal discomfort, are remarkably mild. The only serious effect occurs when nitroglycerin medications and Viagra are used together, which can cause a precipitous fall in blood pressure. I had a seventy-year-old patient who used Viagra at his winter house in Florida. Feeling his oats, he went out for a jog after sex and developed chest pain. In the emergency room he neglected to tell doctors that he was on Viagra. They gave him a nitroglycerin medication and he went right into shock. Fortunately he recovered from the steep drop in blood pressure, but not until after learning a hard lesson. Remember, if you're on heart medicine or about to go on it, ask your doctor if you can also take Viagra.

Dosing. Viagra comes in 25 mg, 50 mg, and 100 mg pills. It's an expensive drug, and many health insurance plans don't cover it. I start patients with the 50 mg dose. If that doesn't work, I put them on 100 mg. If the 50 mg dose does work, I recommend that they try 25 mg. (Many patients, because of the expense, have been using half a pill.)

Sexual Dysfunction in Women

Women experience the same three stages of sexual activity as men — desire, arousal, and orgasm. Medical problems can cause dysfunction in any stage.

The woman's clitoris and labia contain tissue that in some ways functions similarly to the corpora cavernosa of the penis: when the woman is aroused, the tissue becomes swollen. During arousal women also experience increased vaginal secretion and relaxation of the vaginal walls.

Treating Libido in Women
In women the principal sex hormone is estrogen, which plays an important role in the menstrual cycle during childbearing years. Among its other functions, estrogen helps maintain the moisture and thickness of vaginal tissue. As I noted in the chapter on hormone replacement therapy,

estrogen levels take a steep dive after menopause, and without estrogen, women can get a condition called atrophic vaginitis, in which intercourse is painful. Estrogen in the form of pills, skin patches, or vaginal creams can prevent atrophic vaginitis.

However, estrogen alone doesn't do much to kindle sexual desire. What does enhance desire in women is actually a small amount of testosterone or a male hormone similar to testosterone. For women with diminished sexual desire, taking a small amount of male hormone can be very helpful. A pill called Estratest, which contains both estrogen and some testosterone, is now on the market, and other testosterone-like drugs are currently being investigated for their ability to increase libido in women.

The side effects of Estratest are the same as those of estrogen when it is used alone, except that with Estratest a very few women experience increased facial hair or voice deepening.

DHEA (dehydroepiandrosterone) is an over-the-counter medication that contains a chemical precursor of both estrogen and male hormone and has been shown to raise levels of both. DHEA has enhanced libido in some women. The male hormone effect can theoretically stimulate the growth of facial hair, but so far that has not been a major complaint. I believe this therapy holds promise for treatment of sexual dysfunction in both sexes, but more thorough studies on the potential benefits and side effects need to be done.

Treating Arousal in Women

Although the result is not as dramatic as in men, some women have taken Viagra and found that it enhanced sexual pleasure. Viagra is known to increase blood flow to the clitoris and labia. Sildenafil is soon to be marketed in a cream form for women, and a similar chemical in pill form is being evaluated for women. Women on nitroglycerin-containing medication will have to take the same precautions as men.

Enjoying Sex in the Golden Years

In addition to the causes of sexual dysfunction mentioned in this chapter, any number of health problems can throw a monkey wrench into a couple's sex life: cardiac problems, severe arthritis, chronic lung disease, obesity, and alcohol abuse. But for most couples who take care of their general health, sex can be a pleasurable activity well into old age. If you're past sixty and married to the same person you've been with for years, chances are you're hitched for the long haul. The glamour of a date or a weekend getaway when you were thirty-five may have paled, but the love, humor, and shared experiences that have built up over many years can make up for this loss. For the sake of each other, you should try to make yourselves as appealing as possible without resorting to breast implants or toupees. Staying fit, maintaining a sense of humor, and showing affection can do wonders for the libido. A friend of mine from Texas has a wonderful Mexican expression: Cabellos grises no delibitan el deseo — gray hair doesn't weaken desire.

REMEMBER THIS

- Sexual activity can extend through much of the third third of your life.
- The three stages of sexual activity are desire, arousal, and orgasm. Physical or psychological problems can cause difficulties in any stage in either sex.
- In men, low testosterone, lifestyle, or psychological factors can result in a flagging libido.
- Erectile dysfunction is the most common physical problem for older men and the major reason many older couples do not have active sex lives.
- Though the cause of an individual case of erectile dysfunction can be difficult to pinpoint, Viagra has been dramatically successful in treating erectile problems stemming from all sorts of causes.
- The side effects of Viagra are tolerable unless you're taking a heart medication that contains nitroglycerin, in which case you could experience a potentially fatal drop in blood pressure.
- Women have a small amount of male hormone that is partly responsible for their sex drive.
- The use of a pill containing both estrogen and a small amount of testosterone, Estratest, can improve libido in women.
- Estrogen replacement therapy prevents atrophic vaginitis, which is the main cause of painful intercourse in older women.
- Sildenafil (Viagra) appears useful in arousing women and enhancing their sexual pleasure.

CHAPTER 19

INTESTINAL PROBLEMS

The intestinal tract starts at the mouth and ends at the anus. Rather than just a bunch of inert pipes, the intestinal tract is a series of constantly active organs that has its own nerve supply, secretes its own hormones, and can bleed, become infected, and grow tumors. There are literally scores of disorders of the intestinal tract, but the handful of problems I discuss here account for more than 70 percent of intestinal complaints in the third third of life.

Let's start at the top and work down.

The uppermost organ in the intestinal tract is the esophagus, a muscular organ that runs from the throat to the stomach. When you swallow, your esophagus pushes food and fluid down into your stomach.

The stomach is a receiving and temporary storage chamber for food. Digestion starts in the mouth and continues in the stomach, where acid and enzymes turn the food you eat into a thick liquid. This semidigested goo squeezes through a narrow junction called the pylorus to enter the first section of the small intestine, the duodenum, where the process of absorbing nutrients begins. Absorption is completed in the final sections of the small intestine, the jejunum and the ileum.

The unabsorbed residual, including roughage, passes through the small intestine and into the large intestine, or colon. The colon ascends along the abdomen's right side, runs across the upper abdomen, then descends toward the rectum and anus. All along the intestinal tract a muscular wall is constantly propelling food forward, a process called peristalsis.

Gastroesophageal Reflux Disease

The most common problem in the esophagus, and one of the most common complaints seen in general medicine, is gastroesophageal reflux disease (GERD). In this disorder the lower esophageal sphincter, a muscular valve that normally prevents food from coming back up, malfunctions and the stomach's contents flow up into the esophagus. The reflux usually travels only a short distance, producing "heartburn," or a feeling of burning pain or indigestion beneath the breastbone. However, when a person is lying down the reflux may enter the mouth, leaving a sour or bitter taste, or be aspirated into the bronchial tubes, causing a nighttime cough. GERD with aspiration is one of the more common causes of a persistent cough.

What Causes GERD?

One common cause of GERD is a hiatal hernia (*see below*), in which the tissue at the hiatus, or the opening in the diaphragm that leads from the esophagus into the stomach, becomes lax. Ordinarily, the hiatus is tightly clamped; when it loosens, a portion of the stomach pushes up into the chest. A hiatal hernia may interfere with the valve mechanism, causing material in the stomach to flow backward. Surgery to repair a hiatal hernia should only be done if it is causing obstructive symptoms or the reflux is resistant to other treatment.

Many people have reflux without a hiatal hernia, and recent research tends to downplay its role.

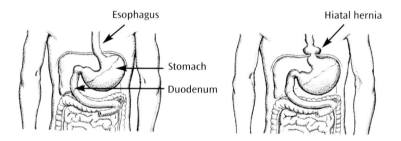

The upper gastrointestinal tract. The normal valve mechanism is often compromised by a hiatal hernia.

Triggers

Most people have GERD symptoms only occasionally. Triggers include:

☐ Large meals
☐ Rich sauces and desserts
☐ Alcohol
☐ Coffee
☐ Chocolate

□ Meals eaten within two and a half hours of lying down
□ Excess weight
□ Cigars and cigarettes

Rich foods relax the lower esophageal sphincter so that food escapes back up, and lying down removes the effect of gravity that aids digestion. Alcohol, coffee, and chocolate stimulate the secretion of stomach acid and can aggravate the situation.

I was on a board that met three or four times a year, and at the end of each session we had a rich banquet that lasted for hours and always ended with a creamy chocolate dessert. Back at my hotel I learned firsthand about the GERD symptoms my patients had complained of.

Treating GERD

If you have an episode only rarely, go easy on the rich food, or take a pre-ventive antacid pill an hour before bed and a liquid over-the-counter antacid like Maalox or Mylanta at bedtime. If the symptoms persist or recur frequently even though you haven't overindulged, you need to see your doctor. The first diagnostic test is usually a barium swallow plus upper gastrointestinal (upper GI) X ray. In an upper GI test, serial X rays are taken as you swallow liquid barium or some other material that will show up on an X ray. This can confirm the diagnosis and rule out more serious problems such as esophageal ulcer, tumor, or strictures.

If reflux is confirmed, the treatment is usually effective. Start with the following measures:

□ Make sure the head of your bed is elevated six to eight inches. You can lift it with books or wooden blocks. A sleeping wedge may help, but extra pillows do not do the job — your head and shoul-ders slip off.
□ Don't eat meals within two and half hours of bedtime.
□ Avoid large or rich meals.
□ Stop smoking — even a rare cigar can bring on reflux.
□ Try to lose weight if you are overweight.
□ Don't wear tight belts or girdles.
□ Avoid alcohol, coffee, chocolate, and very spicy foods.
□ Take an antacid liquid shortly before bedtime if symptoms occur at night, and an hour after meals if symptoms occur during the day.

A measure I have found extremely successful in my patients is to start them on one of the newer, more powerful antacid pills daily: Prilosec (omeprazole) 20 mg or Prevacid (lansoprazole) 30 mg. They are more powerful than the older-generation antacids, have at least as good if not better a record of side effects, and eliminate symptoms more quickly. Once symptoms are under control, I suggest that patients switch to over-the-counter Zantac or Tagamet.

What If GERD Persists?

If your symptoms don't clear up promptly, or aren't gone in two weeks, you and your doctor need to move to a more intensive evaluation. Refluxing acid and bile are a corrosive mixture that can cause ulcers or scarring, sometimes so severe that the lower esophagus becomes partially obstructed. You may need to have an upper endoscopy or esophagascopy. During this test a gastroenterologist, using a fibroscopic tube, examines the lower end of the esophagus and takes a biopsy. An esophagascopy can detect a serious complication of GERD called Barrett's esophagus, in which a healing esophageal membrane is replaced by a different type of cell that may become malignant.

A WORD OF CAUTION

The presence of Barrett's esophagus is reason for careful follow-up by an experienced gastroenterologist. You should take large doses of Prilosec or Prevacid indefinitely and scrupulously follow all other measures to reduce reflux. The Barrett's membranes should be biopsied again every one to three years. If a change called dysplasia occurs, you should have a biopsy more frequently — every six to twelve months. High-grade dysplasia is so likely to become malignant that many experts are advising surgery to remove the lower esophagus. To avoid this radical measure, some patients have had newer laser or other ablative techniques to destroy the dangerous tissue without removing the esophagus. I recommend ablative techniques over surgery in cases of high-grade dysplasia. If you have high-grade dysplasia and an operation or ablative technique is not performed, make sure you're re-examined and biopsied every three months.

Esophageal Motor Disorders

As I noted, the esophagus is not an inert tube; it is a muscular organ with sphincter muscles at either end that move liquids and solids through as you swallow. Relaxation of the sphincters and the propulsive motion of the esophagus have to be synchronized for effective and comfortable swallowing. Lots of things can go wrong with this mechanism.

One problem occasionally seen in people over sixty is achalasia, a condition in which the lower esophageal sphincter doesn't relax with swallowing and the propulsive mechanism is weakened. Using a balloon on an endoscope, a gastroenterologist can dilate the sphincter and give relief for many months or years. This procedure should only be done by a gastroenterologist with experience in esophageal disorders, for even in the best hands, a rupture can occur. Another common motor disorder is esophageal spasm, where the muscles toward the back of the esophagus go into painful, prolonged contraction.

Muscular disorders of the esophagus are hard to categorize, particularly in older people. Numerous disorders cover the spectrum from "too relaxed" to "too spastic" sphincter muscles, or from "too relaxed" to "too spastic" propulsive muscles. Gastroenterologists often have motion picture X rays of the esophagus or sophisticated pressure measurements done to tailor treatment to a specific patient.

How to Swallow Horse Pills

The esophagus can be irritated when a large pill squeezes through. Certain antibiotics, aspirin, nonsteroidal anti-inflammatory drugs (NSAIDs), prednisone, potassium, and iron preparations are particularly irritating. When taking a "horse" pill, you should swallow water or some other liquid first, then the pill, then wash it down with more liquid — lots of it. Always take your pills sitting or standing. If something gets stuck and then passes through, drink a moderate amount of warm water to soothe your irritated tissue.

Ulcers and Gastritis

Stress and worry as a cause of ulcers have been dramatically de-emphasized. The only ulcers in which stress is a significant factor are those seen in patients in intensive care who are under major physical stress, and even then medication may be part of the cause.

What Are the Symptoms of Ulcers?
The classic symptom of ulcer of the stomach or duodenum is localized pain in the mid-upper abdomen or just to the right of the mid-abdomen. The

pain, typically described as a burning or "gnawing," comes on two to three hours after eating or during the night. Eating or taking antacids usually brings relief.

Several other conditions can produce a similar symptom — gallbladder disease, irritable bowel syndrome, GERD, non-ulcer or functional dyspepsia, and superficial gastritis caused by *Helicobacter pylori*.

Testing for Ulcers

If you have a burning or gnawing pain in the abdominal area, your doctor may suspect an ulcer but cannot be certain without an X ray or an upper endoscopy. If you are over sixty it is important to be tested, because other conditions whose symptoms mimic

> **Did You Know?**
> For years, doctors thought ulcers in the stomach and particularly in the duodenum were caused by stress or worry. I remember one patient of mine, a macho executive, announcing, "I don't get ulcers, I cause them." This misconception was corrected when a study demonstrated that the bacterium *Helicobacter pylori* causes almost all duodenal ulcers, most gastric ulcers, and many forms of gastritis. Seldom has one simple finding so rapidly revolutionized the treatment of a common disease. *Helicobacter pylori* probably causes more than half of ulcers; almost all the rest can be attributed to NSAIDs.

ulcer symptoms are more likely. All gastric (stomach) ulcers should be biopsied for possible malignancy. And you should be tested for *Helicobacter pylori*, either through a blood test, a breath test that detects chemicals from the bacteria, or special stains on biopsy tissue taken during an endoscopy.

Treating Ulcers

If the diagnosis is Helicobacter, you should be put on extensive therapy with combination medication for two weeks. I use tetracycline, Flagyl (metronidazole), Pepto-Bismol tablets, and Prilosec, but several other programs are equally effective. After treatment for Helicobacter, a breath test should be done to make sure the bacteria have been eradicated. If not, another two-week program should be started with a medication regimen that includes different antibiotics.

If you're taking NSAIDs when ulcer symptoms appear, these need to be stopped. If you've had a major, disabling condition that you've been treating with NSAIDs, you might try substituting Celebrex or Vioxx a little later, when the ulcer symptoms have subsided. No matter what the cause of the ulcer, Prilosec or Prevacid should be used for at least a month.

A WORD OF CAUTION

If you have *Helicobacter pylori*, everything should be done to eradicate it and to heal the ulcers. Besides being painful, ulcers can erode into blood vessels, causing severe hemorrhage, and they can perforate the duodenal or stomach wall, resulting in peritonitis. Ulcers can also cause swelling and partial or total obstruction of the pylorus.

Another reason Helicobacter should be eradicated is that it may cause cancer. Over the past hundred years in the United States, the incidence of stomach cancer has dropped steeply. This is believed to be the result of better hygiene, which has led to a much lower incidence of infection with Helicobacter.

Intestinal Bleeding

You can bleed from any portion of the intestinal tract. The bleeding can be slow and imperceptible or massive, causing the sufferer to vomit blood or pass blood in the stool.

Upper gastrointestinal bleeding can come from the esophagus, stomach, or duodenum. If blood in the stool is from upper gastrointestinal bleeding, it tends to be tar-black and have a metallic odor. If it is from the colon, it is a bright red or maroon color. Bleeding from the small bowel is unusual. Lower intestinal bleeding, from the colon, can have many causes — a bleeding polyp or cancer, ulcerative colitis, diverticuli (weak spots on the colon wall that erode into blood vessels), and blood vessel abnormalities in the wall of the bowel. Minimal bright red rectal bleeding often signals hemorrhoids or a superficial tear, or fissure, in the membrane inside the anus.

Treating Intestinal Bleeding

If you vomit blood, or have a tar-black stool or a large amount of red blood in the stool, you need to get medical treatment immediately. Any significant gastrointestinal bleeding can be fatal if not evaluated. Gastrointestinal bleeding is usually managed in an intensive care unit where pulse and blood pressure can be monitored and blood tests taken. A small amount of rectal bleeding — spotting on the toilet paper, or a small amount on the stool or in the toilet — should be reported to your doctor. This type of bleeding is not as serious. Your doctor may examine your anus with a short lighted scope — an anoscope — to see if you have hemorrhoids or an anal fissure. If so, you can be treated and after a week or two retested to make sure all bleeding has stopped. If no cause for the bleeding is found, or if after treating for hemorrhoids blood is still seen, or hidden blood is detected in the stool, a colonoscopy should be performed to rule out bleeding polyps or cancer.

Hemorrhoids — engorged or thrombotic veins just inside or just outside the anus — are common and often occur along with a superficial anal fissure. They tend to appear after straining to have a bowel movement, heavy lifting, cycling, or horseback riding. The majority of sufferers respond well to hot baths and creams or suppositories such as Preparation H, Anusol, or Wyanoid. Most important is to avoid further straining. Rarely, a surgeon will do surgery to remove chronic hemorrhoids. In the rubber band procedure, the engorged vein is tied off and eventually falls off owing to a lack of blood supply.

Diarrhea

Diarrhea is a common complaint in the elderly. If diarrhea is acute — coming on quickly and lasting a few days — the cause is usually a viral infection of the intestine, in which case the only treatment is to maintain fluid and salt intake. If severe symptoms last longer than three days, or if there is mucus or blood with the diarrhea, you should contact your doctor and get a stool culture.

Short-term diarrhea can be relieved with Imodium or over-the-counter Kaopectate. If your case is severe, you may require paregoric or Parapectolin. The key is to maintain fluid intake. If you have diarrhea, nausea, and vomiting and cannot keep fluids down, you need to check in to the hospital for intravenous fluid and salt replacement.

Traveler's Diarrhea

About 60 percent of people who travel to developing countries for more than a few days get some form of traveler's diarrhea. Most cases are caused by bacteria — *E. coli*, salmonella, shigella, and the cholera bacillus.

The first principle of prevention is to avoid tap and well water. The only safe drinks are bottled water, cola, tea and coffee made from boiled water, and beer. Washing your hands may not help since the water source could be contaminated. Fruits and vegetables should be cooked or peeled (a banana is safer than lettuce), and all meat should be well done.

I would advise you to bring along:

☐ *The antibiotic Cipro (ciprofloxacin)*. This kills most bacteria. Take 500 mg twice a day for three to five days if you begin to experience symptoms of diarrhea with fever or muscles aches.

☐ *Imodium (loperamide)*. This gives symptomatic relief but should not be taken in the presence of bloody diarrhea, high fever, or severe abdominal pain. Imodium can dry the mouth and exacerbate urinary problems in men.

☐ *Salt tablets*. If the diarrhea is severe, add this to your bottled water and drink plenty of it to rehydrate yourself. You can also restore fluids with soft drinks and salty soups.

Another problem for travelers who visit a national park or wilderness area is diarrhea caused by parasites. Stool examination can confirm the presence of parasites such as giardia, and a colonoscopy can determine whether the parasite has given you inflammatory colitis.

Constipation

More elderly people are bothered by constipation than by any other intestinal problem. The problem isn't, as so many believe, that the bowel stops functioning with age. Constipation results primarily from the use of certain medications and from lifestyle choices — inactivity, a low-fiber diet, or low fluid intake. In the very infirm, the difficulty of getting to a toilet may postpone bowel movements and result in severe impaction.

The best treatment for constipation is not to let it happen. I recommend regular physical activity, a high-fiber diet including bran or bran cereals, adequate fluid intake — and getting to the toilet when you feel the urge. If these lifestyle changes don't do the trick, you could take a bulk agent such as Metamucil or Citrucel, or a stool softener such as docusate. Avoid laxatives if you can.

Chronic constipation, or any change in bowel pattern, should be discussed with your doctor and may warrant abdominal X rays, X rays of the colon, or a colonoscopy. You might be one of the rare individuals with mechanical blockage due to a more serious problem such as an adhesion or a tumor.

Traveler's Constipation

Constipation doesn't just happen at home. During travel you have a different diet and a different schedule, and you may have trouble finding a toilet — all of which can spell constipation.

Here are some suggestions:

- ☐ Eat fruit, properly prepared vegetables, and whole-grain bread.
- ☐ Get plenty of fluids.
- ☐ When traveling by plane, get up and walk in the aisles. If you're in a car, stop every hour or so and walk around for a few minutes.
- ☐ Bring along a little bag of All Bran, or some Metamucil, Citrucel, or docusate.
- ☐ If you have had bouts with constipation that exercise and roughage don't ease, take along some Dulcolax rectal suppositories — but use them sparingly.

THE PROBLEM WITH LAXATIVES

Laxatives used repeatedly tend to do more harm than good. Patients who make a practice of taking laxatives after the bowel has emptied itself may experience chronic mucoid diarrhea as well as sodium and potassium depletion. I had a sixty-nine-year-old patient who I am certain caused her own death through excessive laxative use. She was frequently hospitalized for weakness and low sodium or potassium, but exhaustive testing for abnormalities of the bowel showed no specific disease. Once when I was doing my hospital rounds, her purse, which was lying on the bedside table, fell open and out spilled dozens of Dulcolax tablets, an extremely powerful laxative. Even with psychiatric counseling and repeated hospitalization, she continued her addictive behavior. One day she was found dead in her apartment, dehydrated and potassium-depleted.

The moral of this story: reserve laxatives for an emergency. If you really do suffer from severe constipation, use a Dulcolax suppository followed about thirty minutes later by a Fleet enema. If this brings no comfort, call your doctor.

Diverticulitis

Diverticulitis — infection and rupture of a weak spot or pocket on the colon or bowel — is one of the more common, potentially serious bowel problems in older people (see opposite). Once I had four patients in the hospital at the same time for severe attacks of diverticulitis. The course of this disease varies, with attacks ranging from mild to devastating. The following cases illustrate several of the many aspects of diverticulitis and its treatment.

Intact bowel   Ruptured diverticulum

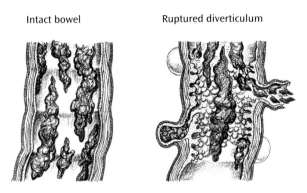

Normal wall of colon *(left)* and colon with intact and ruptured diverticulae *(right)*. The ruptured diverticulum causes diverticulitis.

Jenny

Jenny is sixty-five years old. Several years ago she had moderately severe pain in her lower abdomen. I noted moderately severe tenderness and a slight fullness on pressing the painful area. A scan of the abdomen showed weak spots protruding from the bowel and swelling around one of them. This confirmed diverticulitis. Jenny was started on large oral doses of two antibiotics, cephalexin and metronidazole, and kept on a liquid diet for the first three days of the ten-day antibiotic program. All her symptoms disappeared. Because she has a tendency to constipation, Jenny took to eating bran daily, exercising regularly, and drinking plenty of fluids. She hasn't suffered from constipation or diverticulitis since.

Aaron

Aaron was ninety-two years old and remarkably fit when he awakened one morning with severe pain throughout the abdominal region. Immediately, he went to the emergency room. His abdomen was tender all over and very firm to pressure, and the normal sounds of peristaltic activity were totally absent — classic signs of peritonitis. X rays of the abdomen confirmed this diagnosis and showed free air in the abdominal cavity, signaling a ruptured organ. Although advanced in age, Aaron was strong enough to undergo surgery. Abdominal exploration showed that his ruptured colon had spewed infected bowel contents into the abdominal cavity. The area was cleaned, and a section of bowel around the rupture was removed. The bowel could not be rejoined because the area was infected, so Aaron got a colostomy (an artificial opening in the bowel that empties into a bag outside the body). After a course of IVs and antibiotics, Aaron recovered and adjusted to the colostomy. He has opted not to have more surgery to rejoin the bowel, which would probably have been done in a younger person.

Kerry

Kerry is sixty-three years old. She had ten episodes of diverticulitis over five years, and between episodes often experienced discomfort in her lower abdomen. Several of the diverticulitis episodes resulted in hospitalization for IV antibiotics. One barium enema X ray of the colon showed a massive number of weak spots, mostly clustered in one section of the descending colon. Because the episodes were frequent and severe, and the discomfort suggested smoldering infection, she had surgery to remove the affected part of her colon.

During Kerry's operation, the parts of the colon on either side of the removed section were joined. After surgery Kerry was counseled on diet, but she argued that she "never met a vegetable she liked." However, she did start taking Metamucil regularly, and she's been keeping up her fluid intake and getting regular exercise. So far there have been no major recurrences.

Preventing Diverticulitis

Most Americans over sixty have some protrusions or pockets on their bowel, a condition known as diverticulosis. This is painless and, for most people with a small number of pockets, will never result in the rupture and inflammation of diverticulitis. As far as we know, anything that increases pressure on the bowel can cause the protrusions or pockets to form; what causes them to rupture is hard stools plus pressure.

A British surgeon in eastern Africa, Dr. Dennis Burkett, noted that Africans who lived in rural areas and ate high-fiber diets didn't suffer from diverticulitis; when they moved to the city and adopted a European diet, they developed this disorder at the same rate as people of European descent living in eastern Africa. This sort of anecdotal evidence combined with observations I've made from my own practice suggest that a high-fiber diet with plenty of liquid and exercise can prevent this often miserable disease from developing.

REMEMBER THIS

- Gastroesophageal reflux disease (GERD) is very common and may cause heartburn or a nighttime cough.

- GERD usually clears up if a person takes Prilosec or Prevacid, elevates the head of the bed, and avoids late-night meals as well as certain spicy or rich foods.

- Persistent GERD needs to be treated vigorously to prevent Barrett's esophagus, which can lead to esophageal cancer.

- Almost all ulcers of the stomach or duodenum are caused by either the bacterium *Helicobacter pylori* or NSAIDs.

- Ulcers are treated with antacids, but *Helicobacter pylori* must be eradicated, or NSAIDs therapy stopped or modified, for permanent healing.

- Vomiting blood or significant rectal bleeding are medical emergencies and need immediate evaluation at a hospital.

- Minor episodes of rectal bleeding are most often due to hemorrhoids or an anal fissure, but they need to be evaluated to determine the cause and to make sure the bleeding has stopped.

- Constipation is not an inevitable part of getting older. In most cases it can be avoided with proper diet, added fluid, and physical activity. If something more is needed, bulk agents such as bran or softeners are preferable to laxatives.

- Regular laxative use tends to become habitual and can lead to medical problems such as salt and potassium depletion.

- Diverticulitis is a common problem with complications that may require surgery. A high-fiber diet accompanied by plenty of fluids significantly lowers the risk of diverticulitis.

- In the United States, short-term diarrhea usually stems from a virus and will clear up. If you are terribly ill with diarrhea, you may require IV treatment.

- Your doctor should evaluate persistent diarrhea, which could be caused by parasites or inflammation.

CHAPTER 20

SKIN PROBLEMS

Certain skin problems are much more prevalent in the over-sixty set than in younger people. Some of these problems are merely cosmetic or at worst a nuisance. Others are potentially fatal and have to be treated.

Skin Growths

Aside from my African-American patients, who are much more resistant to skin growths, I've hardly ever examined a person over sixty who did not have some sort of skin growth. The most common lesions are seborrheic keratoses, plaquelike tan or brownish spots. Also, there are many other bumps and nodules that require careful inspection or dermatological consult.

The most common skin nodules or raised areas — or the most important to have examined — are:

□ Basal cell cancers
□ Squamous cell cancers
□ Actinic or sunlight keratoses
□ Seborrheic keratoses
□ Moles
□ Melanoma

The three malignant types — basal cell cancer, squamous cell cancer, and melanoma — are all at least partly caused by sun exposure. Actinic keratosis, which can become malignant, is also caused by sun exposure. Much of the damage is done in the teenage years when kids think being tan is cool. It's not so cool when those lazy hours of lolling in the sun come back to haunt you in later years. But even in advanced age continued exposure, particularly a bad sunburn, can cause damage. I hiked on the snow-covered slopes of Mount Rainier on a very sunny day and neglected to cover part of my temple with sunblock. I ended the hike with a wicked local sunburn and a few weeks later developed keratoses that would probably have become malignant if I had not removed them with Efudex. And that was just one day of sun exposure.

A WORD OF CAUTION

Being a doctor, I knew to remove the keratoses on my temple before they became malignant. You don't have to be a doctor to act prudently when it comes to skin growths. If you've sprouted anything suspicious, don't wait for your periodic exam — call your doctor and schedule an appointment today. Meanwhile, don't forget to slather on sunscreen with an SPF of 30 or more when you go outside, especially if your destination is Florida, Arizona, or the tropics.

Basal Cell Cancer

Basal cell cancer, which used to be called farmer's or sailor's disease, is the most common type of skin malignancy. Growths occur mostly on the face, back of the neck, ears, upper back, chest and shoulders, and back of the hands. They are roundish with a raised, pearly edge and a slightly sunken center that may have tiny dilated blood vessels. Basal cell cancers spread by direct extension only and don't get into the bloodstream or lymph nodes. They are slow growing and most can be surgically removed with a scalpel. If a growth appears on the nose or some other place where a wide excision would be difficult or leave an unsightly scar, Moh's surgery can be performed. This is a highly specialized procedure where repeated thin layers of tumor are removed and examined under the microscope until all the malignant tissue is gone.

Though easily treated, basal cell cancer can become a major problem with neglect. The oldest patient I've ever had died at age 105 after several massive basal cell cancers on her face grew ulcerous and infected. The growths were diagnosed some ten years before that, but Ethel refused to have surgery, thinking something else would kill her before the basal cells progressed.

Squamous Cell Cancer

Squamous cell cancer, much less common than the basal cell kind, is slightly more malignant and in rare cases can spread through blood or lymph vessels to distant parts of the body. Typically the growths appear as raised, reddish plaques, often with thickened, irritated crusts. Some may resemble warts. Your doctor should examine any suspicious or irritated area, and if he or she is not sure it is benign, a biopsy should be performed. I have had three patients with squamous cell cancer that metastasized — spread to other parts of the body — and resulted in death. Squamous cell cancer is usually removed through surgery or with a curette; with early removal, the patient has a 100 percent chance of being cured.

Sunlight Keratosis

Actinic or sunlight keratosis, once known by the derogatory term senile keratosis, is common in the third third. Growths are irritated, rough, raised areas, usually on the face, ears, neck, chest, or back of the hands. Initially small, they are easily removed by surgical scraping or liquid nitrogen. I prefer using a medicated cream called Efudex (fluorouracil). This anti-cancer drug eliminates sunlight keratoses with very little scarring. You have to be careful not to get the cream in your eyes, and you have to put up with scabs over the affected areas, but the scabs disappear after several days. Efudex can also be used to take off very small basal cell cancers.

Seborrheic Keratosis

Seborrheic keratosis is the most common type of skin growth. The nodules, tan to dark brown and slightly raised, look as if they've been stuck on to the back, chest, abdomen, face, or backs of the hands. Sometimes they're confused with melanomas. Unlike sunlight keratoses, seborrheic keratoses don't become malignant, but they are unsightly. If you've sprouted these growths in profusion and it bothers you, a dermatologist can remove them with liquid nitrogen.

Moles

Most of your moles or nevi have formed by the time you turned sixty. If a mole changes — grows darker or larger, or develops spidery extensions in the surrounding skin — then you should have it evaluated. It could be melanoma.

Melanoma

Melanoma is the most dangerous form of skin malignancy, for growths quickly metastasize through the blood or lymph vessels. Any mole that is multicolored or changes color — you may see shades of black, blue, red, white, or purple — or that protrudes into the surrounding skin should be seen by a dermatologist. Melanomas are removed with wide excision; occasionally the physician will do a skin graft to cover the scar. Risk factors are a family history and severe sun exposure.

Dermatitis

Dermatitis can be acute with blisters and oozing, or chronic with redness, fine scaling, and thickening of the skin. Most dermatitis itches. Forms of dermatitis that often afflict older people are:

□ Nummular eczema
□ Stasis dermatitis
□ Contact dermatitis
□ Seborrheic dermatitis
□ Drug-induced dermatitis
□ Dermatitis caused by fungus or yeast

Nummular Eczema

Nummular eczema is a form of dermatitis that starts as round patches (nummular means coinlike). The cause is often unclear, though in older patients dryness tends to be a common trigger. People living in the rural areas around Charlottesville, Virginia, where I trained, called nummular eczema winter itch. Indeed, this condition can be very itchy, and it gets worse with scratching, exposure to dry air, and frequent hot baths. Keeping your house well humidified, drinking plenty of fluid, and using creams such as Lac-Hydrin Five or Keri lotion can help. If the irritated lesions don't heal, try a corticosteroid cream for a few days. You might try over-the-counter hydrocortisone first; if that doesn't work, try a stronger prescription drug. Keep in mind that prolonged use of stronger corticosteroid creams can thin or damage the skin.

Stasis Dermatitis

Stasis dermatitis is an inflammation of the skin of the ankles and lower legs due to poor blood circulation. The ankles are often swollen, and the skin is brown or red and oozing. Open skin can become infected. If the area turns hot and pink, let your doctor know. You'll need antibiotics, and it may help if you elevate your feet, take diuretics to reduce swelling, apply cool, damp to dry compresses, and wear special stockings that your doctor can recommend.

Contact Dermatitis

Contact dermatitis is caused by allergy, most commonly to poison ivy, or chemical irritation, for example, after washing the hands with detergent. The allergic form responds to corticosteroid creams and cool baths — no scratching — but may require a brief course of oral prednisone or Medrol. If you think you've been exposed to poison ivy while hiking or gardening, wash the area thoroughly with cold water and strong soap as quickly as you can. Chemical contact dermatitis often starts clearing up with corticosteroid cream, but it won't entirely disappear unless the contact stops.

Seborrheic Dermatitis

Seborrheic dermatitis, an irritation of oily areas of the skin, often appears with dandruff. Seborrheic dermatitis, which usually appears beside the nose, the eyebrows, and over the breastbone, responds to frequent cleaning with a mild soap, lots of water, and over-the-counter hydrocortisone cream.

Nizoral shampoo, now sold over the counter, is the best dandruff shampoo I've ever prescribed. Even patients who've had refractory dandruff for years have responded well.

Drug-Induced Dermatitis

Skin reactions to drugs can take many forms — spots resembling measles and hives, round patches as in nummular dermatitis, or layers of skin coming off, a serious condition called exfoliative dermatitis. If you're taking a medication and you get a skin rash, let your doctor know immediately. A rash can appear out of the blue, even if you've taken a drug for a while without incident. If the drug has to be stopped, a substitute medication may be available for treating your other condition.

Dermatitis Caused by Fungus or Yeast

Dermatitis caused by fungal or yeast infections frequently appears in moist areas of the body — in the groin, under the breasts, and in the armpits. The rash is itchy and red, often with tiny scales. If you practice careful hygiene, keep the area dry, and use over-the-counter Lotrimin or prescribed Lotrisone, the problem will usually clear up. Occasionally a stronger antifungal agent is needed.

Herpes

The skin can also be infected by viruses. The two most troublesome viral infections of the skin are herpes simplex (fever blisters and genital herpes) and herpes zoster (shingles).

While herpes simplex is somewhat rare in the elderly, shingles is common and can be severe.

CHICKENPOX IN GROWNUPS

Shingles is caused by the varicella, or chickenpox, virus. Most people get chickenpox in childhood and the symptoms go away. However, varicella can lie dormant for as long as seventy years and then suddenly erupt in the roots of sensory nerves. Pain may set in before the characteristic rash of blisters, welts, and scabs. Oddly, shingles almost always appears on one side of the body, anywhere from the scalp to the toes. The pain can be treated with a skin counterirritant, capsaicin, or amitriptyline, Depakote, or Neurontin. Though the rash clears up, in some patients, particularly the oldest ones, nerve pain may become chronic and debilitating, requiring local or spinal nerve blocks.

The typical shingles rash can be treated with soothing creams, steroid creams, or antibiotics in case of secondary infection, but the nerve pain may last for months. Standard therapy is a large dose of an antiviral medication started as soon as the diagnosis is made. I prescribe Zovirax 800 mg five times a day for ten full days. This will reduce the likelihood and severity of pain. If shingles appears in the eye or on the skin nearby, an ophthalmologist should help with the management. If it appears on the face or around the ear, treatment should be very aggressive to prevent permanent nerve damage and facial paralysis.

REMEMBER THIS

- Two types of cancer common in older people are basal cell and squamous cell. Alert your doctor to any reddish, scaly patches or raised areas with pearly borders.
- Basal cell cancer, squamous cell cancer, and melanoma occur more frequently in people who have had extensive exposure to the sun, whether in youth or adulthood. A sunburn is more harmful than mild periodic exposure, but everyone over sixty should use sunblock even during times of brief exposure.
- Actinic keratoses, which are premalignant, can be easily removed.
- Seborrheic keratoses, the most common skin plaques or growths, are usually nothing more than a cosmetic problem.
- Many different drugs can trigger dermatitis. Any rash that appears while you're taking a drug should be reported to your doctor.
- A painful, blistered rash on one side of the face or body is likely shingles and should be reported immediately.

FATIGUE

Sylvia was a seventy-three-year-old widow living with her daughter, who had recently been divorced and moved back into Sylvia's house. Sylvia had a longstanding tendency to an irritable bowel and mild emphysema, although she had stopped smoking several years before. Sylvia said she had suffered fatigue all of her life; shortly after her daughter's divorce this condition grew worse. She felt tired around the clock, particularly in the morning. Though she could fall asleep she slept fitfully and woke up during the night. A thorough evaluation for physical causes of fatigue showed nothing significant. Breathing tests indicated only mild emphysema, not enough to cause tiredness. Sylvia admitted she felt depressed and I prescribed a mild antidepressant. She began seeing a clinical psychologist to help her deal with her personal problems. After about two months she felt better than she had in a long time and much less tired, though not quite as energetic as she would have liked.

A year and a half later, Sylvia came in and said she was tired again, but it was a different kind of fatigue. Though a little tired all the time, she became exhausted when trying to do something as simple as going up a flight of stairs. Sylvia appeared pale, and blood tests pointed to significant anemia. Her blood iron level was low, almost always a sign of blood loss in someone her age. I had a stool test run for blood and it turned up positive. A search of Sylvia's intestinal tract revealed a small, nonmalignant bleeding polyp in the right side of her colon. The polyp was removed, and she received iron therapy to correct the anemia. Sylvia felt well again.

The Causes of Fatigue

Sylvia's case brings out several points about fatigue. First, a careful characterization of the pattern of fatigue is important. Pervasive, constant fatigue, often worse in the morning, may be the result of stress, depression, poor sleep, or all three — that was Sylvia's symptom pattern and diagnosis the first time she complained of fatigue. But fatigue predominantly related to exertion, as in Sylvia's second episode, often has a physical cause.

The causes of fatigue are many and sometimes hard to pinpoint. They include overexertion, insomnia, depression and anxiety, chronic lung disease, hidden malignancies, noninfectious inflammatory conditions, and alcohol abuse. If you suffer from fatigue, all these possible conditions may be running through your doctor's mind as he or she takes your history. Your doctor may also be wondering about:

☐ Blood disorders
☐ Thyroid problems
☐ Congestive heart failure
☐ Infection
☐ Polymyalgia rheumatica

In addition to a full history, your doctor will conduct at least a partial physical exam and some routine blood tests. If nothing dramatic turns up and your activity or sleep habits suggest you are overextended or honestly exhausted, the doctor may talk to you about slowing down or practicing sleep-enhancing techniques (see part 2, chapter 22, "Sleep Disorders").

FEELING FATIGUED? BE SPECIFIC

Though fatigue can be a maddeningly vague syndrome, give your doctor the most accurate possible description of symptoms. Being specific will improve your chances of finding a solution. Tell your doctor:

☐ How long you've been feeling fatigue
☐ How long it lasts, and when it occurs (after exertion only? in the morning only, or also later in the day?)
☐ Whether you're drowsy in addition to being fatigued
☐ How severe the fatigue is, and whether it prevents you from performing activities that used to be part of your daily routine
☐ What other symptoms you have, either when you're fatigued or at other times
☐ How much alcohol you drink and whether you're on medication

---

The type or severity of fatigue, associated symptoms, and preliminary exams may point to a specific physical cause. Fatigue stemming from a physical cause has characteristic symptoms, and it may be helpful to know what your doctor is looking for.

Blood Disorders

Anemia is a common cause of fatigue. The feeling may be present all the time but worse with exertion. A routine complete blood count will indicate whether you're anemic. If so, the doctor will have to pinpoint the cause, for anemia itself has many sources. You may be suffering from iron deficiency due to subtle blood loss, bone marrow failure owing to a vitamin B_{12} deficiency, cancer, leukemia, or a condition called myelodysplasia, in which the marrow doesn't produce red blood cells properly.

A WORD OF CAUTION

Various hidden malignancies may give rise to fatigue or weakness. If no cause for your fatigue can be discerned through a routine physical examination, X rays, or blood tests, you should ask your doctor to consider a CT scan of the abdomen or chest.

If you have iron deficiency and you're over sixty, it is critical that your intestinal tract be looked at to rule out a bleeding polyp or tumor that may be or may become malignant. The evaluation starts with the colon and a colonoscopy. If nothing is found there, your upper intestinal tract should be evaluated.

If you do not have iron deficiency, a bone marrow biopsy may be needed. This is usually performed by inserting a small needle into the upper part of the pelvic bone. The marrow cells can be examined to determine what is causing poor blood production.

Another cause of fatigue — sometimes with dizziness and faintness — is low blood pressure. Some older people may have low blood pressure because of illness, poor fluid intake, or a brain disease such as Parkinson's. Careful attention to fluid and salt intake may be all that is needed, though some cases call for Florinef (fludrocortisone), a drug that causes the body to retain salt and water, or a new drug called ProAmatine (midodrine) that boosts blood pressure by constricting tiny blood vessels. A warning: these drugs can work too well. Florinef can result in too much fluid retention, and ProAmatine can send blood pressure up too high. Keep in close contact with your doctor if you're on either of these drugs.

Thyroid Problems

Thyroid problems are easy to detect with a simple blood test that measures thyroid-stimulating hormone (TSH) from the pituitary gland. High TSH indicates an underactive thyroid, low TSH an overactive thyroid. Either condition can cause fatigue, though in cases of underactive thyroid, fatigue tends to be lethargy or drowsiness, while in patients with overactive thyroid, symptoms are more often jitteriness, weakness, and muscle fatigue induced by activity.

Treatment for an underactive thyroid is easier: one daily pill of inexpensive generic thyroid hormone. Treatment for an overactive thyroid is less straightforward. Certain medications can block buildup of the hormone, but definitive therapy usually involves taking a radioactive substance like iodine that damages the overactive cells. Months or years after radioactive treatment the gland may become underactive, in which case extra thyroid is required to bring TSH levels back up to normal. If you've had radioactive thyroid treatment you're at high risk of developing low thyroid, so you should have at least one TSH test each year.

Congestive Heart Failure

In congestive heart failure, the heart muscle weakens and fluid builds up in the lungs, ankles, or abdomen. In later stages of this disease the body may not get proper oxygenation. Shortness of breath is the most common symptom, but some people complain of fatigue as a major accompanying symptom or even the only symptom. Lying down at night may cause shortness of breath, while sitting may relieve it. (See part 3, chapter 28, "Congestive Heart Failure.")

If during an exam your doctor hears noise in the lower part of your lungs, notes that your liver is swollen because of pressure from the heart, or detects fluid in the ankles, he or she might suspect congestive heart failure. A chest X ray can test for fluid in the lungs, and an echocardiogram can measure the pumping ability of the heart.

Congestive heart failure can be treated with diuretics and medications that relieve pressure on the heart. The sooner it's detected the easier it is to treat. If you experience shortness of breath or unusual fatigue from exertion, see your doctor right away.

Infection

Most infections appear with telltale local symptoms — a cough with pneumonia, for example, or areas of warm red skin with cellulitis. However, some infections are subtler and may only produce a sense of fatigue or exhaustion and a low-grade fever, if even that. Sometimes pneumonia, an abscess in the abdomen, a urinary tract infection, or a heart valve infection causes fatigue without other symptoms. Blood tests, blood or urine cultures for bacteria, or chest X rays may be performed to determine the cause. Fatigue, particularly fatigue with an unexplained fever, should be thoroughly and promptly evaluated; in the elderly, infections can get out of hand rapidly and dramatically.

CHRONIC FATIGUE SYNDROME

Controversy reigns in medical circles over so-called chronic fatigue syndrome. The syndrome is described as recurrent episodes of malaise and pervasive or recurrent weakness and fatigue, sometimes accompanied by a sore throat or the aching muscles commonly experienced in viral infections. At one time, chronic fatigue syndrome was thought to be caused by the EpsteinBarr virus that is responsible for mononucleosis. Today physicians — including yours truly — are more inclined to chalk up much chronic fatigue to stress, anxiety, or depression.

Polymyalgia Rheumatica

Polymyalgia rheumatica (PMR) is a condition in which the muscles' tiny blood vessels become inflamed. More troublesome than the characteristic sore, aching muscles is a general feeling of malaise — weakness, fatigue, and possible feverishness. Though we do know that PMR responds readily to prednisone, we don't know what causes the disease. According to one hypothesis it is an autoimmune disorder, and the body's own antibodies attack the muscles' vascular tissue. Or PMR may be caused by an infection. No organism has been found, however.

Though most people have never heard of PMR, it is quite common in older people, particularly in women over sixty. The last case I diagnosed, in July 2000, was typical. Susan was seventy years old, had been feeling tired for three or four weeks, and for one week had felt as though she had a case of the flu. Before the fatigue set in she had noticed aching across her shoulders, neck, and upper arms, which was beginning to spread to her hips and upper thigh muscles. When I examined her, she looked exhausted and was unanimated. The muscles of her upper torso and upper thigh were tender. I ordered a blood test called a sedimentation rate, which tests for inflammation by indicating how fast red cells settle out from the blood plasma. The result usually doesn't exceed 30 or 40 units in a normal older person; Susan's was sky high at 110.

Feeling almost certain that she had PMR, I started Susan on a low-moderate dose of prednisone, which quickly tapered down to one 5 mg pill per day. I saw her again in ten days. "Doctor, it's a miracle," she announced. She had been free of symptoms within two days of starting the medication.

Prednisone is a "miracle" drug for the treatment of PMR — fatigue can disappear within days of beginning therapy — and it is a useful therapy for other diseases as well. But doctors must be very cautious when prescribing prednisone for older women. Because this drug can cause osteoporosis, muscle wasting, and other devastating problems — and because it is usually taken for at least six months, if not years — the doctor must find the lowest-possible dose that will control symptoms. I try to keep the dose under 7.5 mg. Older women on prednisone should be considered for Actonel to prevent severe osteoporosis.

Other Causes

Though I've mentioned only some of the most common triggers, scores of other illnesses, particularly neurological and muscular problems, can induce fatigue. If you're suffering from this symptom, don't let the fact that diagnosis can be difficult prevent you from seeing the doctor. True, a persistent search for physical causes can be expensive, inconvenient, and uncomfortable, and it may overlook the possibility of psychological causes. And true, a cavalier diagnosis of depression without a full physical evaluation can miss a serious problem. If your physician doesn't make quick headway in diagnosing you, at least make sure that he or she pays attention to both your body and your mind. Anyone who is chronically drowsy or weak needs a full evaluation for physical or psychological causes.

Jet Lag

With increasing numbers of people flying these days, jet lag has become more common. How can you readjust your sleeping schedule? Start on the plane. Avoid drinking too much alcohol, which can disrupt your sleep and leave you dehydrated. To help people slumber in uncomfortable plane seats, I often prescribe a mild, short-acting sedative like Restoril (temazepam) or Ativan (lorazepam), or the sleeping pill Ambien. Remember, if you take a sedative don't have more than a single alcoholic beverage.

If, after an overnight trip, you arrive at your destination in the morning local time, you'll adjust more quickly if you stay up for the day and get to bed early that night. You should be fine by the second day. Though it doesn't yet have the FDA's stamp of approval, over-the-counter melatonin seems to help some people sleep during the first few nights abroad. If not, again, you might try Ambien — but don't take it for more than three nights in a row.

A Final Word

Although the years past sixty are a time when most of us move into slower gear, many people cannot because of financial needs or family responsibilities, or because they are just plain driven. Regardless of the reason, keeping up a forty- or fifty-hour-per-week job can be tiring as you get older. My advice is to pace yourself if you have to work. When you have the option to retire, take stock of your situation. How much stress does your job entail? How much pleasure do you derive from it? If the stress outweighs the pleasure, then retirement may be the thing for you. If not, and you want to keep going, you might consider working part-time.

In gauging the pleasure you take in work, you should factor in the ego element. How will you perceive yourself if you do retire? As someone who had a fulfilling career and deserves a rest — or as worthless? A lot of our self-image stems from work. That's why a lot of elderly people like to perform volunteer work — it gives them a sense of self-worth. But I've seen older people overextend themselves in the post-career plunge to do good. Though in several other chapters I've urged people to get involved in community service, here is the place for a warning: be careful not to take on a volunteer job that is too time consuming or not right for you. Some of the most accomplished and valuable public citizens know when to say no.

As for family commitments, they can be exhausting. Caring for sick or senile relatives easily leads to mental and physical fatigue. I'm amazed that more people don't break under the strain. If you're in this position, make sure you get help and get out of the house from time to time to do something fun. Fatigue may ultimately force the conclusion that it's best for you — and the ill loved one — to transfer the person to a nursing home (see part 3, chapter 24, "Memory Problems.").

REMEMBER THIS

- One of the most common complaints in older patients, particularly those over seventy-five, is fatigue. Fatigue has many causes, both physical and psychological, and they may overlap.
- Constant fatigue suggests a nonphysical cause, though it may be due to a subtle physical illness.
- Fatigue brought on by everyday activities points to a physical cause.
- Older people frequently suffer from PMR. Malaise, fatigue, and muscle aches are the major symptoms. This disease improves dramatically with the drug prednisone.
- Don't be dissuaded by the possible difficulty of diagnosis: both persistent fatigue and fatigue related to exertion are reasons for thorough evaluation.
- When a complete physical evaluation fails to pinpoint a reason, psychological factors such as too much work, stress, and depression should be considered.

CHAPTER 22

SLEEP DISORDERS

Three years ago I received a call from the wife of a seventy-two-year-old man. She wanted me to refer him to a neurologist or a sleep specialist because she thought he was having seizures at night. Bob would grunt, moan, and jerk his arms and legs, and once he had even fallen out of bed.

I felt I should see him before a referral. When they came to the office I took a history from both Bob and his wife, because in my experience a patient's partner often gives a more accurate account of a sleep problem. I asked about alcohol and Bob told me he had two or three drinks each night— "heavy martinis," his wife added. His neurological and vascular exams were normal. I told them he should try not drinking alcohol as the first step; if that didn't work he could see the neurologist. He was to have only one martini a night for three nights, then stop alcohol totally and see me in ten days. Ten days later, Bob was sleeping like a baby and had had no further "seizures." He felt dramatically more rested and agreed to give up martinis, though hadn't ruled out an occasional light scotch.

The elderly person plagued by sleep problems is a common sight in general medical practice, and unfortunately, most cases are neither as dramatic nor as easily treated as Bob's. Sleep problems can't just be attributed to the myth that the elderly sleep less. In reality, most healthy older people sleep about the same number of hours as in their younger years. What changes in advanced age is the quality of sleep. Older people do not get as much deep sleep as they once did. If you're sleepy during the day, you may need more hours of sleep at night.

Sleep Stages

Sleep scientists divide a night's sleep into several stages based on the type of brain waves noted on an electroencephalogram (EEG) recording device and on certain behavior during sleep, such as eye movement. First we enter the brief, half wakeful state of falling asleep. This is followed by four or five cycles of sleep of varying depths that show up as different wave patterns on the EEG. Each cycle consists of two stages, nonrapid eye movement (NREM) sleep and rapid eye movement (REM) sleep.

- Nonrapid eye movement sleep. NREM makes up 75 percent of total sleep time. It occurs first in a given cycle and has its own stages, the last being the time of deepest sleep. As we get older we do spend considerably less time in this period of deepest sleep. As a result, some experts believe, older people need more sleep.
- Rapid eye movement sleep. This final stage of sleep, which makes up roughly a quarter of sleep time, is when your most vivid dreams play out. Sleep specialists believe REM plays an important role in brain reordering. Some research suggests that during REM our brains sort out the events of the day, filing away important or emotionally charged memories and tossing others into the neurological wastebasket.

A new and extremely interesting finding is that the human growth hormone, which builds muscle and helps older people maintain a sense of well-being, is produced mainly during deep sleep. The insomniac or person who sleeps fitfully has lower levels of this hormone and therefore a greater tendency to build fat instead of muscle.

Insomnia

Insomnia, a major affliction in the elderly, is the feeling that you haven't had enough sleep — you're either not sleeping long enough or not deeply enough. You may experience difficulty falling asleep, wakefulness during the night, or early morning wakefulness. How long is long enough? That's difficult to say. Some people feel that less than seven hours is insufficient, while others get by fine on four or five hours. As a rule I advise older people to get at least seven and, preferably, eight hours of sleep a night.

Common Causes of Insomnia
The causes of insomnia are many:

- Anxiety or depression
- Change of schedule

- ☐ Alcohol and caffeine
- ☐ Environmental distraction
- ☐ Medication
- ☐ Smoking
- ☐ Heavy exercise
- ☐ Medical problems

Anxiety or depression. Stress from personal or business worries, grief, or depression can interfere with sleep. Anxiety or apprehension commonly makes it difficult to fall asleep, while depression is more likely to cause wakefulness during the night. People who conduct business affairs close to bedtime, or who habitually stew over family problems in bed, often suffer from insomnia.

Change of schedule. Jet lag or a change in your work schedule, which throws off your biological rhythm, can cause insomnia for a few nights.

Alcohol and caffeine. Everyone knows that caffeine can cause sleeplessness in some people; not all realize that even a single cup of coffee in the morning, or the caffeine in tea, cola, or chocolate, can disrupt sleep. Many people also mistakenly think alcohol will put them to sleep. In truth, alcohol is one of the world's worst sedatives.

> **Did You Know?**
> If you have a drink before dinner or wine with it, you may nod off after eating, and a nightcap might make you mildly sleepy at first. Don't let these soporific effects fool you: research confirms that almost any alcohol, particularly more than two drinks, can interfere with restful sleep during the night. The more alcohol, the worse the sleep problems. In fact, the hangover you get after overindulging comes largely from sleep deprivation.

Environmental distraction. New places, too much light or noise, a noisy or restless bed partner, an uncomfortable mattress, dry air — all can contribute to poor sleep.

Medication. The list of medications that can interfere with sleep is long. Stimulants such as Ritalin, diet pills, antidepressants, excessive thyroid hormone, prednisone, decongestants, and two types of bronchodilators — aminophylline and isoproterenol — can disturb sleep. The antimalaria drug Larium causes so much insomnia that I rarely prescribe it. Even the statin family of cholesterol-lowering agents can cause insomnia in some people.

Smoking. This refers to cigars and cigarettes. Particularly before bed, nicotine can be a stimulant.

Heavy exercise. Strenuous exercise just before bed can be a stimulant and should be avoided if you have trouble sleeping. However, regular exercise during the day, which is a wonderful way to relieve stress, can produce more restful nights.

Medical problems. Painful physical problems such as arthritis and back strain often interfere with sleep. Other sleep disrupters include congestive heart failure, lung problems that cause shortness of breath, acid reflux from the stomach into the esophagus, throat, or mouth, and a prostate problem that forces you out of bed several times during the night.

What Can You Do about Insomnia?

If you want to enhance your sleep, don't take sleeping pills as a first step. If you take pills too often they'll become less effective, and you might end up relying on them instead of tackling the underlying reason for your sleeplessness. Instead, try the following measures first:

- Make sure your bedroom is quiet and slightly cooler than the rest of the house. In the winter, it shouldn't be too dry. If you buy an air conditioner or a room humidifier, check in the store to make sure it's not too noisy. Change mattresses if your bed is uncomfortable.
- Drink no coffee or caffeine-containing drinks after lunch; if this is not successful, cut out your morning coffee or switch to decaf.
- Stop all alcohol for a week, then limit evening drinks to no more than one. Don't drink a nightcap.
- Enjoy some quiet time before going to sleep — read, do a crossword puzzle, or listen to calming music.
- Deal with personal or business problems early in the day; don't stew over them at bedtime. Think of something restful as you try to go to sleep.
- Don't take long naps in the afternoon.
- Exercise regularly, but not after dinner.
- Avoid heavy meals late at night, particularly meals with a high fat content.
- A small bedtime snack may be helpful if you are hungry.
- If you're awake during the night and cannot get back to sleep, get up, go to another room, and read something calming.

☐ If you cannot seem to relax, or if you feel depressed, see your doctor. Insomnia is a common symptom of both anxiety and depression.

☐ Stop all over-the-counter medications and ask your doctor if what is prescribed can cause insomnia.

Sleeping Pills

If you've tried all the above measures and you're still not sleeping well, you should consider medication. However, don't continue it for more than a week or so. Often just breaking a poor sleep cycle can have lasting results, and it can be accomplished without the side effects or addiction associated with long-term use of sleeping pills.

Over-the-counter sedatives. Sominex or antihistamines such as Benadryl may help some people. I advise patients to be very careful with them, however. They can cause somnolence the next day. If you have a prostate problem, definitely avoid antihistamines. About once a year, I have a male patient who needs emergency bladder catheterization because Benadryl or some other antihistamine blocked the nerve stimulus to an already compromised bladder. Furthermore, excessive use of over-the-counter sedatives can cause confusion. A man came back from a week in New England and found his sixty-two-year-old mother totally confused and paranoid. After carefully checking, we estimated she had increased her Sominex from two to about five or six per day. It took almost a week in the hospital before she recovered.

Ambien. My favorite sleeping pill is Ambien (zolpidem), again, however, for short-term use only. It seems as successful in inducing sleep as the benzodiazepine family with fewer short-term side effects and far less potential for addiction. I advise older people to take 5 mg — or better yet, if it works, 2.5 mg — for no more than a week.

Melatonin. Another possible medication is over-the-counter melatonin. Melatonin is a natural body chemical that plays a role in the wake-sleep cycle. Its usefulness as a treatment for insomnia has not been sufficiently tested, though anecdotal evidence suggests that in some people it does enhance sleep. One 3 mg pill a night shouldn't be harmful. Keep in mind, however, that melatonin is not FDA regulated — what you buy may not be pure melatonin.

A WORD OF CAUTION

I've become increasingly leery of using drugs in the benzodi-azepine family, which includes Restoril, Halcion, and Dalmane (sold as sedatives), and Ativan, Valium, and Xanax (sold as tran-quilizers but also used as sedatives). Many people experience a hangover effect with these drugs. And because of their addictive properties, if they're used at all it should be for a few days only. If you must use one, ask your doctor about Ativan or Restoril. They are shorter-acting than most of the other medications in this family and therefore preferable.

Snoring and Sleep Apnea

Snoring and sleep apnea symptoms — noisy, irregular breathing, snorting and choking, and mild sleepiness in the day — are two common sleep dis-rupters. They are often caused or made worse by obesity, alcohol, a local nasal obstruction, or hay fever. Obstructive sleep apnea represents a spec-trum of problems that result from partial or near total blockage of the upper airway during sleep. This condition affects men about four times as often as women and is much more common, and more severe, in over-weight or obese people. Most people with sleep apnea snore, and I tend to consider severe snoring as a possible prelude to apnea. The mechanism is the same — airway obstruction; it is just much worse in sleep apnea.

In sleep apnea, the obstruction may be severe enough to prevent a per-son from taking a breath for the better part of a minute. The person snores, snorts, seems to choke, then has frightening breathless episodes. In even the mildest cases, during the day the person feels sleepy and has dif-ficulty concentrating. In the worst cases, the person falls asleep while eat-ing, walking, or driving.

William

Severe cases of sleep apnea, while not common, can complicate other health problems. Take the case of William, a brilliant retired chemist and inventor with several patents. Despite years of trying to diet, William steadily gained weight and developed diabetes and high blood pressure. On account of "choking," he hadn't been able to sleep on his back for several years. His daughter was worried about the volume and irregularity of his snoring. Sleepiness prevented him from exercising much, and when he came for appointments at my office I always had to wake him from a chair in the waiting room.

Two formal sleep evaluations showed an extreme number of apneic episodes. Surgery to correct a defect of the nasal septum didn't do much good. William had long since stopped drinking alcohol and was using a cortisone nasal spray to try to open the nasal passages. A continuous positive airway pressure (CPAP) breathing device helped a little, but William had difficulty tolerating it. His diabetes and blood pressure were poorly controlled in spite of a multitude of medicines, and he was hospitalized with early congestive heart failure.

While in the hospital, William was fitted for a new type of CPAP machine, one he could better tolerate. He went home and since then his heart condition has improved somewhat. Though he remains in significant jeopardy, the new breathing device seems to have lessened the severity of his somnolence.

> **Did You Know?**
> In many people who suffer from apnea alcohol is a contributory factor. It swells the nasal membranes and may interfere with brain function during sleep.

William's case illustrates many typical aspects of the downhill spiral of severe sleep apnea: obesity exacerbates the apnea, the apnea and resultant lethargy make it impossible to exercise and lose weight, and continued obesity worsens diabetes and high blood pressure, resulting in heart failure. William's lack of deep sleep probably compounded the obesity by decreasing his levels of growth hormone, resulting in less muscle and more fat. Unfortunately for William and many other people suffering from severe sleep apnea, there is no easy cure.

What Can You Do about Snoring?
If snoring is your only problem, I would advise you to:

- Avoid sleeping on your back. You can tie a tennis ball to your back to prevent yourself from rolling into this position.
- Make sure your bedroom is well humidified.
- Stop drinking alcohol.
- Shed some pounds if you're overweight. A 5 to 10 percent reduction in weight often brings results.
- Try a cortisone nasal spray (Flonase, Nasalide, Nascort, or Rhinocort).

If none of these measures stops your snoring, you should see an ear, nose, and throat specialist to be sure there is no blockage that can be corrected.

What Can You Do about Sleep Apnea?

If you have apnea symptoms, you should follow the above advice. If you don't improve promptly, you need formal evaluation in a sleep center. This means being hooked up to an EEG and having your vital signs monitored. If you have enough apneic episodes, you should try the CPAP device. Most people dramatically improve with it, though it can be uncomfortable.

You should also have an ear, nose, and throat evaluation. Many ear, nose, and throat doctors routinely perform an operation to remove the soft palate and loose tissue on the sides of the throat, where the tonsils are. I feel this operation is radical and discourage my patients from having it unless they're desperate. Large studies show that only about 50 percent of the patients who have the procedure improve.

Some people with sleep apnea — less than 10 percent — have some abnormality in the base of the brain where the breathing impulse originates. In this condition, called central sleep apnea, obstruction isn't the problem. Central sleep apnea can be caused by polio, multiple sclerosis, and other forms of atrophy, possibly inherited. People with central sleep apnea are not usually obese, don't snore, and can only be helped with a CPAP device.

SLEEP DISORDERS IN PATIENTS WITH DEMENTIA

Patients with dementia, particularly those with advanced Alzheimer's, often sleep more in the daytime and less at night. In Alzheimer's the normal daily rhythm of brain and hormone chemistry is thrown off, which can result in "sundowning," where the person becomes sleepy and increasingly confused at dusk. Reducing or rescheduling anticonfusion or antidepression medication is a first step. Bright lights through the dinner hour and the presence of a companion to engage the patient in conversation may make sundown come a little later.

Restless Leg Syndrome and Nighttime Leg Cramps

People who have restless leg syndrome feel that they can't keep their legs still in bed. The urge to move them interrupts sleep. Mirapex (pramipexole) and other drugs used for Parkinson's disease can stop this, as can mild tranquilizers and Neurontin, an antiseizure medication.

A much more common complaint is nighttime cramps in the feet and lower legs. These occur when the muscles go into spasm. Cramps can be painful and may result in tight, muscular lumps in the calf. They often occur after a day of more walking than a person is used to. Sodium or potassium depletion may be a factor, and a glass of Gatorade at bedtime may help. Getting out of bed and walking around briefly can help, but cramps sometimes require medication. Quinine dramatically relieves cramps, and if taken for a few nights often keeps them at bay for several weeks. Either have your doctor write a prescription, or try drinking tonic (quinine) water — without the gin — at bedtime.

REMEMBER THIS

- Insomnia is common in older people. Usually the cause is clear.
- Anxiety, depression, habitual stewing about problems at bedtime, medications, caffeine, alcohol, and noisy or uncomfortable surroundings can bring on sleeplessness. Address any of these possible causes before starting on sleeping pills.
- The benzodiazepine family of drugs (Restoril, Ativan, Xanax, Dalmane, Valium) can cause confusion and easily become addictive.
- Snoring and obstructive sleep apnea are common problems in the elderly, often caused or made worse by obesity, alcohol, a local nasal obstruction, or hay fever.
- Sleep apnea produces daytime sleepiness or fatigue and should be evaluated in a specialized sleep center.
- In cases of severe apnea, a CPAP breathing device may be the only solution, and it's a partial solution at best.
- Surgery on the soft palate for apnea is only successful half of the time, and should be considered as a last resort only.

CHAPTER 23

OTHER CONSIDERATIONS AS YOU AGE

"I'll never let myself deteriorate like that," people often think when they witness their parents age. And then it happens to them, the small, inexorable changes in the body signaling that youth is not eternal. As they move out of their sixties and into their seventies, many people finally come to accept the fact that they're no longer middle-aged. Slowly but surely, physical decline overtakes their self-image. They may have receding gums, or deteriorating vision and hearing, and chronic aches and pains that turn the bathroom cabinet into a medicine chest. Sound dismal? It doesn't have to be. If you exercise, eat well, and stay on top of your health, you'll improve your chances of entering old age gracefully and relatively fit.

Maintaining Your Hearing and Vision

There is no more stereotyped image of an old person than someone who constantly needs others to repeat themselves — or shout. Being hard of hearing is embarrassing, frustrating, and socially isolating, but there are ways of coping with hearing loss.

Hearing Loss
Most people past seventy experience hearing loss (presbycusis), but it can occur earlier, especially in people who have had years of exposure to loud noises from guns, music, and machinery such as lawn mowers and chain saws. Typically, this sort of hearing loss occurs in the high-frequency range — you may not always hear Fs, Ss, or certain female voices. Hearing loss from loud noises cannot be restored, but you can protect your ears from further damage by using ear protectors around loud noises. Good-quality noise protectors cost only around ten dollars.

Should you get a hearing aid? That's an individual decision — or a couple decision, since your spouse may be fed up repeating everything she says, or acting as a go-between and translating what other people say to you. Newer aids have arrived on the market that filter background noise so you can use them at social gatherings. They don't detract from your appearance as much as the older generation of aides — and certainly not as much as yelling "What's that?" at a party.

OF SPECIAL CONCERN

Your doctor or an ear, nose, and throat specialist should evaluate sudden or accelerated hearing loss immediately. Two conditions, viral neuritis and persistent bacterial infection, can cause permanent damage if not treated promptly. Impacted earwax also frequently results in rapid hearing loss; fortunately, it is easily treated during an office visit.

Tinnitus

Tinnitus refers to an abnormal sound in the ear — a ringing, hissing, puffing, or buzzing sound. A mild amount of tinnitus is present in most people past sixty. If you're very quiet, you can probably hear a hissing sound in your ears right now. For most of us this background noise isn't a problem. If it bothers you, try stopping aspirin, caffeine, alcohol, or smoking. Interestingly, a hearing aid may also make tinnitus less noticeable because proper hearing may mask the sound. Your doctor can't do much about mild tinnitus; I would only report it if it is very disconcerting or gets dramatically worse.

Guarding Your Vision

Losing your vision is a frightening prospect because it can reduce you to a dependent state. The most common eye problems my older patients suffer from are:

- Cataracts
- Glaucoma
- Macular degeneration
- Vitreous and retinal detachment
- Vascular problems

Cataracts

Cataract, a loss of transparency in the lens of the eyes, is the principal cause of vision loss in older Americans. About half of Americans over seventy-five have at least a mild cataract.

Some people appear to have a hereditary predisposition toward cataracts. Diabetes or long-term use of the prednisone family of drugs can lead to early cataracts. Smoking, prolonged exposure to ultraviolet light, and vitamin deficiencies stimulate cataract progression. Observe these precautions:

- If you smoke, stop.
- Avoid excessive sunlight exposure, and wear a hat and dark glasses in bright sunlight.
- Take a daily multiple vitamin.

There is no medicinal treatment for cataracts. Cataract extraction with artificial lens implantation, one of the most common surgical procedures in the United States, has vastly improved the quality of life for older people. Cataracts should be removed when your vision can no longer be corrected with glasses. Difficulty reading, driving, playing tennis or golf, or watching television are some reasons to discuss cataract removal with your eye doctor.

Glaucoma

In glaucoma, pressure inside the eyeball increases and ultimately damages vision, particularly peripheral vision. The risk factors for glaucoma are hereditary predisposition, African-American race, diabetes, obesity, and eye injury. Most glaucoma is open angle, that is, fluid in front of the lens drains, but slowly, so pressure gradually builds up. If you have open-angle glaucoma, you should have eye examinations every year; borderline elevated pressure should bring you back to your eye doctor much more frequently.

Treatment of both types of glaucoma involves drops, often of the beta blocker family, and possibly a diuretic such as Diamox (acetazolamide), which helps reduce the pressure in the eye. Warning: many medications should not be taken by people with severe glaucoma, including intestinal medicines and certain antidepressants. If you have glaucoma, double-check any new medicine with your ophthalmologist, and always remind the prescribing doctor that you have glaucoma. In some severe cases of glaucoma, laser surgery is performed to open the drainage system.

A WORD OF CAUTION

Most glaucoma is open angle and progresses slowly. Closed-angle glaucoma, in which the fluid cannot drain from the eyeball at all, is a medical emergency. If your eye is painfully red, with the pupil dilated — this may be accompanied by nausea or vomiting — call the doctor immediately. If not promptly treated, closed-angle glaucoma can result in a permanent loss of vision.

In fact, any sudden loss of or decrease in vision, whether total or partial, is a medical emergency and should be seen by an ophthalmologist immediately.

Macular Degeneration

In this condition the macula, a small yellow spot in an area of the retina where central vision is registered, and the surrounding area of the retina undergo a degenerative process that may lead to loss of vision. Vision loss tends to occur in the central field of your vision, with possible patches of loss or distortion throughout the visual field. Some specific areas of macular degeneration can be treated with lasers, but other than taking multiple vitamins that include antioxidants, there is no general treatment. If you are developing symptomatic loss of vision, you should do daily vision checks with an Amsler grid.

Vitreous and Retinal Detachment

The vitreous body is a jellylike material that fills the eyeball behind the lens. As we get older some of the vitreous liquefies, and the liquid may accumulate between the retina and the remaining gelatinous vitreous. With vitreous detachment, you may see a crescent of wavy lines in one part of your visual field or what looks like flashing lights. Usually, vitreous detachment is benign and corrects itself, though in some cases it signals a future full-blown retinal detachment.

OF SPECIAL CONCERN

A retinal detachment, where one layer of the retina separates from an underlying layer, is painless but serious and requires immediate medical attention by an ophthalmologist. A person may see flashing lights or what looks like floating debris, or it may appear as if a windowshade is being pulled over the visual field. Early action may prevent permanent loss of vision.

Vascular Problems

Abnormalities in blood vessels — narrowing, clots, or hemorrhage — can cause various acute vision problems. All should be considered medical emergencies requiring prompt attention to minimize or reverse damage. Only the most serious causes are covered here.

Diabetes. Diabetes, which can damage the blood vessels in the retina, is the most common cause of mid-life blindness in the United States. If you are diabetic, regular eye evaluation by an ophthalmologist may allow for an occasional laser correction of a rupturing vessel, but overall scrupulous control of your blood sugar is the most important preventive.

Thrombosis or clotting of the central retinal vein. This serious problem can occur with high blood pressure, with conditions that increase blood viscosity, and rarely with excessive hormone replacement therapy. A substantial reduction in visual acuity often results. Early intervention to stop secondary damage is important.

Atherosclerotic narrowing of the carotid artery in the neck or inside the skull. This can cause a syndrome called amaurosis fugax — temporary or fleeting blindness — which requires prompt evaluation with doppler imaging of the blood vessels and an MRI of the brain or blood vessels. Severe narrowing of the carotid arteries in the neck can be corrected with surgery. If it occurs further along inside the skull, the use of an anticoagulant such as Plavix or aspirin often prevents a stroke.

Temporal or giant cell arteritis. This inflammatory condition of the blood vessels in the scalp and to the eyes and brain is characterized by headache, tenderness in the temple or scalp, muscle aching, and a flulike feeling. It can cause strokes or permanent or intermittent loss of vision. Treatment with anticoagulants and prednisone will stop the inflammation. It occurs much more frequently in people with polymyalgia rheumatica (PMR).

Guarding Your Teeth

Old age and bad teeth have been assumed to go together for a long time. Shakespeare's soliloquy on aging in *As You Like It* ends, " Sans teeth, sans eyes, sans taste, sans everything." George Washington, the most famous of all Americans, went into old age with wooden pegs to replace his lost teeth.

The two major reasons people lose their teeth are tooth decay (cavities) and periodontal disease.

Tooth Decay

Most of us in our sixties or over now get fluoride protection in our toothpaste and perhaps at the dentist's, but almost all of us in the third third also have dental fillings, whether amalgam, gold, or some form of superplastic. Over time, fillings can loosen or deteriorate, allowing bacteria to creep between the remaining tooth and the filling and causing renewed decay. Talk to your dentist about whether you should have X rays to check for decay under old fillings. Early intervention can save a tooth.

Periodontal Disease

The major reason for loss of teeth in people over sixty is periodontal disease — disease of the gums and around the base and root of the tooth. Periodontal disease refers to infection, deterioration, and retraction of the gums as well as a buildup of plaque and tartar, which erodes the enamel of the tooth, the exposed base of the tooth, and even the bony sockets the teeth sit in. If periodontal disease is uncared for, the teeth may loosen and come out.

> **Did You Know?**
> Gingivitis, a condition in which infected or inflamed gums swell, bleed, and eventually pull away from the base of the tooth, is more common that you might think. About half of American adults between forty and sixty have gingivitis, while three-quarters of people over sixty-five have gingivitis or some other form of periodontal disease. Severe gingivitis may require antibiotics or gum surgery.

Dental plaque is a sticky film of food debris — solidified products of saliva and bacteria — that clings to the teeth and gums. If plaque is not removed in a day or so it begins to form tartar, a hardened, yellow or brownish accumulation of food debris and calcium in the saliva. Tartar can darken and erode tooth enamel. Worse, plaque and tartar working together can cause gum disease and erosion of the socket in the jawbone.

If one or more teeth are just not salvageable, dental implants are probably the best solution. For most people implants are successful and, though costly, carry little downside risk, while a bridge may ultimately damage adjacent teeth.

A preventive program is much easier, cheaper, and dramatically more effective than having gum surgery or dental implants. Your dental hygienist has probably told you more than once, and I'll remind you here: the best way to prevent periodontal disease is to:

☐ Brush regularly after eating
☐ Floss regularly
☐ Use an antiseptic mouthwash daily
☐ Have your teeth cleaned twice a year

Controlling Pain

Pain is what brings most people to the doctor — and pain is what most people are looking to stop. But doctors must be cautious about overtreating pain. Why?

☐ Overtreating pain can mask symptoms and make it difficult to diagnose the underlying cause of pain.
☐ Pain medicine causes short-term side effects such as constipation, nausea, drowsiness, confusion, and slowed breathing. Unless the situation is terminal, the risk-benefit ratio must be carefully considered.
☐ Pain medication is both psychologically and physically addicting. In a person with low-grade chronic pain, excessive use of pain medication may create a problem far graver than the one being treated.
☐ Anxiety and depression often coexist with pain and can make it much less tolerable. Focusing only on the pain and not on the psychiatric symptoms may leave a major part of the problem untreated.

In most cases the need for pain relief is short-lived, and the pain goes away when the condition causing it is treated. In some situations, however, when the condition is chronic or terminal, treatment may be impossible and should be secondary to pain control.

Just the Facts, Ma'am

When your doctor is diagnosing you, the most important information he or she has is how you describe your pain. Be specific about the location of the pain, its nature, duration, and severity, what brings it on, and what makes it better. "I've got stomach pain" is useless when it comes to diagnosis. More like it: "I have pain far down on the left side of my abdomen." Help your doctor, and your doctor will help you.

Arthritic and Other Mild Pain

In general, pain control should start with as little medication and the mildest analgesics (pain reducers) as possible. For nagging arthritic pain, as well as mild postoperative pain or pain from injury, aspirin, acetaminophen, ibuprofen, or the newer nonsteroidal anti-inflammatory drugs Celebrex or Vioxx often help. If none of these works, you might talk with your doctor about more powerful medication in the opium family. Remember, however, that opioids can have powerful side effects and are addictive. Again, starting low and building up is important. You can enhance the pain control without adding to the toxicity if, along with the opioid, you continue aspirin or ibuprofen, or take an antidepressant such as amitriptyline. Amitriptyline effectively controls pain in doses far lower than those used for depression, its primary use.

Chronic Muscle Pain

Most muscle pain stems from a local strain or injury. Physical therapy, massage, hot or cold applications, and avoidance of whatever caused the strain will ultimately relieve it. Many muscle injuries or strains respond to these simple measures, possibly in combination with a mild analgesic to relieve pain or a nonsteroidal anti-inflammatory drug (NSAID). I would recommend that you try local measures before resorting to regular use of NSAIDs. Acupuncture may be helpful in chronic localized muscle pain.

Nerve Pain

In one sense, all pain is nerve pain, since the nerves carry the pain message to the brain. In this context, however, nerve pain refers to conditions in which the primary cause of the pain is pressure on a nerve or irritation of a nerve, as in spinal arthritis with bone spurs. Nerve pain often responds to a regimen of amitriptyline and ibuprofen to start, with one of the milder opioids such as codeine added if the patient requires further relief. Acupuncture, although not universally accepted by American doctors, has been helpful for some of my patients. I have had several patients who have also found relief of chronic nerve pain from either Depakote (valproate) or Neurontin (gabapentin). These are primarily prescribed as antiseizure medications, but they also act to calm nerve activity.

Postoperative Pain

The past few years have seen a vast improvement in the handling of postoperative pain. Patient-controlled analgesia (PCA) is an innovative device that allows patients, within certain limits, to control their own pain medication. With an infusion pump, the patient administers a small amount of intravenous or subcutaneous pain medication. Continuous infusion of a small amount of anesthetic in a catheter placed against the wrapping of the spine — an epidural — has also proven very effective in treating some pain. If you're scheduled for surgery, talk with the surgeon or anesthesiologist about these alternative techniques for controlling postoperative pain.

REMEMBER THIS

- As you move from your sixties into your seventies and beyond, your body will inevitably show signs of wear and tear. Staying on top of your health can improve your chances of aging gracefully.
- Sensory neural hearing loss is common in older people. Though nothing can restore lost hearing, protection from noise exposure may limit progression, and a hearing aid will improve your hearing.
- Sudden or accelerated hearing loss may be reversible and should be evaluated by your doctor promptly.
- Cataracts are extremely common in older people. The only treatment is surgical removal, which should be timed according to symptoms.
- You should have an eye exam at least every two years, and more often if you have borderline glaucoma.
- If you experience sudden or accelerated changes in vision, whether total or partial, it is a medical emergency requiring prompt evaluation.
- Most people who lose teeth over the age of sixty have periodontal disease.
- Periodontal disease starts as bacterial infection in the gooey plaque around the base of the teeth and the gums. Ultimately, the bony sockets are involved and teeth fall out.
- Proper brushing, regular flossing and use of an antiseptic mouthwash, and a professional cleaning every six months dramatically reduce tooth loss in older people.
- Doctors are cautious about overuse of narcotics in nonterminal patients because of short-term side effects and the potential for addiction.
- Combined use of milder pain control medications such as ibuprofen and the antidepressant amitriptyline may prevent or minimize the need for stronger drugs.
- Postoperative pain can be managed by PCA or epidural infusion.

PART THREE

COPING AND CARING

YOU NEVER THOUGHT in your youth that you'd get to this point, but now you've arrived. Congratulations! You officially belong in the ranks of the very old, and you marvel that once upon a time your limbs had the strength to take you running up stairs, leaping over logs, and racing across fields. Over the past decades your body has slowed down maddeningly. While at first you might have raged "against the dying of the light," to quote the poet Dylan Thomas, perhaps by now you have come to accept some of the facts of aging.

The pages that follow are addressed to both patients and their caregivers and families. This section is less about curing than coping. What are you experiencing, or what can you expect to experience, as you age — memory loss, dizziness, urinary problems, congestive heart failure? How can you and your caregivers enhance your safety and your comfort during times of illness and of relatively good health? What can be done to ensure that you meet your death with dignity? My hope is that these pages will shed some light on your condition, whatever it is, and that after reading them you and your caregivers will know a little more about how to make your twilight years as comfortable, peaceful, and fulfilling as you rightfully deserve them to be.

But before we get into specifics, let's talk about your doctor. If you can find a doctor who answers your needs, and if you can work with this person, you've already gone a long way toward enhancing your quality of life in the final years.

Your Doctor

I was once asked to make a house call on a ninety-seven-year-old patient who had been coughing. Evelyn lived in a row house with her ninety-eight-year-old sister. After I had examined Evelyn and prescribed an antibiotic, her sister asked me if I would be her doctor, too. I asked her who her doctor was. She said she hadn't seen anyone since her internist had retired fifteen years earlier. I was astounded — this woman had lived from age eighty-three until ninety-eight without seeing a single medical professional!

If you have good genes and good luck, you could follow Evelyn and her sister's path, but the odds are great you'll have a medical problem in these years. And you'll most certainly have a problem if you aren't plugged into the healthcare system through a primary care doctor.

Why You Need a Primary Care Doctor

Everybody, at any age, should have a primary care physician. If you're over sixty this is even more important, and if you're frail or have a chronic illness, it's essential. The primary care doctor is the person who performs your routine health exams and preventive maintenance. He or she should know you well, because this person will also serve as the quarterback of your medical team. If you're not comfortable with a specialist's advice, or you have conflicting advice from more than one specialist, or you're having trouble weaving your way through complicated insurance matters, your primary care doctor will step in and help.

A general internist is usually the best choice for a primary care doctor. Internists usually have more experience than most family practitioners with the illnesses of older people, although some family practitioners have a special interest in the aged. If you become extremely frail or incapacitated, you might want to switch to a geriatrician. However, most general internists have extensive experience with elderly patients, and what you gain in a geriatrician probably won't compensate for the personal bond you and your current doctor have built up over the years.

Choosing Your Doctor

If you're "shopping" for a new doctor, one of the best sources of information is to ask friends or relatives about the same age as you how they like their doctor. Of course, competence should be the first criterion in making your choice. Make sure your candidate is certified by the American Board of Internal Medicine or another reputable group. If the doctor practices at a leading hospital, and particularly if he or she has privileges at a medical school hospital in your area, this is an excellent sign. Other matters to consider are the doctor's availability and personal manner — is he or she courteous and respectful?

Helping Your Doctor

The first and most important information your doctor gets comes from you. Your doctor will want to know your current symptoms, your history, the medications you're taking, and any bad reactions you've had to medications. When you visit your doctor, bring along a list of the medications you're on with the doses — or better yet, bring the medications themselves. Silly as it may seem, when you dump all your medicine bottles on your doctor's desk, you may be saving yourself a major drug reaction and your doctor a lot of time.

I once took over the care of a woman in her late eighties who had Parkinson's disease, arthritis, low thyroid, depression, congestive heart failure — and to top it all off, a heart arrhythmia. Virginia, who was on twenty-two different medications from various doctors, was becoming sleepy and confused, and was losing both weight and her coordination. Although she had devoted health aides, they weren't all that knowledgeable. When I visited Virginia at home and reviewed her bedside pharmacy, I discovered that she was taking double the thyroid medication and double the heart medication, three different but similar antidepressants, and three different arthritis medications. I stopped all the duplications and reduced dosages for most of the other drugs. Within a week, Virginia's sleepiness, coordination problems, and arrhythmia disappeared, and she regained her appetite.

What had happened to Virginia to bring on so many disabling and life-threatening symptoms? There had been a breakdown in communication among herself, her aides, her primary care doctor, and her specialists — either that, or her primary care doctor was doing a poor job of quarterbacking her medical team.

Be specific. Once you've told the doctor about your medications, you need to present a history of your current problem — and you need to be specific. For example, if you have a pain, try to give the exact location, and describe it. Is it sharp and knifelike, or aching and dull? Constant or periodic? What seems to bring it on — standing up, breathing deeply, eating? Is there anything that seems to relieve it? Be specific about how long you've had the symptom. "Quite a while" isn't helpful to the doctor. That could mean three hours or three months.

If you're having a chronic condition such as high blood pressure monitored, be sure to alert the doctor or doctor's assistant to any changes. Are you doing fine? Then a brief "I've really been active and feel well" suffices. If you're getting a little more short of breath when you take your daily walk, tell the doctor or office nurse. Information like this can often prevent major problems down the road.

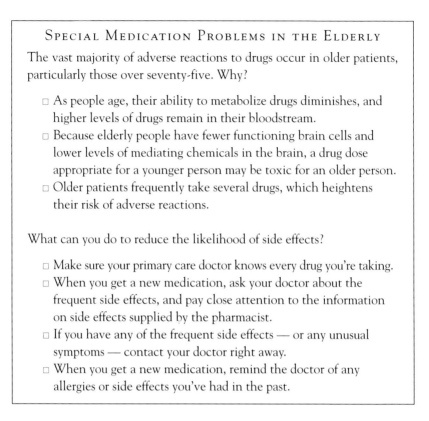

SPECIAL MEDICATION PROBLEMS IN THE ELDERLY

The vast majority of adverse reactions to drugs occur in older patients, particularly those over seventy-five. Why?

- As people age, their ability to metabolize drugs diminishes, and higher levels of drugs remain in their bloodstream.
- Because elderly people have fewer functioning brain cells and lower levels of mediating chemicals in the brain, a drug dose appropriate for a younger person may be toxic for an older person.
- Older patients frequently take several drugs, which heightens their risk of adverse reactions.

What can you do to reduce the likelihood of side effects?

- Make sure your primary care doctor knows every drug you're taking.
- When you get a new medication, ask your doctor about the frequent side effects, and pay close attention to the information on side effects supplied by the pharmacist.
- If you have any of the frequent side effects — or any unusual symptoms — contact your doctor right away.
- When you get a new medication, remind the doctor of any allergies or side effects you've had in the past.

Take charge of your health maintenance. While you're in the doctor's office, don't hesitate to ask about the date of your next exam, test, or shot. I never minded these questions, and sometimes they jogged my memory; on occasion I would discover that indeed it was soon time for Ethel's mammogram, or Ted's cholesterol test, or Gerry's pneumonia shot. Also, as you're leaving the office, make sure you ask when you should come back if the doctor hasn't been specific.

Being an active participant in the maintenance process will give you a greater sense of control over your health. I'm not suggesting that you spend your life dwelling on doctors' appointments and medical tests. One of the points of this book is to help you make the most of your life between jaunts to the doctor. I'm merely recommending that, before seeing the doctor, you devote a few minutes to organizing your thoughts about your symptoms and your health maintenance. This will save you time, money, and effort, increasing the chance of early, correct diagnosis and successful treatment.

CHAPTER 24

MEMORY PROBLEMS

The human brain is a magnificent organ. It weighs about three pounds and packs over 100 billion nerve cells or neurons, 30 billion of them lodged in the cerebral cortex or thinking portion. A dense network of small fibrils called axons and dendrites connects the neurons in a system as complex as the most sophisticated computer. The number of possible interactions in your brain far exceeds the number of particles in the universe!

But your brain isn't a computer made of hardware. It's wet, living tissue. For messages to jump from the axon of one neuron to the dendrites of the next, transmitting chemicals have to be present at the point of transfer, and in just the right amount. The tiny gap at this juncture is called the synapse; the chemicals are synaptic mediators, more familiarly known as neurotransmitters. The chemical that plays the most significant role in the transfer of memory messages is acetylcholine.

It is remarkable that for most of us, the whole neural system remains so balanced, allowing the brain to perform its many amazing tasks. But inevitably, some alterations in mental function do occur with age.

Benign Slowed Recall

To put it simply, brain cells die as we get older. MRI (magnetic resonance imaging) scans show shrinkage in the brains of people past seventy-five, even in people who are functioning well. The normal aging brain experiences a drop in the levels of neurotransmitters, including acetylcholine, which protects against memory loss, and serotonin and noradrenaline, which promote a feeling of well-being. This happens to some degree in all of us, not just people who are demented, delirious, or depressed. Certain conditions, however — alcoholism, Alzheimer's, and a series of tiny strokes — can accelerate brain shrinkage.

Older Brains Slow Down

Mild forgetfulness, slower mental processing, less capacity for spatial perception and complex logical analysis — these are the signs of an aging brain. The most familiar sign, of course, is slower recall, what some people refer to jocularly as "senior moments" and what I call benign slowed recall. I have a good memory and usually win at Trivial Pursuit, even against younger people. The only problem is I take so long coming up with the answers. I get catcalls, hisses, and "Come on Dad, you gotta speed up" exhortations.

Older people are also more easily distracted and need to concentrate more on tasks. Teenagers can listen to rock music and do their homework at the same time — the sort of juggling act older people can't handle. Ease of distraction makes us more likely to misplace our eyeglasses or keys. The things we are likely to forget may be compartmentalized, for example, names. I'll see a patient walking down the street and remember all four drugs he's taking, approximately what his blood pressure and cholesterol are, and when he had his diverticulitis attack — but for the life of me I can't come up with his name.

Slowed recall troubles many people. Is it an early sign of Alzheimer's? Probably not. Alzheimer's, as you'll see later in this chapter, exhibits a pattern of brain changes that differs from the pattern of neurotransmitter reduction at play in benign slowed recall.

How Can You Tell If Memory Loss Is More Serious?

Normal memory loss cannot be differentiated from more serious memory loss with 100 percent accuracy, but there are tip-offs. See the doctor if you or a loved one has:

- ☐ Memory lapses are so frequent they interfere with daily functioning.
- ☐ You don't remember things you should know after you've been prompted or told the answer.
- ☐ Your behavior changes.
- ☐ You get lost or have a great deal of trouble with directions.

Unfortunately, if you do begin to have serious problems such as behavior changes, you may not notice or be greatly bothered. Often it takes a loved one to spot changes requiring medical attention. This is the paradox: if you're bothered by memory loss, it's probably not serious. For the vast majority of people in the third third, forgetfulness is a part of aging, just like loss of strength. Don't worry about it unless it is dramatically worsening.

Is There Something You Can Do to Improve Your Memory?

Absolutely, yes! First, you need to realize that both anxiety and depression can result in some memory deterioration. Ask yourself if you're shouldering unusual stress, or if you're depressed. Pose some of the questions noted in part 2, chapter 16, "Depression," and take measure to address your condition. Second, take care of your health and be sure to exercise. Subtle physical fatigue or low oxygen from a heart or lung problem can make you feel like not even trying to remember things. Be careful with alcohol and medications, particularly sedatives and tranquilizers. Once you've addressed your mental and physical health, you need to find ways to exercise your memory.

GREASE YOUR MEMORY WHEELS

Learning or relearning a language taught back in high school can be fun and sharpen the memory. I had a patient who was wonderfully alert until his death at ninety-four. Thomas had learned French in his eighties and read the newspaper and magazines every day. I thoroughly enjoyed his office visits, but he talked so much about health policy and new medical discoveries, it was hard to get on to the next patient.

As Thomas's case suggests, reading is a good way to grease your memory wheels. Here are some others:

- Playing or learning a musical instrument
- Crosswords, acrostics, bridge, scrabble, and chess
- Using computers to send e-mail, surf the internet, or get your financial information in order
- Doing a volunteer job, particularly one with some intellectual content like preparing a church newsletter, working in a library, or managing the schedule for a free clinic
- Hobbies like carpentry and landscaping that require organizing (completing tasks can give you a positive, "can do" feeling)

Last but not least, if you want to keep your memory honed, you'll need social interaction. When you get together with friends and family, don't just gossip or talk about your health. Try to discuss other subjects — history, art, politics, the environment, any topic that interests you. A book or current events club can be great fun and can improve your memory and communication skills.

Can Medication and Supplements Improve Memory?

Studies haven't clarified the role of medication and supplements in memory. For women, hormone replacement therapy seems to reduce signs of benign slowed recall as well as give some protection against Alzheimer's. Vitamin E probably helps improve the memory. Anecdotal evidence supports the theory that the herb *Ginkgo biloba*, which has very few side effects, may be helpful if you're troubled by memory lapses, but it has not been evaluated in meaningful scientific trials.

Dementia

The whole thrust of this book is that the third third can be one of the richest, most rewarding parts of your life if you take care of yourself. I have to be frank, though: sometimes when I observe previously brilliant patients gradually sink into the hopeless confusion of dementia, my optimism wanes. Is it surprising that, with the possible exception of a grossly debilitating stroke, my older patients dread nothing more than losing their mental faculties to Alzheimer's disease? In the minds of many, the slow loss of autonomy associated with Alzheimer's is synonymous with a loss of humanity itself. But there are lots of things we can do to help people suffering from the diseases collectively known as dementia, and perhaps some things to postpone their onset.

What Is Dementia?

Dementia refers to a collection of diseases associated with acquired, chronic impairment of intellectual function. The dementia patient is deficient in at least three of the following mental activities or states:

- □ Language
- □ Memory
- □ Visual/spatial relationships
- □ Emotions
- □ Calculation, judgment, and abstract thinking

People with advanced dementia suffer from profound deficits in all five areas. Dementia covers a number of distinct conditions:

- □ Alzheimer's disease
- □ Vascular dementia
- □ Dementia with Parkinson's disease

- Lewy body dementia
- Hypothyroidism
- Vitamin B$_{12}$ deficiency
- Chronic alcoholism with dementia
- Severe depression (pseudo-dementia)
- Normal pressure hydrocephalus (an abnormal increase in brain fluid)
- Latent syphilis
- Brain tumor

The first two, Alzheimer's and vascular dementia, account for the vast majority of dementia cases.

Alzheimer's. The brain tissue of Alzheimer's' patients examined at autopsy exhibits specific abnormalities in the brain cells called neurofibrillary tangles and the accumulation of a protein substance, amyloid, on the axons between brain cells *(see below)*. Alzheimer's, which occurs rarely below the age of sixty and occasionally below the age of seventy, becomes much more prevalent in people over seventy. The reason it is a major public health problem — and you're hearing more and more about it — is that as the population ages, this disease is affecting progressively larger numbers of people. Up to 30 percent of those who live past eighty-five will get Alzheimer's disease.

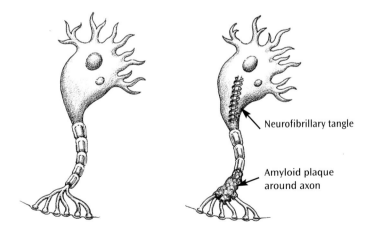

Normal neuron *(left)* and Alzheimer's neuron *(right)*

We know that some cases, particularly early-onset Alzheimer's, may be hereditary, but the cause for the brain changes that occur in the bulk of Alzheimer's patients — in eighty- and ninety-year-olds — isn't understood.

Vascular dementia. Vascular dementia is a catchall phrase for people whose intellectual faculties deteriorate permanently, usually after recurrent strokes. The term multi-infarct (multi-stroke) dementia is becoming more common. The strokes can be either small, resulting from blockage of the tiniest blood vessels, or medium-sized. Dementia from small indistinguishable strokes progresses steadily, while dementia from medium-sized strokes may progress in a more noticeable, stepwise fashion. Other neurological damage such as paralysis or slurred speech may be present.

Many people have both Alzheimer's and vascular dementia, or mixed dementia. The other forms of dementia, though less common, are important to rule out.

How Do You Know If Your Loved One Is Developing Dementia?

This is not always easy to tell. Though most of us worry about memory lapses and slowed recall, very few people are truly demented. Those who are developing Alzheimer's or another form of dementia are brought into my office by a family member. Indeed, if you really were becoming demented, you probably couldn't read this, analyze your own behavior, and report accurately on worsening symptoms. So from here on, I'll be addressing family members, not their demented loved ones.

A WORD OF CAUTION

How do you know if a relative has Alzheimer's or another form of dementia? Here are some telltale signs:

- A rapid acceleration in the number of memory lapses, and many lapses each day
- Major lapses such as forgetting a family reunion or a meal
- Lapses so frequent they begin to interrupt daily routines
- Inability to recall a person or an event after being prompted and told about it
- Behavior changes (moodiness or withdrawal can signal either early dementia or depression — see part 2, chapter 16, "Depression")
- Getting lost while driving in a familiar area

WARNING: DELIRIUM IS NOT DEMENTIA

It's important to know the difference between dementia and delirium, which are often confused. While dementia refers to chronic, slowly progressing disease marked by permanent loss of intellectual function, delirium is a state of disorientation that develops rapidly but can be reversed if the cause is tackled. Delirium most frequently occurs in people with chronic illnesses, particularly those with mild dementia. Typically, a person with mild dementia becomes suddenly and dramatically worse — delirium is superimposed on dementia.

George, an eighty-three-year-old retired lawyer, illustrates one face of dementia. George was in the hospital recovering from diverticulitis. At home he would have a couple of drinks every evening; now in the hospital he wasn't drinking, and he'd been given mild sleeping pills. I checked in on George and he seemed to be alert and recovering well. Then, just as I was about to leave, he said, "I'm disappointed in the security at this hotel. Last night they let in some hit men from the IRS who beat me about the head and shoulders with cudgels." I stopped George's sleeping pills, and fortunately within a few days his mind cleared up.

Classic signs of delirium are disorientation about your surroundings, hallucinations, and paranoia. What triggers this condition?

- ☐ Medications such as sedatives, tranquilizers, and over-the-counter cold remedies
- ☐ Withdrawal from drugs, especially the diazepam family to which Valium belongs
- ☐ Withdrawal from alcohol
- ☐ Infections such as pneumonia, cystitis, or appendicitis (when the elderly get infections, often the only symptom is delirium)
- ☐ Circulatory disorders such as a silent heart attack or worsening congestive heart failure (again, in the elderly delirium may be the only symptom)
- ☐ Dehydration
- ☐ Constipation

This list isn't exhaustive. The causes of delirium are many and often not obvious. Keep close tabs on any change in mental status of an older relative. Calling the doctor and getting prompt evaluation can be life saving.

Screening test for dementia. The Mini Mental Status Examination (MMSE) is a standard test to screen for dementia. The doctor or an office assistant will administer it in a matter of minutes by asking the following questions:

Question	Score
1. What is the day, month, year, and season?	5
2. Where are you — the office, floor, city, county, and state (one point for each correct answer)	5
3. Repeat each word: ball, pencil, tree (words are given to the person separately, with one point for each correct answer)	3
4. Spell world backward. Then subtract 7 from 100 and keep subtracting serially (100-93-86-79, etc.). (If either of these two exercises is performed correctly, patient gets five points.)	5
5. Ask for the words in question 3 again.	3
6. Produce a pen and a watch and see if the patient can name them.	2
7. Ask the patient to repeat "No ifs, ands, or buts."	1
8. Tell the patient to take a piece of paper in his or her right hand, fold it in half, and put it on the floor (one point for each step).	3
9. Ask the patient to read and obey, "Close your eyes."	1
10. Ask the patient to write a sentence.	1
11. Ask the patient to copy a picture of intersecting pentagons.	1

Scoring. If the score is perfect, you can be reassured. If it falls under 25, then a dementia evaluation should begin in earnest. If the score lies between 25 and 30, a repeat test later on would be appropriate. If symptoms persist, more extensive psychological testing may be indicated.

Diagnosing and Treating Dementia

Once dementia is established, you need to try and pinpoint the cause. Treatable causes, though rare, should be ruled out. A thorough evaluation includes blood tests for thyroid, vitamin B_{12}, and syphilis, as well as an MRI of the head, which can help diagnose normal pressure hydrocephalus, rule out a tumor, and differentiate vascular dementia from Alzheimer's.

Normal pressure hydrocephalus is a condition in which improperly draining fluid in the brain cavities damages brain tissue. Patients characteristically have an unsteady gait and lose control of urinary function, often before the dementia has progressed considerably. A permanent shunt to drain the fluid can be inserted in the brain, reversing the condition. The operation is a relatively minor procedure for a neurosurgeon.

Establishing a diagnosis of Alzheimer's disease is a process of exclusion. The doctor can only be absolutely certain of this diagnosis with a brain biopsy sample, which, of course, is entirely inappropriate. In most experienced clinics, however, the diagnosis is about 90 percent accurate. Lewy body dementia may be a form of Alzheimer's, though brain cell changes in the two diseases differ. Lewy body dementia and the dementia of Parkinson's disease may be suspected if the patient's gait and emotional life appear more disrupted than is usual in Alzheimer's. Because treating these diseases is essentially the same as treating Alzheimer's *(see below)*, your doctor doesn't have to be absolutely certain of the diagnosis. Any symptoms of Parkinson's disease or major emotional problems, of course, should be treated.

If the MRI points to multi-infarct dementia and the patient has had other vascular problems, therapy should include aspirin or other anticoagulants, careful attention to blood pressure and other vascular risks, and possibly evaluation of the neck arteries. The drugs used for Alzheimer's don't have much effect on pure vascular dementia, but since many patients have mixed dementia, often those whose MRIs show typical vascular changes are treated for both conditions, that is, with anticoagulants, blood pressure medication, and Alzheimer's drugs.

Can Alzheimer's be treated? Several drugs in the cholinesterase-inhibitor family can benefit people with early or moderate Alzheimer's, when brain cells are injured but not yet destroyed as in later stages of the disease. In early stages when mild injury occurs, the level of acetylcholine that transmits messages from cell to cell falls. This group of drugs raises the level of acetylcholine in the brain and, for a time at least, improves memory and other lost functions. Currently there are three drugs available:

- Cognex (tacrine)
- Aricept (donepezil)
- Exelon (rivastigmine)

Aricept is more effective and has fewer side effects than the older Cognex. I have had little experience with the newer drug, Exelon. Its manufacturer points out that Exelon raises the level of another neurotransmitter as well as acetylcholine, and it's been promoted as helping the behavioral as well as the cognitive problems associated with Alzheimer's. In my limited experience, Exelon causes more nausea than does Aricept. As I mentioned, dementia with Parkinson's disease and Lewy body dementia are so similar to Alzheimer's that Aricept should be tried for all three. All three drugs can cause nausea, vomiting, and bowel problems, and all three can result in sedation or lethargy, making the dementia seem worse. In the advanced state of Alzheimer's when patients have so little acetylcholine left, cholinesterase inhibitors offer minimal benefit.

Additional treatment for Alzheimer's. In addition to the above drugs, there are several medications that may help Alzheimer's patients. These include estrogen, vitamin E, and nonsteroidal anti-inflammatory drugs (NSAIDs) like ibuprofen (see below, "Can Alzheimer's be prevented or postponed?").

People with Alzheimer's often bear the extra burden of depression. Cautious use of antidepressant drugs may help. The selective serotonin re-uptake inhibitor (SSRI) family of drugs seems least likely to have side effects, though they can cause sleepiness or worsen the confusion of dementia. If the patient is hallucinatory or very agitated, calming or antipsychotic medications such as Haldol, Risperdal, Zyprexa, or Seroquel may help. A warning: these drugs can have side effects similar to the symptoms of Parkinson's disease.

Ginkgo biloba, though not proven and not nearly as effective as Aricept, may be beneficial in early-stage Alzheimer's. Because the side effects are minimal, many physicians routinely add it to their Alzheimer's drug regimens. I would absolutely advise against relying on ginkgo alone, however. The Aricept family should be the major treatment.

Can Alzheimer's be prevented or postponed? Though no one can be sure that anything will prevent or delay Alzheimer's, enough convincing studies have been performed to lead most Alzheimer's specialists to recommend the following:

More women than men develop Alzheimer's, and women who have not taken hormone replacement therapy (HRT) have a higher incidence than those who have. Women with a family history of Alzheimer's should take HRT unless there is a major contraindication — and those without such a history should count possible protection against Alzheimer's as a plus in the decision whether to take HRT.

Evidence strongly suggests that people who take NSAIDs for a long time are less likely to get Alzheimer's. These medications may block formation of the amyloid that causes damage and death to brain cells. NSAIDs include over-the-counter Motrin and Nuprin, older prescription drugs such as Arthrotec and Daypro, and the newer Cox 2 inhibitors Celebrex and Vioxx.

Some Alzheimer's researchers advise vitamin E as a preventive. The dose and age at which to begin therapy are controversial. My general advice on vitamins includes 400 I.U. of vitamin E daily. People with an established diagnosis of Alzheimer's should take 1,000 I.U. per day.

The Future of Alzheimer's

Each year in the United States billions of dollars are spent on the care of Alzheimer's patients, who now number about four million. The enormity of the problem has sent expenditures for Alzheimer's research way up in recent years, and now the promise of more effective treatment hovers on the horizon. The complicated mechanism of amyloid accumulation, which seems to cause brain cell damage, offers several excellent targets for drugs that can prevent or arrest Alzheimer's. Another approach is a vaccine that has proven effective in animals and may soon be moved to trials in humans with early Alzheimer's. If and when a drug or vaccine does appear, it will save billions of dollars, save potential caregivers untold hours of agony, and remove a shadow of dread that hangs over everyone in the third third of life. We have enough leads in developing a preventive for Alzheimer's that a research project on a scale analogous to that of the space program of the 1960s seems like reasonable public policy.

Coping with Dementia

In many ways, caring for a person with dementia is more difficult than caring for a person with a severe physical disease. As dementia progresses, the patient may not offer the companionship that a sick but mentally intact person can provide. The spouse or caregiver often feels alone in the struggle, and the fact that dementia is a progressive disease leading nowhere but down takes its toll on even the most stoic or philosophic.

One of the first concerns you should address in taking care of a person with dementia is the doctor. Though in general I don't think it's a good idea to switch doctors, if your doctor lacks experience with dementia, you should consider switching to a neurologist or geriatrician who has a special interest in this area. Or you can stay with your loved one's primary doctor and consult a neurologist or geriatric specialist that he or she recommends. If you live in a large community with a medical school, the neurology department probably has a person on staff with a special interest in Alzheimer's or an Alzheimer's clinic. In any event, you should have your patient see the doctor every three or four months, and much sooner if his or her condition changes.

What to do as Alzheimer's progresses. Alzheimer's is a degenerative disease. Early on, you'll note deterioration of memory, judgment, and possibly language ability. At this stage you should help the patient maintain interests and plan outings or brief trips to see relatives. Keep in mind, however, that environmental changes may compound the patient's confusion. In groups, make sure you include the patient in the conversation. It is a sad but real fact that even the most caring people get caught up in their own conversations and leave the Alzheimer's patient out. As the disease progresses, you might arrange one-on-one visits with relatives so the patient can go over old photographs or review family stories. Monitor the person's hearing closely and have it tested periodically. Even a partial loss of hearing can make the dementia seem worse.

As Alzheimer's progresses, the patient may begin to exhibit psychological or behavioral problems such as paranoia, agitation, or a tendency to roam. Depression may come at any time and should be watched for, especially if the patient becomes much less active. If the patient has a tendency to wander about, take preventive measures such as inserting a double-bolt lock on the door or putting an identification bracelet on the person's wrist. Try and avoid confrontation when the person says something outlandish or heartrending. Responding is a true art. You don't have much leeway — either you correct your patient gently, or you go along with what he or she says. However you respond, do so calmly and reassuringly.

Taking Care of the Caregivers

People who take care of a demented patient in the home spend up to one hundred hours a week on the job. It is an exhausting ordeal, especially for caregivers who are old themselves. If you're a caregiver, let the doctor know how you're feeling. Be on the lookout for signs of depression or fatigue.

You need to get help from a relative, nurse, or sitter who can be with the patient while you take a break and seek out healthy friends to spend time with. Some communities have centers where you can drop off your patient several times a week. Many have trained personnel, and Alzheimer's patients often enjoy the activities. If you're completely worn out, you might arrange to have an experienced caregiver come to your home overnight or for a few days. Another alternative is to have the patient go to a nursing home temporarily so that you can have a few days' respite.

The most difficult decision is when to put the patient in a nursing home. If behavior problems or roaming episodes compromise safety, a nursing home is the only choice. As a caregiver you shouldn't feel guilty about this. Hanging on to home care too long might endanger the patient.

In the choice of facilities, you should try to get one with a dementia unit. Investigate to be sure that the staff truly is trained in dementia. Some states and localities have or are considering regulations defining what constitutes an Alzheimer's or dementia unit. Make sure the facility provides close physician supervision, and that the medical staff includes a doctor with experience in taking care of both the psychiatric and the physical needs of demented patients.

REMEMBER THIS

- Memory lapses and slowed recall are almost universal signs of aging.
- We all have memory lapses. Only if they become dramatically worse should you worry.
- Depression and anxiety may worsen recall.
- Keeping an active mind by pursuing hobbies and intellectual and social activities improves memory.
- Alzheimer's is the leading cause of dementia; vascular disorders are the second most common cause. Some people have both forms of dementia.
- Though rarely, some forms of dementia can be cured. Because the stakes are high, these should be ruled out before the diagnosis continues.
- Aricept and similar drugs can aid memory in the early or middle stages of Alzheimer's.
- Hormone replacement therapy, NSAIDs, and vitamin E may help prevent or postpone Alzheimer's.
- Delirium is a state of disorientation or confusion that rapidly advances but is reversible if the cause is corrected.
- Delirium most frequently occurs in people with chronic illnesses, particularly those with mild dementia.
- Triggers of delirium are numerous and include drugs, alcohol, infections, circulatory problems, and dehydration.
- Report any sudden change in an elderly person's mental state immediately.

CHAPTER 25

DIZZINESS

How many times have I heard it? "Doctor, I'm dizzy." Dizziness is one of those umbrella terms that cover a whole range of symptoms. If you want your doctor to diagnose you correctly, you'll have to be more specific about what you mean. Dizziness can refer to vertigo, unsteadiness, lightheadedness, or fainting — and each of these symptoms, though they may overlap, is associated with a different mechanism.

What to Tell the Doctor

Mild, occasional dizziness or lightheadedness isn't cause for worry, but sudden vertigo, sudden severe unsteadiness, and certainly fainting or near fainting need immediate evaluation in the doctor's office or an emergency room.

The more accurate a picture you give the doctor of your symptoms, the more quickly he or she can diagnose you. Get straight in your mind what to say. Do you feel a spinning or a lurching to one side? Is there associated ringing in the ears or loss of hearing? Do you have double vision (this must be differentiated from a spinning sensation), numbness in the face, any trouble swallowing, or loss of control of an arm or a leg? Does a change in position bring the symptom on? Is it more likely to occur standing up or while turning in bed? If it is episodic, how long do the episodes last? When did you first notice the symptoms? Have you had similar episodes, even in the remote past? Have you had a recent blow to the head?

Testing for Dizziness

It's important that the history be accurate so that the investigation starts in the right direction. You'll want to avoid time-consuming, expensive, unnecessary tests. Your doctor will probably examine you for heart rate

SEVERAL SYMPTOMS, DIFFERENT CAUSES

Vertigo. This is the false sense that you or your environment is moving or spinning. You probably remember it from childhood when you got off the merry-go-round. Vertigo is most often caused by an imbalance in the fluid of the inner ear; if sudden and severe, however, vertigo may be due to a brainstem stroke.

Unsteadiness. This is the feeling that you have to hold on to something to keep on standing. It is often due to a subtle degeneration of some part of the brain or nervous system, or of the blood supply to the parts of the brain that control balance.

Lightheadedness. This is the feeling you have when you get up suddenly from the floor, or after bending over gardening. Mild lightheadedness is usually caused by a benign, transient fall in blood pressure.

Fainting. This covers the spectrum from near fainting to fainting. If you have to sit down to keep from fainting, there may be something seriously wrong — a heart-rhythm disturbance, a drop in blood pressure caused by heat exposure with dehydration, or sudden dehydration due to an acute intestinal virus.

and blood pressure lying and standing. Your ears, nose, and throat will be examined, and you'll be checked for neurological signs such as imbalance and facial abnormalities. After the history and physical exam, your doctor may make a reasonably certain diagnosis, but if he or she cannot, or there is concern about an impending stroke, you may need a CT (computerized tomography) or MRI (magnetic resonance imaging) scan, cardiac monitoring, or special inner-ear evaluation.

Vertigo

Clarence was a sixty-one-year-old retired bus driver with mild diabetes, longstanding high blood pressure, and a weight problem when his wife called one day in a panic. Clarence had had a sudden bout of dizziness. In addition to a tendency to fall to one side, he was experiencing double vision and nausea. I sent them to the emergency room immediately.

Neurological testing showed unsynchronized eye movements causing double vision, plus the eye movements characteristic of an inner-ear or brainstem problem. Clarence fell to one side when trying to stand or walk and had numbness on the other side of the body. A CT scan showed no hemorrhage, but it was felt he had a blood clot in an artery supplying the brainstem. He was immediately treated with heparin, an anticoagulant, to interfere with blood clotting. An MRI and an MRA (a nuclear scan that shows the blood vessels) confirmed a blood clot cutting off one of the small arteries coming off the main artery to the brain. With the anticoagulant Clarence improved over the next forty-eight hours, but since then he has continued to have some unsteadiness and poor coordination. Unable to drive, he walks with a walker and does light household chores. Although his outcome is far from ideal, he may have saved himself from further brain damage by prompt reporting of symptoms.

There are five conditions that cause vertigo:

- Labyrinthitis
- Benign positional vertigo
- Ménière's syndrome
- Acoustic neuroma
- Stroke

Clarence suffered from the last, a stroke of the vertebral-basilar artery.

Labyrinthitis
Labyrinthitis refers to an inflammation of the inner ear caused, it is thought, by a viral infection of the fluid-filled canals in the inner ear, which control your balance. Labyrinthitis is often accompanied by other viral symptoms such as a cold or muscle aching and may occur in several members of a family. The vertigo is mild to moderate and without neurological symptoms. The symptoms usually last one to several days and then clear. Sometimes a blow to the head can result in so-called labyrinthine concussion. If severe, this can require surgical correction.

Benign Positional Vertigo
Benign positional vertigo is a common condition that occurs when calcium particles become dislocated in the canals of the inner ear. Positional refers to dizziness experienced upon a change of position. This condition is usually mild and brief (less than a minute), but it does recur. It often responds to physical therapy maneuvers that help move the calcium accumulation to a less troublesome area of the inner-ear canals. A mild blow to the head may precipitate benign positional vertigo.

Ménière's Syndrome

Ménière's syndrome, which accounts for about 10 percent of vertigo cases, occurs when too much fluid accumulates in the inner-ear canals. Episodes can be severe and are associated with ringing in the ear (tinnitus) or hearing loss. Salt restriction often helps, as do diuretics.

Acoustic Neuroma

In acoustic neuroma a tumor, usually nonmalignant, lies on or near the acoustic nerve going from the ear to the brain. Although this condition is uncommon, it should be considered in all cases of chronic or progressive vertigo. An MRI of the head is the standard way of making the diagnosis. Any tumor must be removed, either by surgery or by external beam radiation or gamma rays, which shrink or destroy the growth. Radiation may be used after surgery to prevent or limit recurrence of the tumor.

Stroke

The anatomy of the circulation and the number of vital nerve centers in a small area of the brainstem make strokes here extremely dangerous. Two vertebral arteries rise along each side of the spine and join inside the skull to form the basilar artery. This supplies the cerebellum, the brainstem, and the nerves to the inner ear. The basilar artery has several small branches, and blockage of any can lead to a disabling stroke. (See part 1, chapter 7, "Stroke.")

OF SPECIAL CONCERN

Stroke of the vertebral-basilar artery is very serious. If you have any of the following symptoms suggestive of stroke — and especially if you have known vascular disease — get to the emergency room at once:

- Sudden, severe vertigo
- Double vision
- A tendency to fall to one side
- Loss of coordination, or the inability to control an arm or leg
- Numbness in the face

Treatment for Vertigo

The definitive treatment of vertigo depends, of course, on the underlying cause, but certain measures can be taken to treat symptoms when they are severe. In the case of viral labyrinthitis, these will keep you comfortable until the symptoms disappear.

For dizziness, the most commonly used drug is Antivert (meclizine) 25 mg every eight hours as needed. A patch called Transderm-Scop (scopolamine) can be applied every third day and may help prevent motion sickness in a vulnerable person who wants to take a cruise or go deep-sea fishing. If nausea is a severe accompanying symptom, you can use Phenergan (promethazine) 25 mg every six hours instead. Beware: all three drugs can cause sleepiness, so you should avoid alcohol. Transderm-Scop can also make urination difficult.

Unsteadiness

Janice was an eighty-three-year-old with high blood pressure who had experienced mild unsteadiness for many years. Recently it had grown worse. She had been a heavy social drinker and once had a seizure, possibly during alcohol withdrawal. I had spoken to her repeatedly about drinking. She said she would "compromise" and have only one drink each evening. I told her the best thing would be to avoid drinking altogether.

Janice's dizziness was not vertigo, simply an inability to walk or stand up without feeling as if she had to hold on to something. As her condition worsened, she went from steadying herself against walls and furniture to using a walker. Her neurological exam revealed that she walked with her feet wide apart and that she couldn't stand alone with her eyes closed or open. In an MRI scan, her brain exhibited some shrinkage and decreased white matter consistent with the closing off of numerous tiny blood vessels.

Janice's age, history of high blood pressure, and long-term alcohol use had caused degeneration of several parts of the brain that maintain normal balance. Medicine for vertigo didn't help, but since coming to see me, Janice has regained a little balance with formal physical therapy.

What Causes Unsteadiness?
When we're standing or walking, our brainstem and certain neuron clusters at the base of the brain and in the cerebellum act like a computer, constantly receiving data from the inner ear, the eyes, and the joints of the hips and legs to help us maintain our balance. The common type of unsteadiness Janice suffered from usually results from chronic degeneration of parts of this "computer" — the brain, spinal cord, or peripheral nerves that control equilibrium. The imbalance may come on suddenly or in a stepwise fashion, and it usually builds up over time. Janice's problem

was exacerbated by alcohol abuse, but many people who are not excessive drinkers have similar if less severe disorders.

If this neurological degeneration co-exists with arthritis or muscle weakness, it can further curb a person's mobility, and the doctor may have trouble focusing on a specific cause. In fact, most cases do not have a single cause, and for lack of better understanding, physicians simply characterize the condition as chronic disequilibrium syndrome of the elderly.

Treatment of Unsteadiness

If you're experiencing unsteadiness you should be evaluated by your primary physician, who may order neurological evaluations to rule out rare treatable conditions such as vitamin B_{12} deficiency or a condition in which cerebrospinal fluid in the brain increases (normal-pressure hydrocephalus).

For most cases, unfortunately, no definitive therapy exists, but you can take certain measures to cope with the condition:

- ☐ Inform your doctor about any medications you're taking, either prescribed or over the counter. Certain drugs can contribute to unsteadiness.
- ☐ Be extremely cautious about your intake of alcohol. If the syndrome is caused by prolonged excessive use of alcohol, you'll have to stop drinking completely, and even then recovery will be only partial. Even moderate drinking can damage nerves and exacerbate the condition. Stringently limit yourself.
- ☐ Seek treatment for arthritic or spinal problems.
- ☐ Engage in regular exercise, preferably under the supervision of a physical therapist. This is the most beneficial treatment in most cases.
- ☐ Prevent falls by having rails installed on walls and stairs and in the bathroom. Throw out slippery scatter rugs.
- ☐ Conquer your vanity and use a cane (some are very stylish), a quad-cane (one with legs), or a walker. One fall can move you from independent living to a nursing home.

Lightheadedness

Lightheadedness is usually positional (experienced on getting up), the result of a transient fall in blood pressure. Healthy young people who suddenly stand up have vascular reflexes that momentarily readjust to send more blood to the brain. In older people, particularly those with vascular disease or on blood pressure medication, these reflexes are not as efficient. Sudden standing, particularly from a lying or relaxed sitting position, can cause transient lightheadedness.

Lightheadedness and near fainting are hard to distinguish, so be careful in reporting the frequency and severity of your symptoms and what triggers them. Transient lightheadedness isn't anything to worry about. If, however, lightheadedness interferes with normal activities, or if you feel that you might faint, you should report it to your doctor.

Treatment of Lightheadedness

Often just standing up slowly and in stages relieves lightheadedness. When you get out of bed, sit on the side of the bed for fifteen or twenty seconds before standing. If that doesn't relieve the symptom, try sitting a little longer. When you get up from a reclining chair or an easy chair, sit upright for a few seconds. Also be cautious when straightening up from a bending position — hold on to something for a few seconds. If you take these precautions and you continue to feel lightheaded, see your doctor. If you're on blood pressure or heart medication, it may need to be adjusted.

In rare cases when lightheadedness is severe and accompanied by a significant fall in blood pressure, you may need to increase your salt intake or take a medication to keep your blood pressure up. The most commonly used drugs are Florinef, which helps the body retain salt and water, and a new medication called ProAmatine (midodrine), which keeps blood vessels constricted. You have to be closely monitored while taking these medications. Florinef can cause too much fluid retention, straining the heart, and ProAmatine can send blood pressure way up.

Fainting

The medical term for fainting is syncope (the e is pronounced), and the term for near fainting is pre-syncope. The cases below represent two common causes of fainting.

Sam

Sam, a sixty-one-year-old, had just come out of a restaurant when suddenly his mouth felt dry, his tongue thick, and he began to vomit profusely. He went to the bathroom and collapsed on the floor. Later, his wife was helping him to bed when he fell down unconscious. When he came to, Sam was pale and weak but able to get into bed with his wife's help, and after resting for an hour he felt slightly better. Gradually the vomiting episodes tapered out. He drank small amounts of water and then some Gatorade. The next day, though tired, Sam was able to resume his usual activities. He was out of town and didn't call a doctor, though he should have, I told him later.

Sam's story is not unusual: Acute gastroenteritis with vomiting dehydrated him and lowered his blood volume and pressure, causing fainting. He was fortunate to get better so quickly.

Kate

Kate was eighty-three years old and lived alone. While on the phone she felt her heart beating rapidly, then she lost consciousness. When she woke up her panicked friend was shouting on the other end of the line. Promptly Kate called me, and I arranged for transport to the hospital where she was evaluated in the cardiac-monitoring unit. Kate had several episodes of very rapid heartbeat — 170 beats per minute — followed by seconds-long interludes with no beats. A cardiac pacemaker to treat the pauses in her heartbeat was implanted just under her right collarbone, and she was started on a medication to prevent the rapid heartbeats. She has had no fainting for over two years.

Kate's case was typical of fainting due to an arrhythmia. She was right to call me. A doctor should evaluate any fainting episode in someone over sixty.

A WORD OF CAUTION

If you feel as if you may faint, or if you do faint, you should:

- Call the doctor right away or have someone take you to an emergency room.
- Lie down, even if it is on the floor, until you feel stable.
- Avoid driving anywhere until the reason for fainting has been clarified, and your condition improves or is corrected.

Testing for Fainting

If you have fainting episodes, you'll be tested first for blood pressure and heart rate and rhythm. If your blood pressure is low, you'll be tested for possible causes such as dehydration and blood loss, conditions that can be corrected. Acute gastroenteritis with vomiting (Sam's situation) isn't the only cause of dehydration, low blood pressure, and associated fainting; this condition can also be caused by overheating with severe perspiration.

If your doctor is concerned about your heart, you may be observed in a hospital on a heart monitor for a day or so to rule out a painless coronary attack or severe arrhythmia. Alternatively, depending on the severity of the situation, you may have a day or more of monitoring at home with a portable cardiogram called a Holter monitor. This pocket-sized device will record your heartbeat throughout the day and night and can print out any abnormalities. If more sophisticated monitoring is needed, your doctor will consult a cardiologist.

Treatment of Fainting Associated with Arrhythmia

If your heart rate is too slow (bradycardia), or if long pauses interrupt it, you may need a pacemaker. If, periodically, your heart is beating too rapidly (tachycardia), you'll probably need medication. Some people like Kate have both types of heart arrhythmia, a condition called tachy-brady syndrome, which often requires both a pacemaker and medication.

The prospect of a pacemaker tends to frighten patients, who feel this is the end of the line. I try to put patients' fears to rest by telling them what a wonderful innovation pacemakers are. The vast majority of pacemaker wearers resume normal lives of vigorous mental and sensible physical activity. If the problem is an abnormal rhythm, and no angina or congestive heart failure is present, the person can play golf and tennis and hike. One morning, by chance, I saw five patients in a row who had pacemakers, and all were leading active lives. In fact, not one of them had come to the office for a problem related to heart rhythm.

If you have a pacemaker, your rhythm should be monitored. This can easily be done by a device that connects to your phone and transmits the rhythm to the cardiologist.

REMEMBER THIS

- Specify what you mean by dizziness when you talk to your doctor.
- Mild vertigo usually results from a problem with the balancing mechanism in the inner ear.
- Sudden and severe vertigo, fainting, or near fainting should be reported to your doctor or evaluated in an emergency room immediately. It can mean a stroke, heart arrhythmia, severe dehydration, or blood loss due to internal bleeding.
- Chronic unsteadiness is often difficult to cure, but physical therapy and correction of other medical problems can help.

CHAPTER 26

URINARY DISORDERS

A delightfully irreverent lady in her mid-eighties summed it up one day: "Dr. Connally, old men can't pee enough, and old women pee too much." When it comes to urinary disorders, the overwhelming problem for men is enlargement of the prostate with decreased bladder capacity, which makes it difficult to empty the bladder, and for women, incontinence or loss of urinary control, which causes leakage and social embarrassment.

There are three major disorders of the prostate: prostate cancer (see part 1, chapter 6, "Cancer"), benign prostatic hyperplasia (BPH), and prostatitis.

WHAT IS A PROSTATE, ANYWAY?

The prostate is a gland, slightly larger than a walnut, that surrounds the area where the bladder opens into the urethra. The prostate's function is to produce the fluid portion of the semen. Spermatozoa come from the testicles through narrow tubes called seminal ducts to the prostate area. Two small sacs to the side of the prostate store the liquid part of the semen and eject it during orgasm or ejaculation. During a digital rectal exam, your doctor can easily feel the prostate.

Benign Prostatic Hyperplasia

This nonmalignant enlargement of the prostate gland should be considered an almost inevitable consequence of a man's living past the age of fifty, about the time it seems to start. The gland, which normally weighs about twenty grams, may quadruple in size, and as it does, it narrows the opening from the bladder to the urethra. The degree of blockage determines symptoms. A very large gland, enlarged mostly backward or in the lateral lobes, may not produce much obstruction, while a gland that is only moderately enlarged, but mostly in the middle lobe, can cause considerable blockage.

As your bladder opening grows narrower, the bladder's wall muscle may thicken and become irritated. Initially this reduces bladder capacity, causing frequent urination, but ultimately the bladder wall dilates and loses its ability to empty. If urinary function is too compromised, back pressure to the kidneys can cause kidney failure.

The Symptoms of BPH

The symptoms of BPH are all urinary, resulting from obstruction and secondary irritation. Typical symptoms of obstruction include:

- ☐ A weak stream of urine
- ☐ Having to strain
- ☐ Intermittent stoppage as you void
- ☐ Dribbling after you void
- ☐ Feeling as though you have not emptied the bladder

The symptoms of irritation are even more troublesome:

- ☐ An urgent desire to urinate
- ☐ Frequent urination (some men have to get up five or more times a night)
- ☐ Painful urination
- ☐ Occasionally leakage when the bladder is full (cold exposure may cause urgency and leaking)

How Is BPH Treated?

If you're getting up just once or twice a night and not experiencing significant frequency or urgency during the day, you're probably better off than most guys your age — keep your fingers crossed. Drinking most of your fluid early in the day, and not a lot after dinner, may help you sleep through the night. If you have to get up three or four times a night, and you start experiencing more frequency or urgency during the day, then you should see your doctor. He or she will take your history, do a digital rectal exam, and get a PSA (prostatic-specific antigen) blood test to make sure there is no cancerous growth in the enlarged gland.

Discomfort or significant inconvenience can be treated initially with saw palmetto. Saw palmetto is an over-the-counter herbal remedy that many urologists are recommending for mild symptoms. The number of patients in my practice who have reported improvement from saw palmetto seems more than can be explained by a placebo effect. I think this herb is a reasonable opening salvo for those with mild symptoms.

The next step, if symptoms are severe or do not improve, is to try one of the three alpha-adrenergic antagonist drugs available for urinary symptoms: Hytrin (terazosin), Cardura (doxazosin), or Flomax (tamsulosin). This family of drugs relaxes autonomic nerve tension at the bladder neck, making urination easier. Alpha-antagonists are effective, but they have to be monitored carefully because they can lower blood pressure and even cause fainting. Its manufacturer claims that Flomax doesn't lower blood pressure as much as the other two drugs do, but like them it has to be started in very low doses and increased cautiously.

Another medication, Proscar (finasteride), interferes with the activity of male hormones, testosterone specifically. Without testosterone stimulation, the prostate gland doesn't grow, and over several months it will shrink. Unfortunately, Proscar may reduce libido and sexual potency.

In one large comparative study, the alpha-adrenergic antagonists proved effective in a larger percentage of men than Proscar did. Because of this, the potential side effects of Proscar, and the long time before symptoms improve with Proscar, I usually prescribe the alpha-antagonists, though several patients on Proscar have had excellent results with no side effects. One other strategy is to start Proscar and an alpha-antagonist at the same time, then taper off the alpha-antagonist after a few months to see how you are doing on the Proscar.

Also, Proscar lowers PSA, which is a marker for development of a prostate cancer. To have this test continue to be a useful guideline for cancer, the PSA result should be doubled when you are on Proscar.

SHRINK YOUR PROSTATE AND GROW SOME HAIR?

Proscar has a beneficial side effect in some men with male pattern baldness. The same drug, finasteride, is sold in a 1 mg dose as Propecia, a hair-restoring agent. If you're taking Proscar, which is sold in a 5 mg dose, you just may grow some hair while you're shrinking your prostate.

When Medications Don't Work

If medications aren't helping you, or the obstruction is causing bladder and kidney damage, you may need to have your bladder opening surgically widened. The classic method is a transurethral resectioning of the prostate, in which prostate tissue is carved or shaved away through the urethra. In recent years less invasive techniques have been developed to reduce obstruction — laser, hyperthermia, microwave, electrical vaporization, ultrasound, and even a freezing procedure. If you need transurethral resectioning, you should discuss the possibility of these new techniques with your urologist or your primary care doctor.

After transurethral resectioning, during ejaculation the stream goes back into the bladder. Incontinence is rare with this procedure. After transurethral resectioning the incidence of erectile problems is about 5 to 10 percent, but because so many older men have erectile problems to begin with, the percentage is hard to determine.

Prostatitis

Prostatitis refers to infection and inflammation of the prostate gland. It is predominantly a problem of younger men, although it occurs in older men with BPH and may aggravate the symptoms. Older guys can be afflicted with either of two types of prostatitis: bacterial or infectious, and nonbacterial.

Jim

Jim is a typical example. At the age of sixty-four, he had a consulting business and frequently drove two hours at a time to see clients. For several years Jim had gone to the bathroom about once each night, twice if he had something to drink before bed. Then over a period of two weeks his nighttime visits to the bathroom escalated, until he was waking up almost every hour, and urination became urgent and slightly painful. Now he had to stop once or twice on his trips to see clients, and he was mildly incontinent on his way to the men's room.

While doing a rectal exam on Jim I performed a prostate massage, putting pressure on the gland to produce a few drops of prostatic fluid. Viewed under the microscope, this appeared loaded with white blood cells, indicating infection. Jim's PSA test was 14, markedly above the normal score of 4.

Jim was started on Cipro, an antibiotic that kills most prostate bacteria, and advised to avoid alcohol and activities like cycling or weight lifting that could irritate the gland. He felt better in two or three days and continued the Cipro for two weeks. Now he was getting up just once at night, and he no longer experienced urgency or frequency during the day. His PSA level eventually came down to 2.9. Jim had bacterial prostatitis superimposed on mild BPH. The sudden worsening of symptoms was typical.

Treating Prostatitis

If urinary frequency and urgency suddenly grow worse, you should see your doctor right away — you probably have bacterial prostatitis. If your symptoms gradually worsen over several weeks, you could have chronic, non-bacterial prostatitis superimposed on BPH, or BPH that has simply taken a turn for the worse. In this case, too, you should call your doctor.

The cause of chronic, nonbacterial prostatitis isn't known. Irritation may be triggered by sexual stimulation without ejaculation, riding on hard bicycle seats or in bouncing sports vehicles, alcohol, and exercise with extremely heavy lifting or straining. I advise patients to avoid these triggers, and mention that sex with full ejaculation may be helpful. Hot baths rather than showers bring relief to some men. In rare cases, a nonsteroidal anti-inflammatory drug (NSAID) is beneficial.

Incontinence

Incontinence, or inability to control urination, occurs in both sexes but is much more common in women over sixty. In men, the problem stems primarily from the blockage and secondary irritation associated with an enlarged prostate, or from loss of control following prostate surgery. In women, incontinence has to do with bladder irritability, loss of control of the stopping mechanism at the urethra, or both.

In women, the two most common conditions are stress incontinence and urge incontinence. Another condition, functional incontinence, afflicts women and men who are paralyzed, demented, or bedridden.

Stress Incontinence

In pure stress incontinence, the person involuntarily loses a small amount of urine with increased pressure inside the abdomen from coughing or sneezing, laughing, vigorous exercise, or just walking up and down stairs. Stress incontinence signals weakness of the pelvic muscles and tissue that support the bladder and urethra, or weakness of the sphincter muscle of the bladder.

Urge Incontinence

Urge incontinence means the urge to void as soon as the bladder feels full. It occurs when the bladder muscle that normally forces urine out becomes overactive. Though this problem is seen in people who have strokes or other neurological problems, it is also common in aging women.

Most patients experience symptoms of both stress and urge incontinence, with excess bladder pressure and a lax holding mechanism.

How Are Stress and Urge Incontinence Treated?

All women with incontinence should have a urine test to rule out urinary infection and a pelvic exam to rule out atrophic vaginitis, urethritis, and major anatomical problems such as a prolapsed bladder or badly sagging uterus. Any infection should be treated, and if the woman is not already on it, hormone replacement therapy (HRT) should be considered (see part 2, chapter 13, "Hormone Replacement Therapy"). HRT, by combating atrophic vaginitis, alleviates frequent urination and tends to strengthen the pelvic support muscles. An estrogen cream may help if there are reasons not to take oral estrogen.

Kegel exercises. If the symptoms indicate stress incontinence, the treatment is weight loss and Kegel exercises to strengthen bladder support muscles. When a woman does Kegel exercises, she contracts the pelvic muscles around the vagina and urethra. Studies have shown that incontinence improves in up to 80 percent of women who perform Kegels properly. The exercise program, which is very simple and can be performed almost anywhere and at any time, should nonetheless be started under the direction of a physical therapist, urologist, gynecologist, or nurse practitioner who has experience in teaching Kegel exercises and doing follow-up.

Medication. If the symptoms are those of urge incontinence, or of mixed urge and stress incontinence, a medication to relax overactive bladder muscles can be beneficial. Detrol (tolterodine) and Ditropan (oxybutynin) were developed specifically for incontinence, though many women do well on traditional therapy with small doses of tricyclic antidepressants, which have a relaxing effect on the bladder.

The most common side effects of Detrol and Ditropan are dry mouth, dizziness, somnolence, blurred vision, and constipation. Paradoxically, some people find they have more difficulty urinating.

When to see the urologist. If you have incontinence and don't see improvement with the above measures, you should see a urologist, if possible one specializing in incontinence. The urologist can measure pressure in your bladder before and during voiding to get a better idea of what additional medications to try and to determine whether surgical correction, such as strengthening the support structures of the bladder or pelvis, might help.

Some large medical centers now have incontinence programs in which urologists and gynecologists work together to evaluate problems. If surgery is called for, the urologist and gynecologist may operate jointly to correct bladder abnormalities and sagging pelvic structures. Pelvic support problems include conditions in which the bladder, rectum, or uterus bulges into the vagina or out of the vaginal opening.

For about 60 percent of women with one or more of these problems, a pessary or donut-shaped device can be inserted high into the vagina to give support, which improves incontinence and discomfort. Pessaries are usually well tolerated, but they have to be removed and cleaned regularly.

Functional Incontinence

People who are demented, paralyzed, or bedridden may develop urinary incontinence for a number of reasons, requiring them to receive full or extra nursing care. The patient may not perceive bladder sensations properly, may have a urinary infection or impacted fecal matter pressing on the bladder, or may not be able to get to the toilet in time.

Not only is functional incontinence uncomfortable and malodorous, but a wet bed increases the risk for groin infection and bedsores. The patient needs regular assistance when going to the toilet or bedside commode, a frequent change of diapers or pads, and careful attention to skin care. Indwelling urinary catheters can easily infect the bladder and should not be used just for convenience. They can be justified if urine overflow is caused by obstruction, or if constant moisture prevents the healing of bedsores.

REMEMBER THIS

- BPH is an almost universal condition in men over sixty. Symptoms vary from mild (getting up once or twice a night) to severe (frequent, painful, and urgent urination or total obstruction).
- A reasonable course of treatment can start with saw palmetto in mild cases. In all severe cases, or if saw palmetto doesn't relieve the symptoms, the treatment is alpha-adrenergic blockers and possibly Proscar.
- Persistent symptoms may call for transurethral resectioning or one of the newer, less invasive procedures to reduce blockage.
- If your BPH symptoms suddenly worsen, you may have superimposed prostatitis.
- Urinary incontinence is extremely common in elderly women. It is usually caused by abnormal spasm of the bladder muscle accompanied by inability to stop the flow of urine.
- Incontinence can be managed with estrogen, treatment of any infection, Kegel exercises, and bladder-relaxing medication.
- If none of these therapies helps, evaluation of bladder pressure by a urologist or urology/gynecology team may help in the search for a solution. Pessaries are often helpful.
- In the extremely frail, neurologically impaired, or bedridden patient, diapers and scrupulous cleaning prevent bedsores. Indwelling urinary catheters can cause infection and should be reserved for significant obstruction or bedsores.

CHAPTER 27

UNWELCOME WEIGHT LOSS

Earlier, I discussed one of the major health problems for people in their sixties — being overweight. For the vast majority of people over seventy-five, however, overweight either isn't a health risk or ceases to be one. That's because as people age, they begin to lose weight. And they don't just lose fat — they lose crucial muscle. Severe weight loss with its accompanying symptoms is called cachexia. (See part 1, chapter 8, the Body Mass Index chart.)

Why is weight loss a concern? First, for some elderly, weight loss and frailty are synonymous. The downward spiral can be hard to escape: loss of muscle makes people weak and tottery, they exercise less, and then they lose more muscle. Second, thin, frail types are more likely to fall and have less padding when they do fall. Last but not least, weight loss can result in a shattering loss of independence.

Celia

Celia was a ninety-three-year-old widow. Except for slightly high blood pressure, she had no major health problems until she fell at age ninety, fracturing two bones in her right shoulder. After surgery her shoulder didn't regain complete function, and Celia had to leave her large apartment and move to a retirement home. She was small at the time of her move — five feet one inch tall and only ninety pounds (down from 120 pounds in her youth).

In the retirement home, despite all our efforts to keep her weight up — vitamins, antidepressants, physical therapy, meals arranged by a dietician, and assistance during meals — Celia's weight dropped to seventy-four pounds. Nothing could put weight back on her. During the last two years of her life she grew more and more frail and required assistance to walk and dress herself. Mentally Celia was sharp. Tests showed no neurological or metabolic abnormalities, just some mild anemia from poor nutrition.

Celia exhibited a pattern of symptoms common in otherwise healthy people over seventy-five: an inevitable, irreversible decline in appetite, weight, and overall well-being, accompanied by some depression.

Why Does Weight Drop in the Elderly?

Older people lose weight for any number of reasons. The logistical difficulty of getting food into the home is one reason. Aged people have a hard enough time just getting across the room, much less navigating through a parking lot with bags in tow. Other causes include:

☐ Normal physical changes of aging
☐ Lifestyle changes
☐ Disease
☐ Psychological factors
☐ Socioeconomic factors

Usually several factors contribute to an individual's weight loss. To try to reverse the trend, doctor and patient need to approach the weight problem from various angles.

Normal Physical Changes of Aging

Certain changes contribute to weight loss after age seventy-five and accelerate after eighty-five. Hormonal and chemical changes in the brain that stimulate appetite become less pronounced, and the satiety mechanism that causes people to feel full and stop eating becomes more active.

We know that certain hormones help the body maintain muscle mass, and that a diminished supply of them can result in weight loss. Human growth hormone (HGH) is currently thought to be the most important of these. HGH levels fall as we get older, as do levels of the main reproductive hormones — estrogen in women (a dramatic drop after menopause), and testosterone in men (a gradual drop).

And for reasons that are not entirely understood, in the very aged the mechanism for building protein — the main component of muscle — slows down. This may be a basic biological change of the aging cell, and may ultimately limit what we can do to help older people maintain or put on weight.

Lifestyle Changes

Weight loss and frailty result primarily from loss of muscle mass, and loss of muscle mass has much to do with lack of muscle-building exercise. From the point of view of prevention and reversibility, this is a critical fact. Even older people who do maintain their weight past seventy-five experience a shift in the balance of fat and muscle, with the scale tipped toward fat. Fortunately, loss of muscle mass, called sarcopenia, can be dramatically reversed or slowed by regular weight-bearing exercise (see part 2, introduction). If you're wasting away, make sure you talk with your doctor about the possibility of a supervised weight-training program.

As people get older and lose friends and loved ones, eating habits change. Dining alone isn't much fun — and doesn't offer much motivation for

> **Did You Know?**
> As I said in part 1, chapter 2, "Cholesterol Problems," though high LDL cholesterol is associated with a significantly higher death rate from heart attacks and strokes, the risk appears to be greater for people in middle age than for the very old. If you're over seventy-five, unless you have extremely high cholesterol (LDL over 200) or known vascular disease, you need to pay much more attention to an adequate intake of protein than to avoiding cholesterol.

preparing food. If you're losing weight, tell your doctor about your diet. For reasons of preference or because it costs less, some elderly have a diet that is too low in protein. We in the medical profession may have encouraged this tendency with our admonitions about high-cholesterol and high-fat foods, which happen to be good sources of protein.

Disease

Chronic obstructive pulmonary disease and congestive heart failure can contribute to weight loss. In both conditions, oxygen flow to the tissues is compromised and the patient has to expend more calories breathing. In someone with congestive heart failure the intestinal tract may be engorged, causing nausea or loss of appetite and reduced absorption of nutrients.

An overactive thyroid increases the body's metabolism and can lead to weakness and weight loss in older people. The usual signs of an overactive thyroid in younger people — fast pulse, prominent eyes, or warm skin — may not be present in older people, so a thyroid test should be done on everyone who is losing weight.

Weight loss may be the first symptom of early cancer, but usually other symptoms point to a local tumor such as abdominal pain, coughing, or enlarged lymph nodes. Advanced cancer may be accompanied by loss of appetite or nausea with severe weight loss. A progesterone-like hormone, Megace (megestrol), may help boost the appetite.

Intestinal problems associated with nausea or appetite loss, abdominal pain, decreased nutrient absorption, or bowel irregularities can cause weight loss. Hidden infections or inflammatory conditions such as polymyalgia rheumatica may contribute to weight loss by reducing the appetite and changing the metabolism so that tissue buildup is diminished.

Any major physical stress such as an operation, a fracture, or a severe acute infection like pneumonia can accelerate weight loss, not just by temporarily interrupting adequate food intake but also by changing the body's metabolism so that for some time after the episode, body tissue breaks down rather than builds up. And, of course, any disease that keeps a patient bed bound for extended periods or that curbs exercise can lead to weight loss.

Psychological Factors

The aged person who suffers prolonged grief or clinical depression may end up shedding vital pounds. While the poor appetite that accompanies normal grief usually improves after a while, appetite loss with full-fledged depression may not correct itself so easily. Depression often complicates weight loss in people with other illnesses or who have difficulty getting food into the home. For some people, weight loss is the result of phobias or misguided medical ideas that led to a lifelong avoidance of certain nutritious foods.

SOCIOECONOMIC FACTORS AND WEIGHT LOSS

Although poverty among the elderly is less prevalent now than in 1965 when Medicare was launched, some people still have difficulty affording all the food they need for a healthy diet. I've had several patients tell me they have to skimp on meals because their medications ate up so much of their pension or Social Security money. Other patients, often because of frailty, simply don't buy or prepare the right types of food. In addition to lack of funds and frailty, ignorance about what makes for a balanced diet can turn the once sturdy silhouette of a grandparent into a rail.

Putting Pounds Back On

In the quest to restore pounds, the two most important steps a person can take are:

☐ Getting regular weight-bearing exercise to overcome muscle loss.
☐ Following the U.S. Department of Agriculture's Food Pyramid, which recommends a diet with balanced food groups. Remember, extra meat is not a problem for the person past seventy-five.

Check your weight or that of your loved one at least every two weeks. It also helps to keep a log that records food intake and appetite. If the scale is drifting downward — and certainly if it registers a loss of eight to ten pounds — contact the doctor to be sure no possible weight-gain measure has been overlooked. Meanwhile, you might consult a clinical nutritionist for recommendations. Dietary supplements such as Ensure or Sustacal can be enormously beneficial in restoring lost weight.

If the doctor rules out a specific illness, including depression, as the cause of weight loss, it's time to move into the next phase of treatment. Consider every factor that can possibly be changed. Can you or your loved one easily get food? Is help needed with preparation? Are there physical problems — perhaps dental or visual, or problems related to arthritis — interfering with eating? Meals on Wheels or a visiting health aide might remedy difficulties with food procurement and preparation. Dentures or vision correction may help the feeding problem. If you've tried all these things and weight loss and inadequate nutrition persists, then an assisted living center or nursing home may be the only answer.

Are There Medications to Help Control Weight Loss?

Several appetite-stimulating medications have been tried without much success. A drink before meals — for decades, an old standby was a glass of sherry — doesn't do much good. As mentioned, if appetite loss arises from cancer, Megace may help.

Anabolic drugs to "build up" the body have a spotty record but should be considered. Both estrogen in women and testosterone in men help build and preserve muscle mass. Levels of estrogen drop dramatically when a women goes through menopause (see part 2, chapter 13, "Hormone Replacement Therapy"). In addition to preventing osteoporosis and heart disease, preserving muscle mass is a major reason that women take hormone replacement therapy.

At around age seventy-five, men have about one-half the level of testosterone they had at twenty. Replacement can increase muscle strength and bulk. Because of the risks, however, most doctors reserve testosterone for a few select patients, usually those whose levels are extremely low. The main concern is that testosterone can stimulate the prostate, exacerbating prostate cancer and benign prostatic hyperplasia.

Moreover, testosterone, whether taken by pill, injection, or skin patch, can depress the body's own testosterone; as the outside source is withdrawn, the body may have virtually no testosterone left.

If someone getting over a severe illness is weak and underweight, one of several anabolic agents similar to testosterone may be given for the short term: Winstral (stanazol), Oxandrin (oxandralon), or Androl (oxymetholone). These are the body-building steroids some young athletes use, and the side effects can be serious. They include prostate cancer growth and prostate enlargement in men, and voice deepening and the growth of facial hair in women. In large doses, anabolic steroids can produce something akin to a manic state. These drugs should be strictly limited to short-term situations such as convalescence after surgery.

A more realistic possibility is the hormone precursor dehydroepiandrosterone (DHEA), the chemical building block of estrogen and testosterone that is available over the counter. Studies have shown that DHEA promotes muscle bulk and strength, and so far there have been no major reports of problems. I would reserve it for a person who is actively losing weight. DHEA shouldn't be taken regularly since its long-term side effects are unknown.

CAN HGH MAKE SUPERMEN OUT OF THE ELDERLY?

You might recall human growth hormone, which I mentioned earlier in this chapter. Our levels of HGH tend to taper off in advanced age. Recent work indicates that HGH plays a major role in preserving muscle size and strength as we get old. In studies at the University of Virginia, HGH injections produced dramatic improvement in muscle strength and bulk and overall physical robustness in men in their seventies and eighties.

Because it is made up of large molecules (polypeptides), HGH has to be given by injection several times a week. At one time, it could only be gotten from cadavers; then in the mid-1990s HGH became available through the manipulation of bacterial DNA. It is still very expensive — approximately $14,000 a year for the required number of injections. As you can guess, the pharmaceutical industry is scrambling to develop an oral form of the active portion of the HGH molecule. If this effort succeeds, it will make Viagra, Prozac, Lipitor, and Celebrex look like small-scale pharmaceutical bonanzas by comparison — and would mark a huge improvement in quality of life for the third third.

REMEMBER THIS

- After age seventy-five, weight loss and muscle wasting are common and often result from a combination of physical, psychological, and socioeconomic factors.

- Regular weight-bearing exercise and a balanced diet are the first steps to restoring or maintaining a healthy weight.

- Keep close tabs on your weight or that of your elderly loved one, and report what's happening to the doctor.

- Dietary supplements such as Sustacal and Ensure may help restore lost pounds.

- Severe weight loss often signifies that an older person should move into an assisted living center.

- Aside from estrogen replacement in women in whom it is not contraindicated, current hormone therapies have worrisome side effects or are not practical. DHEA, available over the counter, may be helpful in maintaining or building muscle in the elderly, but its long-term effects are unknown.

- HGH, if it can be developed in a convenient and affordable form, could be an extraordinary boon to geriatric medicine.

CHAPTER 28

CONGESTIVE HEART FAILURE

Congestive heart failure (CHF) is a condition in which the heart muscle no longer has the strength to meet the body's needs. Because the heart cannot pump the way it used to, not enough blood moves forward to supply the body, and some blood backs up. The failing heart causes fluid buildup in the limbs and internal organs. The person becomes weak, easily exhausted, short of breath, and often swollen, and may suffer from secondary failure of organs such as the kidneys or liver. Sometimes brain function is impaired.

I discussed heart disease in general in part 1, chapter 1, "Heart Disease," but I revisit the topic here because advanced CHF is one of the most common disease processes people have to contend with in their twilight years.

Although by definition CHF occurs in a diseased heart in which the damage has usually already been done, we can still deal with the symptoms effectively. In the past five years, newer approaches to the treatment of CHF have for the first time changed the overall death rate, reducing annual deaths by 10 to 25 percent. More importantly, they have dramatically improved patients' symptoms and quality of life. If you learn a few basic facts about living with CHF and work closely with the doctor, you can add months or years of comfort to your life or the life of the older person you're caring for.

> **Did You Know?**
> About 10 percent of people over eighty years old have CHF, while only about 1 percent of the population between the age of fifty and sixty-five do. There were 875,000 Medicare admissions for CHF in 1999 alone. Approximately 4.8 million Americans suffer from this disease, and 75 percent of them are over sixty-five.

What Happens in CHF?

When the heart muscle weakens, two events occur. First, your heart cannot pump enough blood to take care of your body's needs; you feel weak and easily fatigued. Second, when your kidneys don't receive adequate blood they secrete a hormone that causes the body to retain salt and water, increasing the amount of fluid in circulation. This, on top of a weak, failing heart, causes fluid to build up in your limbs and in your lungs and other internal organs. Your neck veins may also become distended because of back pressure from the weak heart.

Symptoms include shortness of breath — initially with severe exertion, then with mild exertion, and ultimately even at rest. Often it becomes difficult to sleep lying flat in bed, and you may need to prop yourself up with two or three pillows. Some people have to sit up at night because of sudden severe shortness of breath coming on while they're asleep. Usually, but not in everyone with CHF, the feet and ankles swell. In many people the swelling is noticeable throughout the body — feet, ankles, legs, abdomen, and neck.

In severe progressive CHF, the intestinal tract may become swollen and oxygen starved, causing loss of appetite, nausea, and weight loss. Poor circulation to the muscles causes weakness and easy fatigue, and decreased circulation to the brain may result in confusion or somnolence.

How Does Your Doctor Know You Have CHF?

As with any diagnosis, your doctor will start with your history. The symptoms above are very strongly suggestive of CHF, but the doctor can come closer to a definitive diagnosis by hearing noise at the base of the lungs (rales) or a peculiar "gallop" sound in the heart, and by confirming swelling in the ankles or distension of the neck veins. A chest X ray shows the heart to be enlarged and may also reveal a distinctive pattern of fluid in the lungs. Another test is the echocardiogram, in which sound waves reflect off the heart to give a picture of its size and tell about its function. Echocardiograms, frequently performed by cardiologists, determine the percentage of blood in the heart pumped out with each beat, a very good measure of heart weakness.

Once it is established that you have CHF, the doctor has to determine two things: what disease process caused the heart to weaken in the first place, and what tipped you over and caused immediate significant symptoms. The echocardiogram can usually identify the disease process. Are there weak spots in the heart wall consistent with coronary disease? Is the heart symmetrically dilated, as in a primary heart muscle disease (cardiomyopathy)? Are the valves so defective they are making the heart muscle work overtime and fail dramatically?

Treating CHF: The First Step and Beyond

Before anything specific can be done to try and correct the underlying disease, the heart needs to be stabilized, and there are several medications that can help.

If you are so sick you require hospitalization, oxygen and intravenous diuretics — usually Lasix (furosemide) — are administered, then several drugs are added. The Lasix usually needs to be continued orally once you have left the hospital. If you can be treated as an outpatient, the same order of drugs should be used. It is now accepted that everyone with CHF should have a drug in the ACE inhibitor family and that most should have a drug in the beta blocker family, particularly in cases associated with coronary disease.

Once your condition stabilizes, you have to follow these guidelines:

☐ Avoid strenuous activity. Moderate activity is helpful unless you are suffering from extremely severe failure or you become significantly worse. Working with a cardiac rehabilitation team in a large hospital can help you determine the right amount of exercise.

☐ Limit salt in the diet. I had a patient who went back into severe symptomatic CHF for unexplained reasons every three or four weeks. I saw him at home as his wife was setting up for their monthly bridge group, laying out pretzels and potato chips in abundance. He did not add extra salt at meals but loved the snacks.

☐ Avoid alcohol. Alcohol in large quantities can cause direct damage to the heart muscle, and even small amounts of alcohol can weaken a heart muscle already damaged by another process. (See part 2, chapter 17, "Alcoholism and Alcohol Abuse.")

☐ Avoid extremely large meals, which put increased demands on the heart.

☐ Report worsening symptoms promptly, especially increased fatigue, shortness of breath, or swelling. This means something is going wrong!

☐ Avoid medications that can make CHF worse, especially non-

steroidal anti-inflammatory drugs (NSAIDs), calcium channel blockers, and prednisone.
□ Follow your medication program closely. Stopped or missed medications are a frequent reason for worsening symptoms.

The Good News on Treatment

In the past few years, we've made a lot of progress in our ability to reduce symptoms and improve the quality of life of even severe CHF patients. The generally accepted drugs that should be prescribed or at least considered by your doctor are:

□ *ACE inhibitors*. These reduce pressure on the heart and make it more efficient.
□ *Aldactone (spironolactone)*. This is a mild diuretic that seems to help kidney function and interferes with the process of fluid retention. Recently, it has been added to the drug program of almost all CHF patients.
□ *Lasix (furosemide)*. This is a potent diuretic, and you will probably need potassium replacement pills when taking it. Your potassium needs to be checked frequently, because kidney failure or Aldactone can make your blood potassium go too high.
□ *Beta blockers*. These drugs reduce strain on the heart but in rare cases may weaken the heart. If your doctor adds a beta blocker to your drug regimen, you need to watch your symptoms carefully and report any worsening.
□ *Digoxin*. This is a modern form of digitalis medication, which was used for "dropsy" (CHF) in the late eighteenth century. It used to be the main weapon against CHF, but is currently a second-line drug.

Why Does CHF Suddenly Get Worse?

If you and your doctor cannot figure out why you suddenly took a turn for the worse and landed in the hospital, it is likely to happen again, soon after you're discharged. Lots of things can trigger "decompensation" with dramatic worsening of symptoms.

Actions you may have taken, such as:

□ Stopping or missing medications
□ Taking medications that can cause fluid retention

☐ Eating too much salt
☐ Drinking too much alcohol
☐ Overactivity and lack of rest

Complicating medical conditions, such as:

☐ A new coronary, or worsening coronary circulation
☐ A heart arrhythmia
☐ A blood clot going to the lungs
☐ Other illnesses that stress the heart such as anemia, fever, or an overactive thyroid

---

A WORD OF CAUTION

If a person with CHF experiences worse symptoms, the doctor must be alerted right away. Are any of the symptoms associated with decompensation? Prompt attention to changing symptoms is the most important step you can take for yourself or the CHF patient you're concerned about.

Long-Term Prognosis

Patients with CHF can live for several years if they follow the above rules and work very closely with their doctor, and if every effort is made to keep any underlying coronary disease from progressing. I have had patients travel to Europe or Hawaii without worsening symptoms, and many people are able to play golf (in this case, I certainly advise using a cart). One patient continues to do very well in national amateur seniors competition three years after he first had CHF symptoms.

The medications I've described have been shown unequivocally to reduce invalidism and hospitalization for CHF patients and to improve quality of life dramatically, often for several years.

The Final Stages

In the final stages of CHF, patients often experience a severe and rapid decline. Death is usually from an arrhythmia and frequently occurs outside the hospital. While the final stages can be difficult, with care all CHF patients can be made comfortable. There are few if any situations in medicine where close cooperation between patient or caregiver and doctor is more important.

Patients should make frequent office visits to have medication effects and symptoms monitored. If the heart is terribly dilated and flaccid, Coumadin — an anticoagulant — may prevent a stroke from an embolism, a blood clot that travels from the heart. This medication requires close supervision.

Because of decreased circulation to the kidneys and the possible side effects of ACE inhibitors and diuretics, the patient must also have blood tests to determine kidney function and sodium and potassium levels. When diuretics have to be pushed to much higher doses, there is a very thin line between too much residual fluid in the circulation and actual dehydration. This tenuous situation must be watched. Another problem with terminal CHF is nausea, loss of appetite, and loss of weight. In monitoring all of these problems, daily weight checks at home can be very helpful to the doctor. Ultimately, oxygen use at home or in the retirement home may be required.

More and more people with terminal CHF have chosen not to enter the hospital, and I'm always flexible about managing the situation wherever the patient and family feel most comfortable — especially when further therapeutic measures aren't going to do much to improve the situation.

Although hospice care in the home was initially envisioned for terminal cancer patients, it is legal under Medicare and sensible in certain cases to use hospice nursing for terminal CHF. Oxygen, a hospital bed, and sedatives or medication to improve "air hunger" (severe breathlessness) should be part of the therapy. If the physical arrangements at home are adequate, and if responsible, knowledgeable caretakers are available, terminal care at home may be preferable.

REMEMBER THIS

- Approximately 4.8 million Americans suffer from CHF, and 75 percent of them are over sixty-five. CHF is a common terminal illness in the very elderly.
- Newer drug programs including ACE inhibitors, beta blockers, Aldactone, and carefully monitored diuretics and potassium can help patients maintain an acceptable quality of life for many months or several years.
- Avoidance of alcohol and excess salt, cautious, moderate exercise, and prompt reporting of worsening symptoms are critical in maintaining quality of life.
- As the disease reaches a near terminal state, comfort can be improved by close cooperation with the doctor in monitoring symptoms and medications.
- Once the disease is terminal, home care is an acceptable alternative to hospital admission. Adequate caretakers and medical supervision, oxygen, a hospital bed, and sedatives and narcotics can be obtained through the doctor or a hospice agency.

CHAPTER 29

COMFORT AND SAFETY

One of the most rewarding experiences of my medical practice has been making house calls. And that's not just because when you take care of a lot of old Washingtonians, you see interesting things, like the photograph on the bedside table of a 103-year-old Russian-born patient of mine, showing her in her youth with Tsar Nicholas II's mother. The real reward of house calls is the insight it gives me into my aged patients' quality of life.

Because of my busy schedule, I limit calls to disabled, demented, very frail, and bedridden elderly who don't live too far from my office. It's easier to see these patients at home than in the office, where the difficulty of lifting them on to the examining table and undressing them can be formidable.

Visiting a patient on his or her own turf — seeing the bed, the toilet facilities, how well the person gets around — helps me assess the situation and advise the family on caregiving, assisted living, nursing home care, and end-of-life decisions. The visits have taught me a lot about good home care and what can go wrong. From my experience with house calls, I can say that the single biggest mistake people make is this: hesitating to get more help when it is needed, or to move a loved one into assisted living where more help is available.

What can you do to make your life, or the life of your loved one, comfortable and danger-free? Let's start with some simple safety measures that everyone past seventy — and many in their sixties, if they have problems like arthritis — should follow.

Making the Home Safe

Each year, more than one-third of people over sixty-five fall down. The older and more frail you are, the more likely you are to sustain an injury from a fall: about 10 percent of people in nursing homes who fall, and some 5 percent of people who fall in their own homes or apartments, become seriously injured. Injuries include hip fractures, concussion, and subdural hemorrhage (bleeding between the skull and the brain).

Most falls in the elderly result from medical problems — fainting, unsteadiness, diminished reflexes, muscle weakness, poor vision, and a host of other neurological problems. Often falls occur when a senior citizen overdoes it. One eighty-four-year-old patient broke his arm toppling off a ladder while using a chainsaw to prune a tall tree! People in advanced age and their caregivers should use common sense — and common sense means following simple safety precautions.

HOME SAFETY RULES

☐ Be extremely careful on ladders, and don't use chairs or boxes as ladders.

☐ To prevent dizziness, sit on the side of the bed, or sit forward in an easy chair, for a few seconds before standing.

☐ Pay close attention on stairs and keep one hand on the railing. If there is no railing, have one installed.

☐ Get rid of all scatter or throw rugs, and have all slippery floor areas and stairs covered with stable carpet.

☐ All well-traveled areas, particularly stairs, should be well lighted and clear of clutter.

☐ Have lift or hold bars installed in all bathtubs and showers.

☐ Keep rubber-backed mats on all bathroom floors.

☐ If the person is very unsteady, have a seating arrangement in the shower.

☐ Install a raised toilet seat.

☐ Changes in floor levels should be marked — yellow tape is the best color.

A physical therapy or home safety consultant can evaluate the patient and the environment and make specific recommendations such as the use of canes, walkers, and bedside commodes. This person may help your older relative become a little more mobile, for example, by recommending a device for picking up objects on the floor.

Driving

One of the hardest blows for an older person is being advised to stop driving — words that spell a loss of autonomy and mobility. Deprived of their driver's license, some of my patients have sunk into depression. It's a cruel fact of life: some people just don't belong on the road. Better to face up to the fact now than to wait until an accident occurs.

In the case of early dementia, when the driver shows signs of getting lost or becomes totally befuddled at an intersection, the keys should probably be taken away. For the frail, neurologically impaired but mentally intact older person, the decision may be more difficult. If you're concerned about a loved one's driving, get in the car and carefully observe the way he or she navigates.

ROAD ALERT

Should you or your senior citizen give up the car keys? Here are some warning signs:

- ☐ Difficulty driving at night or in bad weather
- ☐ Difficulty turning, particularly left turns
- ☐ Hitting curbs
- ☐ Moving into wrong lanes or difficulty changing lanes
- ☐ Not appreciating a possibly dangerous situation
- ☐ Scrapes or dents on the car
- ☐ Driving too fast or too slow
- ☐ Confusion, inappropriate anxiety, or anger when driving

What to Do with the Driving-Impaired

If an elderly loved one shows any signs of being driving-impaired, make arrangements for a road test. If the score is low, then you owe it to the driver and to everyone else on the road to advise against further driving. Tickets for moving violations, accidents, or getting lost may be a good opportunity to step in. If the elderly person is not convinced and continues to drive, you should enlist the help of the doctor. Tell the doctor exactly what you observed, and let him or her use a medical exam as a lever to convince your relative not to drive.

What if the patient fails to comply? In that case, the doctor can refuse to sign the medical form for re-licensure when it comes due. Of course, it may not be due — which presents another obstacle. In rare instances, I have written letters to the Bureau of Motor Vehicles to have dangerous drivers' permits revoked.

If the difficulty is restricted to vision problems at night or in inclement weather, you get the older person to agree not to drive in those specific circumstances.

A WORD OF CAUTION

Some people, under pressure from an elderly loved one anxious to hold on to his or her freedom, compromise and get the person to agree to drive only in the neighborhood or to the grocery store. Stick to your guns. Seniors incapable of driving most places can get into terrible trouble at any intersection or in any parking lot, even familiar ones. Remember, there are no safe places for neurologically impaired drivers.

Tough Love

I learned my lesson about tough love several years ago when an elderly man said he would rather see me than one of the older doctors in our practice. This was fine with the older doctor, who couldn't have been busier. "Watch out, though," my partner warned. "That patient once switched to me because his previous doctor refused to sign his driver's license renewal form." Lo and behold, on his second visit to me, Gary whipped out his renewal application and said, "By the way, will you sign this?" Clearly, he was unsteady and impaired. "No, sir," I replied, and urged him not to drive. Rejecting my advice, Gary went to his winter home in South Carolina, found a neurologist to sign his form, and somehow got a license there. One day shortly afterward, when he was scheduled for an office visit, I heard sirens blaring. Apparently Gary had caused a four-car smash-up at one of the busiest intersections in downtown Washington. Fortunately no one was seriously hurt or killed, but the family was liable.

Sometimes we have to practice tough love. Yes, hanging up the keys forever can be devastating to seniors — all the more reason to devote extra attention to them, to chauffeur them, to plan diverting activities, in short, to do everything you can to make them feel they are not headed for a hermit's life.

Care of the Bed-Bound Elderly Patient

Taking care of a relative who is unable to get out of bed, or transfer from a bed to a chair, without assistance can be extremely taxing. Before considering home health care, you need to settle several issues.

Should You Provide Home Care?

If the person has had a stroke or a major fracture, or has an advanced neurological disorder such as Parkinson's disease, you should establish whether he or she even wants to be at home. People with major cognitive impairment may not really know the difference between home and a nursing home. Do you want your relative at home because you would feel guilty sending him or her to a nursing home or an assisted-living center? Do you realize that home care can be a round-the-clock responsibility? Having a severely disabled relative at home will be like having an infant in the home again — one that's heavier and much less cute.

Another question to ask yourself: Does the doctor agree to home care, and is he or she willing to direct it? Unless you have a large family with a responsible member in the home at all times, you'll require help from visiting nurses and other home therapy assistants. Few if any insurance policies cover the expenses of full-time comprehensive home care, which can cost as much as $100,000 a year.

If You Decide on Home Care

Deciding on home care is just the beginning. Now you have to judge the suitability of the home environment. Is the physical setting appropriate for home care? You'll need a hospital bed, possibly a bedside commode, and space for whatever medical equipment or supplies are needed.

Should the doctor inform you that physical therapy will greatly benefit your patient, consider a rehabilitation facility. Physical therapy at home tends not to be as intensive as therapy offered in a skilled-care nursing home.

Remember to keep detailed records of medication dosing. Sometimes licensed practical nurses or home health aides who care about the patient will keep reliable records. In some areas, you can find visiting registered nurses who will supervise health aides in the home and set up monitoring systems for medication, skin care, and exercise.

Bedsores and Flexion Contractures

Two problems commonly seen in the bed-bound are bedsores and flexion contractures. Bedsores (decubitus ulcers) usually arise from pressure on the buttocks, hips, lower spine, or heels when the patient remains too long in one position. The pressure interferes with local circulation. Sores in the hip and pelvic area are more likely, and less likely to heal, if the skin is constantly wet (see part 3, chapter 26, "Urinary Disorders"). If the patient develops bedsores from bedwetting, you might consider using an indwelling urinary catheter.

Treating bedsores. Bedsores are a hundred times easier to prevent than to heal. How can you diagnose and treat them? Look for skin redness that doesn't go away with pressure, or for superficial erosion of the skin. These are the earliest signs of bedsores and they require prompt, sustained care. Duoderm or Tegaderm protective skin covering can help reverse bedsores at this early stage. Pharmacies also carry a large array of protective pads and mattresses to prevent bedsores. If there is the slightest concern about a bedsore, make sure the visiting nurse or doctor sees it.

OF SPECIAL CONCERN

Bedsores, if neglected, can penetrate the skin to the subcutaneous tissue or muscle. In this case your patient may need hospital care. At the very least, a visiting nurse should use an antibiotic cream and medication to remove dead tissue. When severe bedsores become infected, it raises the possibility that fatal bacteria will enter the bloodstream. Keep your doctor abreast of worsening bedsores.

Flexion Contractures

In *The Wizard of Oz*, the Tin Man had a bad case of flexion contractures. Any joint held in a flexed position and not stretched out every day can become stuck in that position. Flexion contractures, to put it simply, are stuck joints. These can make mobilization and bed care extremely difficult. All bed-bound patients should have their elbows, shoulders, hands, knees, and hips stretched out gently every day — a small price to pay for the benefit it reaps. A visiting nurse, doctor, or physical therapist can teach caregivers range-of-motion stretches in just a few minutes.

Does Your Loved One Need Assisted Living?

The decision whether your relative should enter an assisted-living facility or a nursing home is momentous and has to be individualized. Too often, older people are put at great risk because those responsible for their care don't insist on a safer environment. In making a decision, you and your family will have to consider the following issues:

- The functional status of the person
- The availability of helpers at home, either family members or outside assistants
- The physical environment of the home

▢ The quality of available assisted-living or nursing facilities
▢ The financial resources available for home care or assisted living
▢ The person's emotional attachment to home
▢ The person's cognitive ability to appreciate familiar surroundings

Of course, functional status can vary widely from person to person. The following questions should help you gauge your loved one's degree of independence:

▢ Can the person move about, get in and out of bed or a chair, bathe, or get to the toilet without assistance?
▢ Is the person continent, or are accidents frequent?
▢ Can the person feed him or herself?
▢ How is food purchased, brought to the home, and prepared? Are meals nutritious?
▢ Can the person keep track of medications without assistance?

If your answers point to problems in just one or two areas, you might take some simple corrective actions. Meals on Wheels and an occasional visit from a nurse or home care aide may be enough to keep your relative safe and sound at home. If, however, problems begin to pile up and your relative becomes more and more dependent, you should bite the bullet and seriously consider moving the person to an assisted-living facility or a nursing home.

A functionally impaired senior living alone should remain at home alone only when financial resources make round-the-clock, in-house help possible. If the senior lives with other members of the family, the home should be large, and there should be a responsible family member or health aide present at all times.

One excellent alternative to home and nursing care that has grown popular in recent years is the graduated-care, or assisted-living, facility. This offers the elderly person a certain degree of autonomy — for example, he or she may start out in an apartment equipped with a buzzer in case an on-staff nurse is needed. The facility will arrange outings for residents who remain mobile and offer meals in a dining hall for residents who aren't up to cooking for themselves. As residents age and become less independent, they move to wings of the facility that offer intensified levels of care.

People with dementia, particularly those who live alone, often have to be forced to move to a protected environment. When a social worker visited one of my patients and found nothing in her refrigerator but uncashed Social Security checks, we had to arrange for a court-appointed legal guardian to force her into a nursing home.

I hope, if your loved one will be entering an outside-care facility, that the transition is easier. Of course for anyone, moving from home to an outside facility is unsettling if not downright traumatic. To smooth the way, bring as many familiar pictures and pieces of furniture as possible, and arrange for frequent visits from family and friends after the move. Try to make the new environment as much like home as you can.

REMEMBER THIS

- Falls are the major safety risk for mildly impaired older people at home, but they can be avoided with safety measures.
- The decision to revoke an impaired person's driver's license is difficult, but one that family and caregivers must make for the good of the person and the community.
- Continuing home care for very frail, disabled, or bedridden people, though possible, requires abundant human and financial resources plus a backup system of physician and nurse supervision.
- Bedsores and flexion contractures are common afflictions of the bedridden elderly. An ounce of prevention is worth a pound of cure.
- The decision whether to move a person to a nursing home or an assisted-living facility has to be individualized. Too often, older people are put at great risk because those responsible for their care don't insist on a safer environment.

CHAPTER 30

DEALING WITH DYING

"The wise man looks at death with honesty, dignity and calm, recognizing that the tragedy it brings is inherent in the great gift of life." These words of essayist and philosopher Corliss Lamont speak to the heart of many elderly people who have come to this last stage of life. My oldest patients don't fear death; they do, however, fear a painful, struggling, undignified process of dying. Many worry that "the doctors" — the impersonal medical establishment — will take control of the situation and keep them needlessly alive on machines.

It doesn't have to be this way. There are a number of measures doctors and family members can take to ensure the right of the elderly person to a dignified death in a safe and comfortable environment.

Mark

Mark was eighty-six years old, a retired orthopedic surgeon. Following the death of his wife several years earlier, he had sunk into a depression that medication and grief counseling had only partially alleviated. Recently Mark had moved from home into an assisted-living facility. He had severe chronic lung disease and heart arrhythmia, was on oxygen, and got around in a motorized chair — his "scooter." After developing moderately severe pneumonia, similar to cases he'd already had several times, Mark was hospitalized. Despite two days of antibiotic therapy he took a turn for the worse, and because he needed more oxygen, I mentioned the possibility of his going on a ventilator in the intensive care unit (ICU) if the situation didn't improve.

Mark had talked to me repeatedly about not wanting to be kept alive if he was terminally ill. "Sometimes depression makes people feel that life isn't worth it," I said. "You should talk it over with your children." As I was leaving the room Mark, who had been raised in the South, said he'd chosen me as his doctor because I was a Virginian. "I know the Yankees would put me in the ICU, but I thought you wouldn't," he said. I laughed and went back to his bedside, assuring him that neither I nor my Northern colleagues had any intention of putting him in intensive care against his will.

The next morning Mark's son was in the room and I reviewed the situation for them — Mark's worsening condition and quality of life. We agreed not to put him in intensive care. "How about stopping these damned antibiotics?" Mark said. I agreed. We kept the oxygen on, gave Mark sedatives for breathing comfort, and he died peacefully the next afternoon with his son and daughter by his side.

Mark was not only a patient but also a friend whom I'd occasionally seen at social events or professional meetings. I was sad that we couldn't do more for his depression, but I feel that we handled his physical illnesses and his death properly.

You Are in Charge

Mark's case brings out a point you should know: You — or if you're impaired, your family or designated agent — are in charge. Your doctor has a legal and moral obligation to treat you or not treat you according to your wishes. Of course, if you refuse entirely reasonable treatment, or insist on a futile continuation of therapy, the doctor can resign from your case after arranging alternative care, but this almost never happens; most doctors and their patients come to a meeting of the minds.

What Are Your Doctor's Responsibilities?

Besides following your directions on the intensity of care, your doctor has three major responsibilities:

☐ To ensure that all proper, reasonable medical treatments are given, after thorough consultation with specialists. I never withheld or withdrew treatment unless another physician, usually a specialist in the disease threatening my patient's life, had evaluated the person and concurred that the disease was terminal. This is a legal requirement in some states and a requirement in most hospitals.

☐ To be just as careful with pain and comfort measures as he or she would have been with measures to try to improve or cure your problem. In recent years the medical profession has begun to prescribe pain medication more liberally for terminal patients. But patients and their families deserve the opportunity to say meaningful good-byes to one another, and no doctor wants to send a patient into a coma unnecessarily — a possibility with too much pain medication. Feedback from family members regarding any discomfort, breathing difficulties, or nausea the patient may be experiencing will help the doctor in deciding whether to adjust the dosage up or down.

☐ To work with you and your family in making specific decisions. This sort of cooperation can only succeed in an atmosphere of mutual trust. Here the doctor goes beyond just the technical aspects of the case.

Before Therapy Is Withheld

Above all, when dealing with life-threatening illness, the doctor needs to know what your wishes are — how intensive you want the treatment to be. I once had a ninety-three-year-old patient with colon cancer, and I advised against surgery because she had heart problems. She said she wouldn't mind dying during the operation — she just didn't want to die of cancer. We went along with her wishes, and she survived the operation.

Ideally, you'll be in a position to communicate your wishes to your doctor when the time comes for momentous decisions. However, because elderly sick people are often incapacitated, you should have an advance directive as well as a person — spouse, child, or trusted friend — designated to make medical decisions for you. This person has "medical power of attorney."

CHARTING YOUR COURSE: THE ADVANCE DIRECTIVE

An advance directive can never be comprehensive enough to cover all eventualities. I recommend that you give general guidelines to the physician, the family, and the person with medical power of attorney. A general directive might read like this:

"If my physician, after appropriate consultation, believes my condition to be terminal or incurable, or highly likely to leave me permanently helpless or severely mentally dysfunctional, I direct that alleviation of pain and other discomfort take precedence over all other medical considerations. I further direct that in these circumstances no life-support treatment or devices be used to prolong my life."

You may want to specifically address such things as artificial feeding or the use of ventilators. In my experience, however, a blanket statement of the patient's wishes gave me enough to work with in consulting with family members and charting the patient's course.

Making Specific Decisions

When it comes time for you or your family to make a decision on a specific treatment, the doctor will give you his or her opinion on two main aspects of the case: the short- and long-term prognoses, and the patient's likely quality of life after the illness, as compared with before the illness.

The Prognosis

What are your short- and long-term prognoses? The answer will shape your and your doctor's decision. In the case I mentioned, Mark's lung condition deteriorated after each infection. He was on oxygen full time and couldn't summon the energy to walk. The pulmonologists and I agreed that his overall condition would never improve.

One central question, particularly in patients who have multiple life-threatening problems, is how likely they are to survive the ICU. Dr. William Knaus, when he was the director of the ICU at George Washington University Hospital, did an analysis of who survived the ICU. He assigned a score for age, the body systems involved, and the severity of the patient's condition (such as how much oxygen was required and how was the heart functioning), then gave a percentage range of how likely it was that the person would get out of the ICU and improve. Knaus's score system is helpful in determining how likely a person is to come out of the ICU alive, and therefore whether a person should even be considered for the ICU. Of course, this sort of decision can't be entirely reduced to percentages — it is part science, part of the art of medicine. Any decision about whether to put someone in the ICU needs to be discussed calmly and carefully with the doctor, with Knaus's score system as part of the decision-making process.

Quality of Life

What was your or your loved one's quality of life before the illness, and what is it likely to be after the illness? Certainly, advanced dementia is an almost universal reason for limiting treatment to comfort measures. Mild dementia or extreme frailty are factors to consider when deciding whether to limit treatment. In advising families about treating an acute illness like pneumonia in an extremely frail or mildly demented patient, the doctor has to weigh how much the current illness will worsen the patient's overall condition later. Mild pneumonia might be treated with antibiotics and fluids. Severe pneumonia, however, requires the use of a ventilator in the ICU; since such dramatic treatment would probably weaken the patient and diminish his or her quality of life afterward, most doctors would advise

CODE STATUS

One decision hospitals are now requiring at the time of admission is "code status." Code status allows the attending physician and on-scene hospital staff to make certain life-and-death decisions. For example, if a patient has a cardiac or respiratory arrest, code status can help determine whether the person should be resuscitated. Consider this: only 1 or 2 percent of people over ninety who suffer a cardiac arrest live more than a few weeks after hospitalization. The aged, injured body cannot tolerate the emergency measures required for treatment — a breathing tube, chest pumping, electrical defibrillation, intravenous and ventilator hookups.

My advice to all people over ninety, and to all in their eighties with severe chronic medical problems such as emphysema, advanced heart disease, or cancer, is to have the initials DNR (do not resuscitate) put on their chart. Most patients and family members welcome this approach.

against use of the ventilator, or would recommend that the ventilator be stopped if after a few days the patient doesn't improve.

Because each patient's situation is unique, decisions based on quality of life are by nature subjective. When the wishes of the patient are unknown, I try to put myself in the person's shoes, and I ask any decision-makers in the family to imagine themselves in the person's shoes. Of course, family members are more likely than I to know what the patient would want; the final decision rests with them.

When Family Members Disagree

In most cases when family and doctor take into account the patient's wishes, prognosis, and quality of life, everyone is comfortable with the resulting decision. However, differences of opinion sometimes exist within a family.

A retired seventy-one-year-old nurse was unmarried and lived in an apartment with her ninety-one-year-old mother, Lottie, whom she had been taking care of for ten years. Lottie had congestive heart failure, diabetes, and impaired mental status from several small strokes. After developing severe pneumonia, she was hospitalized. Her only other child, who lived in Chicago, flew to Washington when she learned of the hospitalization. She had talked by phone with her mother occasionally but had not been to Washington for several years. Lottie's condition deteriorated in spite of antibiotics. The pulmonologist, the cardiologist, and I all advised against moving her to the ICU or putting her on a ventilator. Her nurse daughter agreed wholeheartedly. But the sister from Chicago would have none of this; she "loved her mother and wanted everything to be done." In my opinion, the sister was making an eleventh-hour effort to assuage years of guilt over not helping care for her mother. After much difficult, intense discussion, we got the sister to agree, and a few days later Lottie died peacefully, without artificial measures to extend her life.

Had Lottie arranged for an advance directive, and had she designated a medical power of attorney, this roadblock could have been avoided. Fortunately, the Chicago daughter did come around and see our side of the argument; if she hadn't, we would have had to convene the hospital ethics committee, bring in lawyers, and precipitate a giant controversy. The loser would have been Lottie.

A WORD OF CAUTION

Everyone over sixty should have an advance medical directive and should designate a medical power of attorney. Equally important, all family members should understand the wishes of the person and, as far as possible, be in agreement long before it is time for critical decisions. It is the responsibility of the person given power of attorney to discuss the subject with the rest of the family. Don't let the guilty-sister-from-Chicago syndrome tear your family up.

Other Difficult Decisions

Earlier, I mentioned the decision whether or not to resuscitate. Two other decisions often have to be made when the very frail become severely ill: whether to use a feeding tube, and whether to opt for surgery.

Feeding Tubes

What if someone has a stroke or other neurological problem that makes swallowing difficult or dangerous because of repeated aspiration into the lungs? The most common procedure for this condition is the percutaneous endoscopic gastrostomy (PEG), in which a small incision is made into the stomach and a tube is inserted so that liquid food can be supplied. Though a PEG insertion is relatively minor, the decision whether to perform it is one of the more difficult in medicine. If the tube isn't put in, the patient will either die of malnutrition or get recurrent aspiration pneumonia, which is usually fatal.

Of course, every case has to be individualized. In general, I encourage patients who are alert and can make their own decisions to go with the procedure. If they are mentally impaired and clearly not improving, I advise that sedatives be administered for comfort and that no food or fluid be given. Sometimes I suggest a temporary feeding tube through the nose and down the esophagus to buy some time; we can wait a little and see if the neurological condition improves. But using the PEG procedure in a permanently comatose or terminally demented patient seems against all reason.

Surgery

Should major surgery be done on a very old or very infirm person? The doctor, if possible the patient, and the family need to consider the degree of trauma from the surgery, possible alternative treatments, and again, the expected quality of life afterward. Unless the surgery is likely to be brief and the objective is easily achievable, I usually advise simply using comfort measures.

Physician-Assisted Suicide

Yvonne had just turned ninety when she brought me a booklet from the Hemlock Society and asked for a stash of barbiturates to keep around so she could commit suicide conveniently. She was lonely, her nearest relative was a nephew, and a close companion had died two years before. One of the problems with her request, besides the legal one, was that she was not very sick. Yvonne had some back pain from osteoporosis and a great deal of gas, but no major progressive or life-threatening disease. I refused her request.

Later, because of more back pain and troublesome urinary incontinence, Yvonne didn't want to go out, so I saw her at home. In her bedroom she had a bulletin board with a picture of Dr. Kevorkian and an inscription, "I wish he were my doctor." Another publication from the Hemlock Society was produced, and she asked me again for a lethal amount of medication. Again I said no.

About two years later, Yvonne vomited a large amount of bright red blood and was admitted to the hospital. In her room, with her nephew present, I told her that she almost certainly had a bleeding ulcer and that we could probably stop the bleeding, but she would need transfusions and a gastroenterologist to tell us where the blood was coming from. She said she didn't want any treatment; her nephew agreed and said he would take legal action if she were treated against her will. I said that wasn't necessary, that I would do nothing against her will. I made sure both of them understood this was probably a treatable condition — that we could probably stop the bleeding in a matter of hours or a day or so. They still refused treatment, so I complied and Yvonne died of the intestinal bleeding the next morning.

What Is Physician-Assisted Suicide?

I present this case to highlight an important point about physician-assisted suicide, that is, an action directed by a physician specifically to cause a patient's death. The withholding of medical therapy because the patient doesn't want it — or in other cases, because it is deemed futile — is not physician-assisted suicide and is within legal guidelines. Nothing was done to hasten Yvonne's death; I simply acceded to her wishes not to be treated.

Another important point: treatment given primarily to alleviate pain or severe shortness of breath — what doctors call air hunger — in a terminally ill patient may contribute to that patient's death, but it is not physician-assisted suicide. Imagine a case of a terminally ill lung cancer patient who has already braved the ordeal of chemotherapy and various other therapies with only modest results, and who finally refuses to continue treatment. Say this person wanted morphine to relieve the pain, and I gave it to him knowing that the morphine might shorten his life. This would not be physician-assisted suicide. Why? Because the medication was given to alleviate pain, not to cause the patient's death. Giving medicine to alleviate the symptoms of a terminally ill patient who is suffering pain, severe breathlessness, or some other discomfort is an entirely legal and widely accepted practice.

> **Did You Know?**
> According to medical ethicists and the courts, it is not physician-assisted suicide if:
> - Medical therapy is withheld either because the patient doesn't want it, or because it is deemed futile.
> - Causing the patient's death is not the reason a treatment is given.

A Few Thoughts about Physician-Assisted Suicide

Currently, Oregon is the only state — and the Netherlands the only country in the world — where physician-assisted suicide is legal. At this point,

I feel it would do more harm than good if more states passed laws to allow physician-assisted suicide. Why?

A physician's active assistance in suicide is almost never warranted by the medical situation. As the story of the retired orthopedic surgeon Mark illustrates, people who are truly terminal will die naturally. We simply have the means with narcotics, sedatives, tranquilizers, and oxygen to keep them comfortable. In all my years of practice, I've never seen a sick patient, other than one with severe depression, who wanted to die who was not already very near death from the disease. All my colleagues and I had to do was keep them comfortable and nature took its course. My terminal patients were almost all old and suffering from organ failure.

Legalized physician-assisted suicide opens up the possibility of killing someone whose problem may be complicated by a temporary state of depression or loneliness. It is likely that the primary problem of one of Dr. Kevorkian's patients was depression.

Active measures can be taken to combat the poor self-image that often leads to thoughts of suicide. Many older people who become physically disabled suffer a loss of self-worth and don't want to go on living. A number of patients have expressed to me the feeling that their families would be "better off" without them. Family members need to be aware of these feelings and to counteract them by giving the elderly person more attention, asking his or her advice, including the person in family decisions, encouraging interests. The "better off without me" feeling may need to be confronted directly. Simply telling a person that it's not true may allay anxiety. If you have an ill relative who's feeling worthless, combat the Dr. Kevorkian syndrome by reassuring the person with words and actions that he or she is loved and valuable.

Legalized physician-assisted suicide would be a radical departure from the medical profession's traditional reverence for life and could be a slippery slope. What would the next move be? Getting rid of the demented and the lonely? Where would the line be drawn? If, as a profession, we do as good a job in alleviating terminal pain and suffering as we have done in preserving life, and if we reserve lifesaving technology only for those who want it or can truly benefit from it, we don't need new laws for physician-assisted suicide.

CHOOSING THE PLACE OF DEATH

More older people are dying at home now than thirty years ago, and unless a person requires complicated medical attention or technical therapies, death at home is often preferable, certainly for the emotional comfort of the patient.

Most large metropolitan areas have home hospice services with nurses experienced in terminal care. This arrangement, plus a health aide or practical nurse in the home and proper equipment, is usually all a family needs.

Some people are apprehensive about the logistics of an older person dying at home. In most jurisdictions, it is simply a matter of the hospice nurse or the doctor seeing the person to certify the death, then notifying the medical examiner that the person has been under his or her care, and that the death was from natural causes and was expected. The medical examiner gives permission by phone for the death certificate to be issued, whereupon the funeral director can come and take the body.

Emotional and Spiritual Support

When a patient is on the verge of death, the doctor can help by doing everything he or she can to make the patient comfortable. With patients I've known a long time, I try hard to say something that will give them a lift — some emotional comfort or an ego boost. But there is only so much a doctor can do, even after a long relationship. The real summing up takes place between the family and the patient, sometimes in concert with a member of the clergy.

One fear people have who are terribly ill and know they are dying is dying alone. In a moving article about the death of his father, Dr. Theodore Tsomides writes that his father expressed a wish not to be "left alone in the corner to die." Both with words and your reassuring presence, you can remove this fear. Make sure you communicate the gravity of the patient's condition to other family members, who can lend a helping hand. Unfortunately, it can be hard to predict the time of death. Family shifts will keep the patient from feeling isolated. You don't need to talk — your presence alone, and your help, will probably suffice.

In the final days and hours, all of us would like our loved ones and closest friends to be present for a summing up and a loving good-bye. A dying person cherishes brief, one-on-one visits from family members and close friends. Visits tell the person that his or her life was well lived. And the few words exchanged in a person's last hours are words that other family members will remember forever. If the person dying is very old or has been ill for a long time, the anguish won't be so great. The emotional intensity of dying will arise not from anguish, but from the mutual expressions of love and appreciation that are the ultimate mark of humanity.

REMEMBER THIS

- You and your family need not fear loss of control over your medical treatment. Doctors are bound, both legally and ethically, to treat terminal patients only as vigorously as they wish.
- Everyone should have an advance medical directive and a medical power of attorney.
- Specific decisions on aggressive treatment for the very old have to be individualized. Limiting treatment to measures providing physical and mental comfort is often the most humane choice.
- Treating pain or breathlessness in a terminally ill patient with drugs that may secondarily hasten death is legal.
- Before critical decisions have to be made, family members should understand and reach agreement about the patient's wishes regarding artificial life support.
- The final days and hours of a person's life are critically important to everyone in the family. Families should make every effort to keep the dying person from feeling alone, and to send a message that his or her life has been well lived and meaningful.

For readers who want to explore individual topics in depth, I've arranged sources in three separate lists. The first list covers recent significant review articles from established medical journals that can be found at medical libraries or through Internet sites such as the National Library of Medicine (see below for Web address). The second list mentions helpful, medically accurate books for lay readers, and the third includes Internet sites that present further information about some of the topics covered in this book.

Articles

Campion, E.W. "Aging Better." New England Journal of Medicine 338 (April 9, 1998): 1064-66. Efforts to reduce mortality also dramatically improve the quality of life.

"Executive Summary of the Third Report of the National Cholesterol Education Program (NCEP) Expert Panel on Detection, Evaluation, and Treatment of High Blood Cholesterol in Adults." New England Journal of Medicine 285 (May 16, 2001): 2486-97. The latest compendium of cholesterol advice.

Felson, D.T., et al. "National Institutes of Health Conference on Osteoarthritis Part 2: Treatment Approaches." Annals of Internal Medicine 133 (Nov. 2000): 726-37. The best recent review of treatment for osteoarthritis.

Fuster, V., et al. "Pathogenesis of Coronary Disease: The Biological Role of Risk Factors." Journal of the American College of Cardiology 27 (1996): 964-1047. This is a classic review of the connection between risk factors and coronary atherosclerosis.

Greenland, P. "Beating High Blood Pressure with Low Sodium DASH (Dietary Approaches to Stop Hypertension)." New England Journal of Medicine 344 (January 4, 2001): 53-54.

Hart, R.G., et al. "Atrial Fibrillation and Thromboembolism: A Decade of Progress in Stroke Prevention." Annals of Internal Medicine 131 (Nov. 2, 1999): 688-95.

"Joint National Committee on Prevention, Detection, Evaluation, and Treatment of High Blood Pressure: The Sixth Report." Archives of Internal Medicine 157 (1997): 2143. Detailed recommendations.

Marley, J.E., et al. "Nutrition in the Elderly:U.C.L.A Conference." Annals of Internal Medicine 109 (Dec. 1, 1998): 890-904. A slightly old but extremely thorough article on all aspects of nutrition in older people.

Morrison, R.S., et al. "Survival in End-Stage Dementia Following Acute Illness." Journal of the American Medical Association 284 (July 5, 2000): 47-52. This article presents scientific data that heroic actions with advanced dementia patients accomplishes little.

O'Connor, P.C., et al. "Medical Progress: Patients with Alcohol Problems." New England Journal of Medicine 338 (Feb. 26, 1998): 592-602. An excellent review of the whole spectrum of alcohol-related problems and therapy.

Sacco, R.L., et al. "Update on Antiplatelet Therapy for Stroke Prevention." Archives of Internal Medicine 160 (June 12, 2000): 1579-82. An excellent review of aspirin and other anticlotting agents to prevent stroke.

Sobel, B.E. "Acute Myocardial Infarction." In Cecil Textbook of Medicine. Philadelphia: W.B. Saunders, 2000. As good a review of the issues surrounding the treatment of coronary attacks as one can find.

Steinhauser, K.E., et al. "In Search of a Good Death: Observations of Patients' Families and Providers." Annals of Internal Medicine 132 (May 2000): 825-32. This provides insights from a careful scientific observation of what families and caregivers do right and wrong.

Theroux, P., and Fuster, V. "Acute Coronary Syndromes." Circulation 97 (1998):1195-1206. This discusses angina and impending heart attacks.

Tolle, S.W., et al. "Oregon's Law In-Hospital Death Rates: What Determines Where People Die and Satisfaction with Decisions on Place of Death?" Annals of Internal Medicine 130 (April 20, 1999): 681-85. This article helps in deciding on where terminal care can best be given.

Tsomides, T. "Reflections on Death." Annals of Internal Medicine 134 (Feb. 6, 2001): 246-48. This is a moving account by a physician of his father's death.

Vita, A.J., Terry, R.B., et al. "Aging, Health Risks, and Cumulative Disability." New England Journal of Medicine 338 (April 9, 1998): 1035-41.

Wiese, J.G., et al. "The Alcohol Hangover." Annals of Internal Medicine 132 (June 6, 2000): 897-902.

Books for Lay Readers

Bales, C.O., Feinglos, M., and Plaisted, C.S. Eating Well, Living Well with Diabetes. Viking, New York: Duke University Medical Center, 1997.

Beasley, J.D. How to Defeat Alcoholism. New York: Random House, 1989. This book contains excellent suggestions on how to curb drinking and how to deal with true alcoholism if drinking cannot be controlled. Ignore the diet advice.

Benson, Anna, and Benson, Cynthia. Firm for Life. New York: Broadway Books, 1998. Excellent review of good dieting principles and an easy-to-follow fitness program.

Kwiteravich, P.O. The Johns Hopkins Complete Guide to Preventing and Reversing Heart Disease. Roseville, California: Prima, 1998.

Mace, N.L., and Rabins, D.V. The 36-Hour Day. 3d ed. Baltimore: Johns Hopkins University Press, 1999. A classic on how to deal with a family member who has dementia.

Morgan, S.L., and Weisner, R.L. Fundamentals of Clinical Nutrition. 2d ed. St. Louis: Mosby Yearbook, 1998. An excellent primer on nutrition.

Newman, D.K. The Urinary Incontinence Sourcebook. Los Angeles: Lowell House, 1997. A thorough discussion of the problem, plus Kegel exercises and biofeedback.

Walsh, P.C., and Worthington, J.F. The Prostate. Baltimore: Johns Hopkins University Press, 1995. A review of the issues surrounding prostate cancer and benign enlargement of the prostate by one of the country's eminent urologists.

Yannios, T. The Heart Disease Breakthrough. New York: John Wiley, 1999. A more extensive presentation of prevention and early treatment of heart disease.

Internet Sites

AARP
http://www.aarp.org

Alcoholics Anonymous
http://www.alcoholics-anonymous.org

American Diabetes Association
http://www.diabetes.org

American Heart Association
http://www.americanheart.org

American Stroke Association
http://www.strokeassociation.org

National Institute on Aging
http://www.medlineplus.nlm.nih.gov

National Institute of Diabetes and Digestive and Kidney Disorders
http://www.niddk.nih.gov

National Institutes of Health
http:///www.nih.gov/health/

National Heart, Lung and Blood Institute
http://www.nhlbi.nih.gov

National Library of Medicine
http://www.nlm.nih.gov

National Sleep Foundation
http://www.sleepfoundation.org

Substance Abuse and Mental Health Services Administration
http://www.samhsa.gov

INDEX

acarbose (Precose), 45
ACE inhibitors, 35, 48, 287
acetaminophen (Tylenol), 116–17, 153, 165
acetazolamide (Diamox), 235
acetylcholine, 255
achalasia, 201
acoustic neuroma, 263
actinic keratosis, 210, 212
Actonel (risedronate), 133, 135–36, 221
acupuncture, 165
adenocarcinoma, 71
advance directives, 301
African-Americans, 30, 39, 42, 45, 48, 61, 68,
   76, 129, 235
albumin (microalbumin), 48
alcohol
   acetaminophen and, 116–17
   alcoholism and alcohol abuse, 117–18, 179–87
   blood pressure and, 34
   cancer and, 71
   cholesterol and, 25–26, 28
   congestive heart failure and, 286
   depression and, 171
   GERD and, 199
   insomnia and, 226, 227
   osteoporosis and, 129
   pneumonia and, 109
   sexual dysfunction and, 191
   unsteadiness and, 265
   weight problems and, 95, 96
Aldactone (spironolactone), 287
alendronate (Fosamax), 133, 135–36
allergies, 103, 214
Alzheimer's disease, 3, 141, 170, 181, 231,
   251–52, 255–58
Amaryl (glimepiride), 44, 46–47
Ambien (zolpidem), 221, 228
amitriptyline (Elavil), 48, 175
amyloids, 77, 251, 256, 257
anabolic drugs, 281
anal fissure, 203–4
analgesics, 239, 240
androgens, 142
Androl (oxymetholone), 282
anemia, 5, 218
angina pectoris, 10
angio-edema, 35
angioplasty, 12–13, 14–15
annual evaluations and exams, 4–6, 66, 68–69
Antabuse (disulfiram), 186
antacids, 199–200
antibiotics, 85, 108–9, 110, 120, 205, 207
anticholinergics, 101
antidepressants, 170, 174–76, 190, 192–93, 256
antihistamines, 109–10, 228
Antivert (meclizine), 264
anxiety, 182, 226, 239, 249
appetite suppressants, 96–97
ARBs, 35–36
Aricept (donepezil), 255–56
arrhythmia, 8, 10, 15, 180–81, 268, 288
arterial disease, 15–16
arteriograms, 11–12, 16

arteriosclerosis, 15–16
arteriovenous fistulae, 77
arthritis, 122, 150–57, 227
arthroscopy, 156
Asian Americans, 129
aspirin, 12, 14, 27, 68, 76, 80, 85, 117, 165, 234, 255
assisted living, 296–98
asthma, 52, 102–3
atherosclerosis, 4, 8, 9, 28–29, 33, 40, 77, 237
Ativan (lorazepam), 221, 229
atorvastatin (Lipitor), 23, 26–27, 282
atrophic vaginitis, 142, 144, 194–95
autoimmune reactions, 119

back pain, 158–67, 227
Barrett's esophagus, 200
basal cell carcinoma, 71, 210, 211
bedsores, 295–96
benign prostatic hyperplasia (BPH), 62, 269–72
benzodiazepines, 229
beta agonists, 101
beta blockers, 12, 35, 171, 235, 287
beta cells, 39, 40
biguanides, 45
biphosphonates, 133, 134–36
bladder cancer, 70, 74, 119
blood clots, 16, 18, 79–80, 84–85, 89, 145–46,
   148–49, 237, 289
blood disorders, fatigue and, 218
blood profile, 5
blood transfusions, 115
body mass index (BMI), 89, 90
bone densitometry, 137
Bontril PDM (phendimetrazine), 97
brain, 33, 82–84, 140–41, 181–82
breast cancer, 53, 58, 64–67, 74, 89, 144, 147, 148
breast exam, 5
breast tissue, 143–44
breathing problems, 10, 89, 100, 108, 229–30
bronchial dilators, 101
bronchial infections, 52, 102
bronchitis, 52, 98–99, 101–2, 110
bupropion (Zyban), 56
bypass grafts, 16

caffeine, 199, 226, 227, 234
calcitonin, 133, 136
calcium, 96, 131–32, 136
calcium channel blockers, 35, 286–87
cancer, 3, 52–53, 57–74, 89, 122, 161, 279–80.
   See also specific types
canes, 265
cardiac arrhythmia, 8, 10, 15, 180–81, 268, 288
cardiomyopathy, 180
cardiovascular disease. *See* heart disease
Cardura (doxazosin), 271
caregivers, 258–59
carotid artery, 237
cataracts, 235
Celebrex, 155, 202, 240, 256, 282
Celexa, 175
cephalexin, 207
cerebellar degeneration, 182

N. THOMAS CONNALLY, M.D., F.A.C.P., received his medical degree from the University of Virginia and has practiced general internal medicine in Washington, D.C., for thirty-two years. Among other positions, he has held clinical faculty appointments at George Washington University and Georgetown University medical schools, and has served as chief of the department of medicine at Sibley Memorial Hospital and as a trustee of the American Society of Internal Medicine. He was appointed by two Virginia governors to the University of Virginia's Board of Visitors, and he chaired the committee that has oversight of the University of Virginia Hospital and the medical and nursing schools.

Dr. Connally has frequently testified before congressional committees on health policy and has lectured and written about health-care costs, the role of the primary care physician, end-of-life issues, and the doctor-patient relationship.

In 1976 Dr. Connally was named the Young Internist of the Year by the American Society of Internal Medicine, and in 2000 he received the prestigious Laureate Award from the American College of Physicians for clinical excellence and leadership in his profession.